Business Result

Upper-intermediate | Teacher's Book

John Hughes

OXFORD
UNIVERSITY PRESS

OXFORD
UNIVERSITY PRESS

Great Clarendon Street, Oxford OX2 6DP

Oxford University Press is a department of the University of Oxford.
It furthers the University's objective of excellence in research, scholarship,
and education by publishing worldwide in

Oxford New York

Auckland Cape Town Dar es Salaam Hong Kong Karachi
Kuala Lumpur Madrid Melbourne Mexico City Nairobi
New Delhi Shanghai Taipei Toronto

With offices in

Argentina Austria Brazil Chile Czech Republic France Greece
Guatemala Hungary Italy Japan Poland Portugal Singapore
South Korea Switzerland Thailand Turkey Ukraine Vietnam

OXFORD and OXFORD ENGLISH are registered trade marks of
Oxford University Press in the UK and in certain other countries

ISBN: 978 0 19 476816 0 (book)
ISBN: 978 0 19 476815 3 (pack)

Printed in China

ACKNOWLEDGEMENTS

Accompanying Teacher's DVD produced by: MTJ Media, Oxford, UK

*The author and publisher would like to thank the following for their kind assistance with
the accompanying Teacher's DVD*: Rebecca Turner, Simon Howells, Penny McLarty,
Stephan Brandt, Manuela Vatana Soares, Kyushick Lee (Bruce), Begüm Kazak,
Erika Valenzuela, Fabio Massimo Parenti, Melissa Fusari, Catriona Davidson
(The Eckersley School of English, Oxford, UK), Tim Bird (British Study Centres,
Oxford, UK), David Newton (OISE, Oxford, UK), Julia Ward (OISE, Oxford, UK),
Judith Bolt (King's School, Oxford, UK), Meriel Steele (Oxford English Centre,
Oxford, UK)

Contents

Introduction

The course

Who is Business Result for?

Business Result is a comprehensive multi-level course in business English suitable for a wide range of learners. The main emphasis is on *enabling* your students; helping them to communicate more effectively in their working lives.

In-work students

Unlike many business English courses, *Business Result* addresses the language and communication needs of employees at all levels of an organization who need to use English at work. It recognizes that the business world is truly international, and that many people working in a modern, global environment spend much of their time doing everyday tasks in English – communicating with colleagues and work contacts by phone, via email and in a range of face-to-face situations such as formal and informal meetings / discussions, and various planned and unplanned social encounters. It contains topics relevant to executive-level learners, but doesn't assume that the majority of students will be international managers who 'do business' in English – the activities allow the students to participate in a way that is relevant to them, whatever their level in their company or organization.

Pre-work students

Business Result can also be used with pre-work students at college level. The course covers a variety of engaging topics over the sixteen units, so students without much work experience will receive a wide-ranging overview of the business world, as well as acquiring the key communication skills they will need in their future working lives. Each unit in this *Teacher's Book* contains suggestions for adapting the material to the needs of pre-work students.

One-to-one teaching

Many of the activities in the book are designed for use with groups of students, but they can also be easily adapted to suit a one-to-one teaching situation. Notes in the individual *Teacher's Book* units offer suggestions and help with this.

What approach does Business Result take?

Business Result helps students communicate in English in real-life work situations. The priority at all times is on enabling them to do so more effectively and with confidence. The target language in each unit has been carefully selected to ensure that students will be equipped with genuinely useful, transferable language that they can take out of the classroom and use immediately in the workplace.

The course recognizes that, with so many businesses now being staffed by people of different nationalities, there is an increasing trend towards using English as the language of internal communication in many organizations. As well as learning appropriate language for communicating externally – with clients or suppliers, for example – students are also given the opportunity to practise in situations that take place within an organization, such as informal meetings, job appraisals or social chat.

The main emphasis of the course is on the students speaking and trying out the target language in meaningful and authentic ways; it is expected that a large proportion of the lesson time will be spent on activating students' interest and encouraging them to talk. The material intentionally takes a communicative, heads-up approach, maximizing the amount of classroom time available to focus on and practise the target language. However, you will also find that there is plenty of support in terms of reference notes, written practice and review material.

The syllabus is essentially communication-driven. The focus on *Business communication skills* as the core of each unit ensures that students are provided with a range of phrases they can use immediately, both in the classroom and in their day-to-day work. The topics in each of the sixteen units have been chosen because of their relevance to modern business and the world of work. Vocabulary is presented in realistic contexts with reference to authentic companies or organizations. Grammar is also a key element of each unit, ensuring that students also pay attention to accuracy and become more proficient at expressing themselves clearly and precisely.

Student's Book

The Student's Book pack

The *Student's Book* pack offers a blend of classroom teaching and self-study, with an emphasis on flexibility and time-efficiency. Each of the sixteen *Student's Book* units provides around four hours of classroom material with the potential for two to three hours of additional study using other components in the package.

There are no long reading texts in the units, and with an emphasis on listening and speaking, written exercises are kept to a minimum. Instead, students are directed to the *Practice file* at the back of the book; here they will find exercises which can be used as supplementary material in class or for homework, as well as more extensive grammar notes.

Encourage your students to look at and use the *Interactive Workbook* on CD-ROM – there are cross-references at appropriate points in each unit. Here they will find a range of self-study material to help them review, consolidate and extend their learning.

Writing is a feature of the course, but is not part of the main *Student's Book* units. The *Interactive Workbook* has an email writing section with exercises and model emails related to the content of every unit. There is also a writing file on the *Business Result* website.

Key features of a unit

Each unit has three main sections – *Working with words, Business communication skills* and *Language at work* – dealing with core vocabulary associated with the unit theme, key functional expressions and related grammar. Each main section ends with a short fluency task to enable students to personalize the target language. Each unit ends with a *Case study.*

Unit menu

This lists the key learning objectives of the unit.

Starting point

Each unit opens with some lead-in questions to raise awareness of and interest in the unit theme. Use these questions to help you to establish what students already know about the topic and how it relates to their own working lives. They can usually be discussed as a class or in small groups.

Working with words

This first main section introduces key vocabulary in a variety of ways, including authentic reading texts, listenings and visuals. Students are also encouraged to look at how different forms of words (verbs, adjectives and nouns) can be built from the same root, or find common collocates that will help them to expand their personal lexicon more rapidly. This section also offers opportunities to work on your students' reading and listening skills. There is a glossary of all target lexis, plus other reference vocabulary, on the *Interactive Workbook* in both PDF and interactive formats.

Business communication skills

This section focuses on one of four broad communication themes – meetings, presenting, exchanging information and socializing. These are treated differently throughout the book so that, for example, students are able to practise exchanging information on the phone as well as face-to-face, or compare the different language needed for giving formal and informal presentations. Typically, the section begins with students listening to an example situation (a meeting, a presentation, a social encounter, a series of phone calls). They focus on *Key expressions* used by the speakers which are listed on the page. They are then given the opportunity to practise these in various controlled and more open work-related tasks.

Practically speaking

This section looks at various useful aspects of everyday communication from a 'how to' perspective. It covers some of the more informal, but very practical aspects of social interaction in the workplace – for example, catching up with colleagues, reassuring and sympathizing or making people feel relaxed.

Language at work

This section focuses on the key grammar underpinning the communication skills section that precedes it. The grammar is reviewed from a communicative point of view; this will meet your students' expectations with regard to learning form and meaning, but also reminds them how the grammar they need to learn commonly occurs in business and work situations. Grammar is taught at this later stage of the unit in order to link it meaningfully to the previously taught vocabulary and phrases.

Case studies

All units end with a *Case study*. This gives students an opportunity to recycle the language from the unit, demonstrate progress and use their knowledge and ideas to resolve an authentic problem or issue. The *Case studies* have been compiled using authentic content and the contexts connect with the unit theme. The content is accessible, and preparation time is minimized by including only as much information as can be assimilated relatively quickly in class. Even so, you may wish to optimize classroom time even further by asking students to read the background material before the lesson.

The *Case studies* follow a three-part structure.

Background – a short text (or texts) about a real company, product or related situation.

Discussion – two or three discussion questions on key issues arising from the background information and associated issues, providing a natural bridge to the task.

Task – a discussion, meeting simulation, or series of tasks, aimed at resolving a core issue related to the case and providing extended practice of the target language of the unit.

Tips

Commonly confused language or language points which may cause difficulty are anticipated by short, practical tips.

Additional material

At the back of the *Student's Book*, you will find the following sections.

Practice file

This provides unit-by-unit support for your classroom work. Each file provides additional practice of target language from the three main unit sections, *Working with words, Business communication skills* and *Language at work*. This can be used in two ways:

For extra practice in class – refer students to this section for more controlled practice of new vocabulary, key expressions or grammar before moving to the next stage. The optimum point at which to do this is indicated by cross-references in the *Student's Book* unit and the teaching notes in this book.

For self-study – students can complete and self-check the exercises for review and revision outside class.

Answers for the *Practice file* appear on pages 123–127 of this book, and on the *Interactive Workbook*.

Information files

Additional information for pair work, group activities and case studies.

Useful phrases

Lists of phrases relating to the *Practically speaking* sections.

Audio script

Interactive Workbook

This is a self-study component on CD-ROM. It contains

- interactive *Exercises* and *Tests* for each unit, with answers
- interactive *Email exercises*, plus a sample email for each unit
- interactive *Phrasebank* – students can create their own personalized 'Phrasebook'
- interactive *Glossary* for students to test their vocabulary
- reference *Glossary* in PDF format, both unit by unit and A–Z
- *Student's Book* grammar explanations in PDF format
- *Student's Book* Audio in MP3 format.

For additional practice material, refer your students to the website at **www.oup.com/elt/result**.

Teacher's book

What's in each unit?

Unit content

This provides an overview of the main aims and objectives of the unit.

Context

This section not only provides information on the teaching points covered in the unit, but also offers some background information on the main business theme of the unit. This will include reference to its importance in the current business world as well as a brief discussion of related issues, such as cross-cultural awareness or technology. If you are less familiar with the world of business, you will find this section especially helpful to read before starting a unit.

Teaching notes and answers

Notes on managing the *Student's Book* exercises and various activities are given throughout, with suggested variations that you might like to try. You will find comprehensive answers to all *Student's Book* exercises, as well as notes on possible responses to discussion questions.

Extension

With some students it may be appropriate to extend an exercise in some way or relate the language point more specifically to a particular group of students. Suggestions on how to do this are given where appropriate.

Extra activity

If you have time or would like to develop further areas of language competence, extra activities are suggested where they naturally follow the order of activities in the *Student's Book*. For example, the *Teacher's Book* may suggest additional comprehension tasks to provide more listening practice and exploit a particular listening activity more fully. Alternatively, if your students need to write emails, extra follow-up ideas are provided.

Alternative

With some students it may be preferable to approach an activity in a different way, depending on their level or their interests. These options are provided where appropriate.

Pronunciation

Tips on teaching pronunciation and helping students improve their intelligibility are provided where there is a logical need for them. These tips often appear where new vocabulary is taught or for making key expressions sound more natural and fluent.

Dictionary skills

It's helpful to encourage students to use a good dictionary in class and the relevant notes suggest moments in the lesson when it may be helpful to develop your students' skills in using dictionaries. They also offer ideas on how new language can be recorded by students appropriately in their notebooks.

Pre-work learners

Although most users of *Business Result* will be students who are already in work, you may also be teaching classes of students who have little or no experience of the business world. Where necessary, you may want to adapt certain questions or tasks in the book to their needs, and extra notes are given for these types of learners.

One-to-one

In general, you will find that *Business Result* can be used with any size of class. However, with one-to-one students you will find that activities which have been designed with groups of students in mind will need some adaptation. In this case, you may wish to follow the suggested alternatives given in this book.

Feedback focus

Throughout the course, students are involved in speaking activities using the new language. You will want to monitor, correct and suggest areas for improvement as well as acknowledging successes. During and after many of the freer practice activities it will be helpful to follow the guidelines in the teaching notes on what to monitor for and ways of giving feedback.

Watch out

This is a note to highlight any potentially problematic language points, with suggestions on how to pre-teach certain vocabulary or clear up misunderstandings.

Photocopiable tests (pages 88–119)

There are two types of test to accompany each unit. These can be administered at the end of each unit in order to assess your students' learning and allow you, the student or the head of training to keep track of their overall progress.

Progress test

Each of these sixteen tests check key vocabulary, key expressions and grammar for the unit. They provide a final score out of 30. Students will need between fifteen and twenty minutes to complete the test, although you can choose to set a time limit that would be appropriate for your students.

Speaking test

To help you assess communicative performance, students are given a speaking task that closely resembles one of the speaking activities in the unit. Students get a score out of a possible ten marks.

How to manage the speaking test

In most cases, the speaking test is set up as pair work. The pairs carry out two role-plays: Student A is assessed in the first, Student B in the second. The marking criteria require students to perform five functions in the conversation and it is advised that you make students familiar with these criteria beforehand. You can grade each of the five functions using a straightforward scoring system of 0, 1 or 2, giving a final score out of ten. This kind of test can be carried out during the class, perhaps while other students are taking the written progress test, or you can set aside a specific time for testing.

Note that if testing is not a priority, the role-plays can also be used as extra classroom practice without necessarily making use of the marking criteria.

Teacher's Book DVD

The *Teacher's Book* at each level of *Business Result* is accompanied by a *DVD* which demonstrates how sections from the *Student's Book* can be used with a typical group of students. It addresses key issues relevant to the level and looks at various classroom approaches. The *DVD* also includes commentary from teachers and one of the *Student's Book* authors, and addresses many of the questions that teachers have to ask themselves when starting a new business English course. The *Upper-intermediate DVD* uses sections from *Student's Book Unit 2* and *Unit 4*.

There are a number of different ways to use the *DVD*.

Orientation through the course

Watching the *DVD* is a fast way to familiarize yourself with the course – how the course is organized, its approach to business English and ways of using the material in the classroom.

Supporting new teachers

If this is your first time teaching business English, you will find the *DVD* especially helpful. It provides guidance, advice and tips on the difference between general English and business English, and suggests approaches to working with business English students.

Teacher development

You may be a more experienced teacher, in which case the *DVD* will address many issues you are already familiar with, but perhaps never have the opportunity to discuss with fellow professionals.

Teacher training

Directors of Studies or teacher trainers will be particularly interested in using the *DVD* as part of a complete teacher-training package. Each *DVD* forms the basis of a training session lasting approximately 45 minutes. You can use the *DVD* in different segments with ready-to-use worksheets (with *Answer key*) on pages 128–136 of this *Teacher's Book* and training notes that are available from the *Business Result* website (see below). Simply photocopy the worksheets and download the training notes to use in conjunction with the *DVD* in your staff training and development sessions. Note that *DVDs* at other levels of *Business Result* address different business English themes; together, the *DVDs* from the different levels form an entire training package in teaching business English. See the website for more information.

Teacher's website

The Teacher's website can be found at www.oup.com/elt/teacher /result. It contains a range of additional materials, including

- needs analysis form – for use at the start of the course
- downloadable diagnostic test
- progress test record
- course management & assessment tools
- DVD training notes
- wordlists
- additional activities
- writing file.

Using the course

How to use *Business Result*

From start to finish

You can, of course, use *Business Result* conventionally, starting at *Unit 1* and working your way through each unit in turn. If you do so, you will find it works well. Each section of the unit is related thematically to the others, there is a degree of recycling and a steady progression towards overall competence, culminating in the *Case study*. Timing will inevitably vary, but allow approximately four classroom hours for each unit. You will need more time if you intend to do the *Practice file* activities in class.

The 'fast-track' option

If you have less time, and wish to focus more on developing your students' communication skills, create a 'fast-track' course using the central section of each unit, *Business communication skills* and the *Case study*. This will still provide a coherent balance of input and output, and students will spend more of their time actively engaged in using the language. You should find with this option that each unit provides at least two hours of classroom material.

Include *Practically speaking* if you wish – allow approximately 20 to 30 minutes extra. If your students need grammatical support or revision, use as much of the *Language at work* section as you feel is appropriate, or refer students to the reference notes in the *Practice file*.

Mix and match

If your students have more specific needs and you would like to 'cherry pick' what you feel are the most interesting and relevant sections of the book, this approach should work well. You will find that all the sections are essentially free-standing, despite being thematically linked, and can be used independently of the rest of the unit. Mix and match sections across the book to create a course that is tailored to your students' needs.

The Expert View from Cranfield School of Management

Cranfield University School of Management is one of the world's leading business schools, and one of only a small number of schools worldwide designated as 'triple-accredited'. It offers a widely respected international MBA programme, as well as a range of MSc and Executive Development courses.

The partnership between OUP and Cranfield provides authentication for key aspects of the course material, particularly the *Case studies*. Each *Case study* is accompanied by a brief commentary on the topic or issue covered. These short texts are written by members of the School of Management academic staff, leading practitioners in their field, and in some cases by former course participants who work in international business. They offer insights and advice on the *Case study* theme. There is also an introductory section in the *Student's Book* which includes information about Cranfield and some biodata on the contributors.

Further information about Cranfield programmes can be found at: www.cranfield.ac.uk/som

1 | First impressions

Unit content

By the end of this unit, students will be able to
- talk about first impressions
- introduce themselves by email
- make a follow-up call
- arrange to meet a business contact
- exchange contact details
- talk about their work and company using the present simple and continuous.

Context

The topic of *First impressions* will relate to your students not only at an individual level, when one person meets another, but also at a company level, where a client gets an impression of the whole company.

Companies can use many 'instruments' as part of presenting a certain image, which are both tangible and intangible. The tangible physical factors include such things as business cards, brochures, publicity materials and even the premises from which the company operates. All will affect our view of the business. In addition, there are the intangible factors such as professionalism and reputation, and the warmth of our welcome in reception. Many of your students may even be learning English as part of the company's need for staff to be able to communicate confidently with overseas visitors and give a good impression.

With international settings, first impressions are affected by cultural differences; the impression one nationality or culture gains can be different to another so it's wise for a company to be culturally aware of the messages it is giving.

The first part of this unit opens up the discussion of giving good first impressions including the issue of culturally adapting websites to meet the needs of different local cultures. Students will then practise the necessary communication skill of meeting people for the first time and networking. If you are starting this unit on a new course with new students, you might want to exploit the context for students to get to know their peers. You can encourage students to work with different people in the classroom in order to achieve a sense of 'team spirit' and collaboration as quickly as possible.

Starting point

Discuss these two questions as a class. You could adapt or extend **2** by asking students to think of five words that describe the impression they think visitors and clients have of their company. You could also ask students how important they think the following are for first impressions.
- atmosphere of company / building
- relationship between colleagues and / or management and staff
- customer service
- company values
- efficiency

> ### Possible answers
> 1 Answers will vary, but students might say that the business is modern and forward-thinking, that it wants to create an impact and be noticed and that it values innovation.
> 2 Answers will vary, but students might say that first impressions range from professional, relaxed, friendly, formal or distant.

Extension

Ask students: *Do you give a different impression when speaking a foreign language?* This is a good moment, if it is the beginning of the course, to get students talking about how they use English and why it is important. Find out if they need English to improve the image of their company.

Pre-work learners

Students could consider what impressions they and others have of their school or college. Discuss what image the brochures and building give.

Working with words

1 Students quickly read the text to answer the two questions.

> ### Answers
> 1 No. A company's image is not based on a single factor but on the total impression created by a variety of factors.
> 2 the culture of clients or customers

Watch out! Students might ask about some vocabulary in the text. Note that most of the difficult vocabulary is dealt with in **3**. Deal with a question by giving a brief answer or asking another student to give a definition.

2 Students read the text again and can answer the questions in pairs. For question 3, refer students to the second half of the text and discuss whether they have similar examples to those of the Finns, Ghanaians and Qataris. Answers to question 4 will depend on how experienced your students are.

Answers

1 The text mentions business card, glossy brochure, fashionable display. Students might add publicity and advertising, reception area, meeting rooms, car parking, behaviour of staff, e.g. telephone manner and attitude to visitors.

2 'Intangibles' refers to those things which cannot be seen or touched. Added to those in the text, students might suggest areas such as attitude to staff development, the staff's approach to their work, level of corporate entertainment and attention to detail and quality.

3 Students match the words to the definitions and can compare answers in pairs.

Answers

1	extravagance	5	innovation
2	creativity	6	reputation
3	professionalism	7	principles
4	rapport	8	tradition

Pronunciation

Ask students to identify how many syllables are in each word in **3** and to mark the word stress. Drill the words as necessary.

Answers: _extravagance (4) creativity (5) professionalism (6) rapport (2) innovation (4) reputation (4) principles (3) tradition (3)._

4 Point out that the words in _italics_ complete phrases from the text, e.g. _project an image_. Students can refer to the text to check their answers. Draw students' attention to the fact that the words in 1–5 are common verb + noun combinations whereas 6 is a phrasal verb.

Answers

1	project	4	build
2	have	5	taken
3	creates	6	come

5 Students work in pairs and take turns to ask and answer the questions in **4**. Encourage them to use the nouns in **3** in their answers where possible.

Watch out! If this is the first lesson with a new class, don't assume all students will be familiar with working in pairs. You may need to set it up carefully and even explain the rationale.

Extra activity

01▷ In **6**, students need to listen and make notes on quite a lengthy listening. If students aren't confident with listening at this early stage of the course, write the following questions on the board and play the listening once. Students only need to listen for short answers (shown in brackets).

1 _Which markets do Western companies want to break into? (Asian)_
2 _What do these companies want Zhifu's help with? (websites)_
3 _Is it enough to translate a site? (no)_
4 _What is important to understand when designing a website? (local culture)_
5 _Where should you start the process of making a website for the Asian consumer? (from the beginning)_

6 01▷ Ask students to read the two questions before listening. If some of your students have international experience with websites or advertising, ask them to comment on what they think the answers might be in the listening.

Answers

1 Zhifu says that, as in traditional advertising, some things are more effective in some cultures than others.

2 Websites for Western consumers have lots of words and facts and are often quite complex. Websites for Asian consumers tend to be more simple, functional and less ostentatious. Asian consumers also prefer sites where you can bargain.

7 Students match the adjectives.

Answers

1	reliable: trustworthy	7	practical: functional
2	unsuccessful: ineffective	8	complicated: complex
3	showy: ostentatious	9	simple: modest
4	positive: favourable	10	effective: successful
5	costly: expensive	11	over confident: arrogant
6	mistrustful: suspicious	12	cautious: wary

Dictionary skills / Pronunciation

Students will find it helpful to use dictionaries for the task in **7**. If up to this level, your students have only used bilingual dictionaries, this may be a good moment to introduce them to monolingual dictionaries and show how they can be used for checking words. As an extra task, ask students to underline the word stress in each word (see _Answers_ above). Drill these words as necessary.

8 Students do the activity in pairs. Some of the answers for question 1 are quite clear. For example, *reliable* is universally a positive adjective. However, being *cautious* can be both positive and negative depending on the context and possibly the culture. Where students don't agree, discuss the word and its different uses.

> **Probable answers**
> **positive:** reliable, trustworthy, positive, favourable, practical, functional, simple, effective, successful
> **negative:** unsuccessful, ineffective, showy, costly, expensive, mistrustful, suspicious, over confident, arrogant
> **potentially both positive and negative:** ostentatious, complicated, complex, modest, cautious, wary

When students discuss questions 2 and 3, it may be helpful to have examples of websites to refer to. If you have access to computers in the classroom, students could show each other different websites. If students work for companies with websites or study at colleges with a site, they could assess the websites with their partner.

>> If students need more practice, go to **Practice file 1** on page 102 of the **Student's Book**.

9 After students have worked through each of the tasks, they can present their views and ideas to the rest of the class.

Pre-work learners

Most of the criteria in **9** will apply when discussing a place of study, so students should be able to discuss these with reference to their college.

ⓘ Refer students to the **Interactive Workbook Glossary** for further study.

Business communication skills

1 As a lead-in, discuss how much students use email at work. Brainstorm reasons why they send and receive emails. Ask them to look at the email to Mr McFee and say how formal it is. In terms of formality, how similar is it to the emails they send and receive? Note that emails can be seen as less formal than letters but the register here is normal for day-to-day business.

Students read the email and can compare their answers for 1–3 with a partner.

> **Answers**
> 1 from Sean's former colleague
> 2 to help with the renewal / design of a website
> 3 call or email to arrange a meeting

2 02▷ Students listen and answer the questions.

> **Answers**
> 1 It's a follow-up call to the email Sean sent to Ivan.
> 2 They arrange to meet to discuss things further.
> 3 Ivan is going to be in Berlin the day after tomorrow.

3 Students can work alone to match the phrases.

> **Answers**
> 1 a 2 c 3 e 4 b 5 f 6 d 7 g

4 02▷ Students listen out for the phrases to check their answers.

Watch out! Explain the meaning of *provisionally* (= for the present time, but it might change).

5 Students categorize the phrases. They can check their answers by referring to the *Key expressions* list.

> **Answers**
> a 1a, 4b   b 2c, 3e   c 5f, 6d, 7g

6 03▷ Students listen and answer the questions.

> **Answers**
> 1 Catherine, Ivan Formanek's assistant, is calling to confirm the meeting on the 13th.
> 2 She will email a map and directions.
> 3 public transport

Tip You could refer students to the use of *actually* here and compare it with *currently* (from audio 02▷).

7 03▷ Students listen and make a note of the phrases used.

> **Answers**
> 1 a Can you tell me how I get to Simply Speaking? Is it best by taxi or public transport?
>   b There's a train that leaves at 3 o'clock.
>   c Will I have time to catch that one (or should I take a later one)?
> 2 a Let me know where you're staying and I'll email you a map and directions from your hotel.
>   b Let me know if you need a taxi and I'll book one for you.

>> If students need more practice, go to **Practice file 1** on page 102 of the **Student's Book**.

Alternative

Note that some students may find it hard to listen and make a note of phrases without listening a number of times in exercises like **7**. To make things easier, students could find and underline the phrases in the *Audio script* or tick the phrases they hear in the *Key expressions* list.

8 Students work alone and prepare their email. Ask them to write the email on a piece of paper rather than in a notebook as they will exchange the email with a partner.

Pre-work learners

Students can think of a scenario in their private life or related to their studies. However, if they need help, suggest they imagine they work for a corporate training company. They write an email to a prospective client who might be interested in courses on presentation skills.

9 To help students to structure their calls, talk through each stage and elicit possible phrases to use. Make sure they are aware they can use the *Key expressions* list to help.

Feedback focus

Give feedback on correct or incorrect use of the phrases and how students structured their calls. At the end, students can comment on their calls and say where they felt they had particular difficulty or success.

(i) Refer students to the **Interactive Workbook Email** and **Phrasebank** sections for further study.

Practically speaking

1 04▷ As a lead-in, ask students how they prefer to exchange contact details, both personally and professionally. Students then listen and answer the questions.

> **Answers**
> **conversation 1:** 1 business card   2 phone
> **conversation 2:** 1 text   2 mobile / text
> **conversation 3:** 1 business card   2 email

2 Students listen again and categorize the phrases. They can check their answers in the *Useful phrases* on page 134.

> **Answers**
> **a** 3, 5   **b** 2, 6, 7   **c** 1   **d** 4

3 If students still don't know everyone in the class, they can use their own identity and details in this activity. However, you could also ask students to make notes on a new identity. They write a name, a number and an email. They could even prepare home numbers and emails as well as those for work. As an alternative, in their groups of four, they could talk in pairs and then change partners to give the contact details of the other person they were talking to.

Language at work

1 As a quick review of the two forms, ask students to read a–i and identify the tenses before answering 1–9.

> **Answers**
> **1** d **2** e **3** b **4** g **5** h **6** a **7** c **8** f **9** i

▶▶ If students need more practice, go to **Practice file 1** on page 103 of the **Student's Book**.

2 Students prepare questions for each of the areas. Make sure they use a variety of present simple and continuous forms.

> **Possible questions**
> Who do you work for?
> Which department do you work in?
> What are you responsible for?
> What are you working on at the moment?
> What's your typical day? / What do you do each day?
> What are you doing next week at work?
> How are your English studies going?
> Do you often use English for your job?

3 Students take turns to ask and answer the questions in **2**.

Feedback focus

The focus here should be on accuracy with the tenses both in terms of the questions asked and the responses.

4 Note that this question asks students to say which phrases they would *normally* expect to appear with the tenses. It's feasible that all of them could appear in present simple or a range of other tenses including the future, conditionals, past tense, etc.

> **Answers**
> **present simple:** generally speaking, on the whole, once a week, most of the time, every winter, once in a while, as a rule
> **present continuous:** for the moment, at the moment, for the time being, tomorrow afternoon, right now, currently

5 You might like to give a few examples from your own life to illustrate the activity. For example:
I'm teaching here for the moment.
Once a week I go to the cinema.

6 This activity gives students a chance to finally get to know everyone in the class and find out about each other's companies. Students will need a little time to prepare and then the presentations can be given to the rest of the class. Set a time limit of 1–2 minutes for each talk. At the end, if a presenter hasn't mentioned all the points listed, other students can ask questions to find out the answers or anything else they would like to know about the speaker.

Feedback focus

Listen and make notes on any problems with the tenses presented in **1**. Write any problematic sentences on the board and discuss and correct them.

ⓘ Refer students to the **Interactive Workbook Exercises and Tests** for revision.

Case study

Background

This *Case study* presents a networking organization which helps small companies to promote their business. The topic allows students to consider the advantages of this type of business networking. The *Task* enables students to practise the language of the unit within the context of forging new business relationships.

Allow a few minutes for students to read the text about BNI and be prepared to answer any questions about vocabulary, e.g. *forge* = make or develop.

Discussion

1, 2 Discuss the two questions as a class or in small groups.

> **Possible answer**
> **1** It provides a cheap and easy way of promoting a business; groups are local and regional so you are likely to meet customers in your geographical area and you don't have to spend too much time; there is opportunity for cross-promotion as other businesses, e.g. prospective suppliers, can be recommended.

Task

Students work in groups of four. Each student chooses a company in the *File* or you can allocate these to make sure each student has a different company.

1 Allow students time to read their information and prepare a 60-second speech.
2 After listening to all the speeches, each student decides which company they would like to forge a link with and why. You may have to intervene here so that each company has a potential partner. Note that there are some obvious ways in which some of the companies could collaborate. You should make notes on the effectiveness of the speeches but may wish to keep your comments until the end of the activity for feedback, when you can also comment on the follow-up calls.
3 Students now pair up with the student from their chosen company, e.g. Languages Today pairs up with Sitemagic.com. Students make their follow-up phone calls.
4 Students simulate a face-to-face meeting to discuss how they can help / promote each other's business.

Alternative

Divide the class into four groups and allocate a company to each group. The presentation is shared between all members of the group so everyone has a chance to say something. For the phone calls, each member of the group can pair up with a member of the chosen company (it doesn't matter if the outcome of the phone call is different from pair to pair). Groups should then reform back to their original 'company' group and meet with all the members of their chosen company to discuss how they can promote each other's business.

Variation

If many of your students are from different companies, they could use information about their own companies rather than referring to those in the *File*.

One-to-one

Your student can read the *Background* and then you can do the *Discussion* questions together. For the *Task*, refer to the *File*, but ask the student to read about Sitemagic.com and you will represent the translation company Languages Today. You should both make your 60-second speech in which it should be clear how the two companies could work together. Then have the telephone call in 3 and meet to discuss as in 4.

>> Unit 1 **Progress test** and **Speaking test**, pages 88–89

2 | Motivation

Unit content

By the end of this unit, students will be able to

- talk about motivation at work
- make small talk
- exit a conversation
- use questions forms.

Context

The topic of *Motivation* may apply to your students in different ways. For management, the issue is how to make staff work more effectively and find ways of ensuring they continue to give 100%. For staff, motivation may be a question of how much they are paid or what the perks and benefits of a job are.

However, what motivates us is more complex than simply money or bonuses. Psychologist and business management theorist Frederick Herzberg discovered that factors such as working conditions, salary, status and job security do not necessarily lead to higher levels of motivation, though without them there will be dissatisfaction. In fact, achievement, recognition, career advancement, job interest and satisfaction are the factors which will bring about staff motivation.

Since Herzberg's famous article on his findings *One More Time, How Do You Motivate Employees?*, other studies show that motivation is also affected by an employee's cultural background. For example, a recent study of motivation with Chinese workers showed that personal loyalty from the manager and organization was rated more highly than how interesting the work itself was. This was especially true of older workers. If you have a mixed-nationality class, this is perhaps an area you could explore and discuss.

While the first part of this unit deals with the language students will need to discuss motivation, the unit also prepares them for making small talk in social situations. To support this communication skill, there is a review of question forms within a social context. When students reach the *Case study*, they will need to think about the reasons for low staff morale and how to improve motivation in a realistic setting.

Starting point

Discuss the two questions as a class or students can work in pairs or small groups to decide what motivates them and what else could be added to the list. Some other possible things to add include: *bonuses, a company car, a pension, praise, travel, holidays, a good boss.*

Pre-work learners

Ask students what motivates them to study for their current qualification or what motivates them to learn English, e.g. *If I speak English, I'll get a better job with better pay and perhaps have the chance to travel ... .*

Extension

Ask the class to complete and discuss the following.
1 Put the list of things in **1** in order of importance from 1 to 8 (1= most important, 8 = least important).
2 Compare your results with the rest of the class.
3 What is the best reward / greatest incentive you have ever had at work?

Working with words

1 Allow time for students to think about their answers to these questions and then discuss as a class.

> **Answers**
> 1 'A reward' in business often refers to something financial though it can mean anything you receive because of something you have done. 'An incentive' refers to something that makes you want to work harder. This may be a cash reward or perk of some kind but the incentive could also be wanting to please someone or to make the company more successful.
> 2 Answers will vary according to students' jobs and types of business.

2 Allow students about two minutes to read.

> **Answer**
> The text is negative about cash incentive schemes but is positive about incentive schemes which offer non-cash rewards.

3 Students read again and can compare answers to questions 1–3 in pairs. Discuss the final question as a class.

> **Answers**
> 1 They help companies achieve their goals by improving performance, boosting staff morale and fostering company loyalty.
> 2 They give employees real symbols of achievement which can be shown to others and are a 'guilt-free reward'. They are seen as having a greater value and can benefit the employee's family.
> 3 They can just 'disappear' or be spent on paying bills (so mean less than non-cash rewards).

4 Students find the words in the text to match the definitions.

Answers
1 motivate staff
2 achievement
3 boost staff morale
4 recognition
5 improve performance
6 incentive schemes
7 benefit
8 non-cash incentives
9 foster company loyalty
10 annual bonuses

5 05▷ Write the table frame from *Answers* below on the board for students to copy. When they listen, they can use it to make notes and you can write their answers on the board afterwards.

Answers

	Claudia	Peter	Macie
Job	sales rep selling soap, shampoo and toiletries	manager of a car dealership	flight attendant
Benefits / rewards / incentives	BlackBerry and laptop, company car, commission of 15%, merchandise, vouchers, social events	sales competition with prizes, reward vouchers (hot-air balloon trip, spa treatment), special trips, training / staff development, staff discount	reduced fares for the family, compensation plan (profit-sharing scheme, non-contributory pension plan, medical insurance), attendance rewards, on-time bonuses
Other factors	meeting new people, travel, autonomy, being acknowledged and recognized for achievements	positive feedback, praise	travel and seeing different countries on long-haul flights, senior management comes round and thanks staff personally

6 Before starting, check students understand the difference between *material* and *non-material* benefits:
material = you can see / touch them
(e.g. money, possessions)
non-material = you can't see / touch them
(e.g. good feelings).

Answers
1 company car, commission, staff discount, attendance reward, on-time bonus, compensation plan, private medical insurance, non-contributory pension plan
2 autonomy, feel valued, be acknowledged, appreciation, positive feedback, (personal) development, praise, satisfaction

Dictionary skills

There are a number of words / phrases in this list or in the listening that may cause students difficulty and they will find it useful to use a dictionary. As a starting point, ask them to look up the following words and identify what type of word they are (adjective or noun).

commission (noun), compensation (noun), contributory (adjective), fulfilment (noun), autonomy (noun), acknowledged (adjective)

You could also ask students to find other forms of the words, e.g. *to compensate, to contribute, to fulfil, to acknowledge.*

Pronunciation

Students can also check which syllable is stressed in these words.

Answers: *commission, compensation, contributory, fulfilment, autonomy, acknowledged.*

7 Be aware, when you set up this activity, that if your class contains employees from the same company with different employment contracts, some students may feel uncomfortable about discussing contracts. Remind students that they should discuss only what is the standard norm in their own countries and not be specific about details.

Pre-work learners

You may wish to miss out **7** with these learners though they should be able to discuss question 3 with reference to their future choice of career.

» If students need more practice, go to **Practice file 2** on page 104 the **Student's Book**.

8 Allow about 15–20 minutes to complete this activity. Make sure groups nominate someone to take notes on their ideas so they can present them to the class at the end.

Feedback focus

As you listen to the discussion in **8** or the presentation of each group's decisions at the end, make notes on any incorrect usage or pronunciation of the vocabulary in the section. Set aside a few minutes afterwards to draw attention to meaning or use and drill any difficult pronunciation.

ⓘ Refer students to the **Interactive Workbook Glossary** for further study.

Business communication skills

1 As a lead-in, ask students to close their books and work alone for a couple of minutes. They should write three tips for a business traveller who is meeting colleagues or clients in their country for the first time. The tips could refer to conversation, dress, customs and formalities. Students can compare their tips in pairs. Then ask them to read the small talk text in the *Student's Book* and see if it contains any similar ideas to their own.

Students discuss each tip in the text and try to reach final agreement on which five are the most useful. With a mixed-nationality class, this activity should raise many cultural issues relating to what is / isn't appropriate when making small talk. For example, tip 1 suggests that using first names (*Hi, I'm Jules …*) is acceptable. In some cultures this may not be the case.

2 06▷ Students answer the two questions for each conversation.

> **Answers**
> **conversation 1: 1** The first speaker uses a number of the tips including 1, 3, 9 and 10.   **2** The conversation fails because the second speaker answers briefly and makes no effort to develop the conversation (tip 6).
> **conversation 2: 1** Both speakers follow a number of the tips including 2 (repeating names) and 5 (flowing conversation). **2** The conversation is successful because of this.
> **conversation 3: 1** This conversation is a good example of two people finding a shared experience (tip 4) and tips 1, 5, 6 are used.   **2** The conversation is successful because of this.
> **conversation 4: 1** Adam quickly starts describing problems and reasons for being depressed (tip 8).   **2** The conversation is unsuccessful because of this and Adriana quickly uses an exit strategy.

3 06▷ Allow time for students to read questions 1–8 before listening. Note that listening and writing out phrases can take time, so students may need to hear the conversations more than once (also see *Alternative* on page 11).

> **Answers**
> 1 Hello, I saw you … but I didn't have a chance to speak to you. I'm Harry.
> 2 Well, it's been nice talking to you. / You don't mind if I go and get myself a coffee? / See you later.
> 3 Hi, I don't think we've met. I'm Paolo from …
> 4 Hi, nice to meet you. I'm Sonia from …
> 5 That's amazing! / What a coincidence!
> 6 Good evening … / How lovely to see you here.
> 7 She responds by saying: Oh dear. / Oh, I'm so sorry to hear that.
> 8 Look, I have to go … / Catch you later.

Extra activity

06▷ Play the listening again and ask students to write down any more phrases (other than those in **3**) they think are useful for making small talk. Alternatively, ask them to underline the phrases in the *Audio script* at the back of the book.

4 07▷ Students listen out for and number the phrases. Discuss how these phrases help the conversation flow. Note that some show interest or surprise (*What a coincidence! / Really?*), some are asking questions (*Don't you … / … by the way?*) and others link information and ideas (*So … / In fact … / Apparently …*).

> **Answers**
> **a** 5 **b** 1 **c** 7 **d** 3 **e** 4 **f** 6 **g** 10 **h** 12 **i** 2
> **j** 9 **k** 11 **l** 8

Tip Refer students to the use of *well* and *so*. To illustrate how these words are used, you could play audio **07**▷ again as the speakers use them.

>> If students need more practice, go to **Practice file 2** on page 104 the **Student's Book**.

5 Students work on improving conversations 1 and 4 which are unsuccessful. In conversation 1, Alessandro only uses short answers and doesn't try to extend the dialogue. One way to solve this would be to give extra information, ask questions and show interest. In conversation 4, Adam goes into too much detail about problems and doesn't ask anything about Adriana.

6 This is free practice, with students starting and maintaining a conversation. To add realism to the task, ask students to stand as if at a conference. With large classes, you could suggest that when students feel they have finished a conversation with one partner, they should use an exit strategy to end the conversation and move on to another person.

Feedback focus

Give feedback on phrases used during the conversation in **6**. If you have video equipment, you could record the students' conversations and afterwards comment on appropriate body language as well as conversation content. If students have difficulty with exit strategies, note that this skill is dealt with in *Practically speaking*.

(i) Refer students to the **Interactive Workbook Email** and **Phrasebank** sections for further study.

Practically speaking

1 08▷ Allow time for students to read 1–5. Elicit any follow-up phrases they think would make the phrases more acceptable. Then play the listening for students to make a note of the phrases actually used.

> **Answers**
> **1** My parking ticket runs out in five minutes.
> **2** But I'll come back when I've seen them.
> **3** I missed lunch because of the conference call.
> **4** Excuse me, I really must go and speak to him.
> **5** I'll call you tomorrow though.

2 Students look at the four situations in the *File* and choose two each. Before role-playing the situations, they could discuss appropriate phrases to use in each case and then try using them at the end of their small talk. The *Useful phrases* at the back of the book will be helpful to refer to.

Language at work

Extra activity

06, 07▷ Ask students to close their books. Play the listenings again, and ask students to note down any questions they hear. Students could work in pairs to do this with each of them listening, writing and working together afterwards to try and make a list of ten questions. They then compare their answers with the list of questions at the beginning of this section.

---

1 Students read the questions and categorize them.

> **Possible answers**
> **1** h, i **2** a, c, d, e, g **3** b, d, f, h **4** f

Tip Students will find it useful to refer to the *Tip* on question use here. You could ask them to suggest some example questions for each use.

2 This is intended as a review of how to make questions. You may wish to write the structures on the board (see *Answers*) or refer students to the language notes in *Practice file 2*. Use question 2 to draw attention to the difference between subject and object questions and note that questions tags are looked at in further detail in **4**.

> **Answers**
> **1** ***Wh-* questions**
> Subject questions: *Wh-* + main verb + object = *Who told you?*
> Object questions: *Wh-* + auxiliary verb + subject + main verb = *Who did you come with?*
> ***Yes / No* questions**
> *Do* + subject + main verb + object = *Do you live in Italy?*
> Auxiliary + subject + main verb + object = *Have you spent much time in India?*
> **2** subject – g; object – c
> **3** by using rising intonation at the end of the sentence to make it a question
> **4** These questions make use of question tags and the expected answer is *yes*.

>> If students need more practice, go to **Practice file 2** on page 105 the **Student's Book**.

3 Students prepare questions and can compare them with the rest of the class afterwards.

> **Possible answers**
> **1** What time does my flight leave? / What kind of hotel am I staying in? / Whereabouts in the city is it?
> **2** So, it's €200? / Delivery is 5 days, is that true? / Did you say there'll be a delivery charge of €8? / The guarantee's a year, isn't it?
> **3** You went to my college?
> **4** Are you here for an interview? / Have you done this kind of job before?

Extra activity

As students tell the class their ideas for questions, you could write them on the board and make any necessary corrections. Then students work in pairs and practise using the questions on the board in mini role-plays based on the four situations in **3**.

---

4 Before you start, check or introduce the basic rules for question tags (see the language notes in *Practice file 2*). Draw students' attention to the example dialogue. Note that if the first verb is positive, the question tag is negative and vice versa.

Watch out! Note that questions tags are typically used by native speakers. Students at this level may have met them before, but usually find it hard to produce them when speaking.

> **Possible answers**
> 1 That wasn't …, **was it**?
> 2 The negotiations have been …, **haven't they**?
> 3 The manager was …, **wasn't he**?
> 4 The meeting won't …, **will it**?
> 5 Emily's looking …, **isn't she**?
> 6 You're going …, **aren't you**?
> 7 Ken can't …, **can he**?
> 8 Nobody got …, **did they**?

Pronunciation

Note that we often use question tags to check and confirm. In this case, the intonation will fall:

That wasn't a very interesting presentation, was it?

However, if rising intonation is used over the tag, this indicates the speaker is less certain of what the answer is:

The meeting won't finish late, will it?

It is probably more important that your students can recognize this difference rather than produce it. However, to practise using the intonation patterns, you can drill sentences 1–8 in **4** with their tags and practise the falling intonation, and then drill again with rising intonation.

5 Students use the *File* to have two conversations. They will need time beforehand to prepare their questions.

Feedback focus

Monitor for and give feedback on correct question forms. With stronger groups, you could also comment on the use of appropriate intonation with question tags.

ⓘ Refer students to the **Interactive Workbook Exercises and Tests** for revision.

Case study

Background

This *Case study* presents a situation where a company is experiencing staffing problems and needs to find ways to increase motivation. The topic allows students to consider the reasons for low staff morale and lack of motivation. The *Task* enables them to practise some of the language in the unit within the context of devising a plan of action to solve the company's staffing problems.

Allow a few minutes for students to read the text about Palmate Hellas and be prepared to answer any questions about vocabulary.

Discussion

1, 2, 3 Students discuss these questions as a class or in small groups. The questions will revisit some of the issues at the beginning of the unit.

> **Possible answers**
> 1 Reasons may include: low pay, poor working conditions, lack of feedback and praise, no rewards or incentives, no prospect for promotion.
> 2 In the case of Palmate Hellas, the HR Department is advisory so departments are not following guidelines for motivating staff. This suggests that it is important. (Students may be able to describe any guidelines at their company.)
> 3 Low priority is given to personal development of staff, and hours are fixed (no opportunity for flexible working).

Task

Put students in groups of four and give each student a letter, A–D. Students turn to the relevant *Files*.

1 Allow some time for reading the information. Students also need to think of questions to ask each other based on the table.
2 While listening to each other answer questions, students complete the table.
3, 4 The group discussion and drafting should last about twenty minutes. Groups could formally present to the rest of the class or two groups could work together to compare ideas. The class (or two groups) should decide on the five best ideas for Palmate Hellas. Feedback can be given on the effectiveness of the presentations.
5 Students compare their ideas with the real solution.

One-to-one

Your student can read the *Background* and then you can do the *Discussion* questions together. Next, the student can complete the table in stage 2 of the *Task* by reading each of the *Files* alone. When the table is complete, discuss ways to solve the staffing problems together.

❯❯ Unit 2 **Progress test** and **Speaking test**, pages 90–91

3 | On schedule

Unit content

By the end of this unit, students will be able to

- talk about managing projects
- ask for and give an update in a meeting
- make and respond to suggestions
- catch up with colleagues
- update on current projects using the present perfect and past simple.

Context

It is often said that management is based on four stages: assess, plan, do and evaluate. This is certainly true of managing projects. Many projects fail or come up against problems because most emphasis is placed on the 'doing' stage – carrying out the tasks required to complete a project. However, experienced project managers know that equal importance should also be given to the stages before and after in order to ensure project success.

Assessing what is required, followed by a period of planning, will let a manager know how many people, what expertise and how much money will be needed. Afterwards, the manager needs to evaluate how effective the work has been before possibly proceeding to the next part of the project.

Not all of your students will necessarily be managers and they won't always be in charge of major projects, but much of their work will include completing minor projects or being involved in the process. They will also be used to working in teams and collaborating on projects, perhaps with companies in other countries.

The first part of this unit looks at some of the problems relating to managing projects and presents vocabulary for discussing the progress of projects. Students move on to develop their skills in meetings and focus on the language for giving an update on progress. The *Language at work* section focuses on the key grammar used for talking about the recent past and giving updates. The *Case study* allows students to practise the language of the unit within the context of project scheduling.

Starting point

The issues relating to these questions are explored in more detail in *Working with words*, so the discussion at this stage can be general and help students think about how the topic relates to them. For **3** and **4**, encourage students to tell the class about any projects they are currently involved in. If they don't work, they could describe projects in their home life such as redecorating the house or planning a wedding.

Possible responses

1 Key factors may include staff, budget, planning, expertise, realistic aims.
2 A project can be completed on time and within the budget. On the other hand, it might run over schedule or require extra money.

Working with words

1 Students can work in pairs or small groups to brainstorm their ideas. Write up a list on the board before comparing students' ideas with those in the text.

2 Students discuss and think of possible solutions for each of the five problems. Again, make a list of the ideas on the board. These can then be compared to the ideas in the text in **3**.

3 Students match the solutions to the problems. Afterwards, discuss the solutions and see how they compare with everyone's suggestions in **2**.

Answers
1 C   2 A   3 D   4 E   5 B

Extra activity

The texts in **1** and **3** both contain a number of useful words which students may not be familiar with. As an extra vocabulary activity, write these definitions on the board and ask students to find the words in the two texts (shown in brackets).

1 *shortage or not enough (lack)*
2 *very important (vital)*
3 *when things stop or don't work effectively (breakdowns)*
4 *a fixed amount of money for something (budget)*
5 *ideas or plans in case something goes wrong (contingency plans)*
6 *the opinion people have about you or your company (reputation)*
7 *correct and precise (accurate)*
8 *prediction or plan for the future (forecast)*
9 *the planned direction (track)*

4 Students categorize the phrases and can compare with their partner to check they agree. Note that *budget constraints* is the main phrase which could be both. For someone in finance, a project with budget constraints is more likely to be successful. However, someone on the project might see the constraints as a cause of lack of success.

Pronunciation

Ask students to underline the word stress in these words from **4**.

> un*rea*lis*tic*, *bud*get, *sched*ule, *ac*curate, *fore*cast, *plan*ning, con*straints*, *dead*line

5 The verbs in this activity form verb + noun collocations which appear in the earlier texts.

Answers
1 resolve	4 allocate
2 prioritize	5 make
3 keep	6 check

6 Students can do this in pairs.

Answers
1 run	4 set
2 stay	5 keep
3 check	

Extra activity

To extend practice of verbs and collocates, write these verbs on the board: *take, spend, make, monitor, finish*. Ask students to find phrases with these verbs in the text in **3**.
> Answers: *make sure, take time, spend longer, make it to market, monitor performance, finish ahead of schedule*.
Then ask students to think of two more words or phrases that will collocate with the verbs.

Dictionary skills

A good dictionary will supply more information with these verbs and many of the collocations in **4–6** will appear. Students could be encouraged to use the dictionary to find and check their answers.

» If students need more practice, go to **Practice file 3** on page 106 of the **Student's Book**.

7 Students read about the project in the *File* and discuss it in pairs. They should make a list of what went right and wrong before making some suggestions for better management. For example, the cost of the work was over budget and it was completed behind schedule, and checking details carefully would help in future.

8 Based on all the ideas and discussion in this section, groups make a list of key factors for managing a successful project. Make sure they use the vocabulary from the section in their presentations.

Feedback focus

Make notes on any difficulties in **7** and **8**, and then conclude this section with feedback on pronunciation and use of the words and phrases.

ⓘ Refer students to the **Interactive Workbook Glossary** for further study.

Business communication skills

1 As a lead-in, ask students to work in pairs. They have two minutes to list all the features on their mobile phones, e.g. texting, games, Internet, etc. See which pair has the longest list. Next, give them another two minutes to think of new features they would like manufacturers to add to their mobiles. Collect their ideas for a 'super mobile' on the board.

09▷ Students read the *Context* to understand the background for the listening. Also allow time to study the agenda for the meeting. Expect to play the listening twice.

Answers
2 has a realistic schedule and extra time has been planned
3 booked two weeks ago
4 already received offers, most within budget, final choice not made yet
5 problem with handset battery life – can run out in six hours
6 may have to reschedule

2 09▷ After students have listened and done 1–3, they can compare their answers with the *Key expressions* list. Note that a number of the phrases include the present perfect tense, which is dealt with later in this unit.

Answers

1 How are things with …? / How's the … coming along? / How far are you with …? / How does your side of things look?
2 So what do you mean exactly? / So what you're saying is …? / So the real problem lies with …?
3 Up to now … / We've set … / We're on track. / He booked the venue two weeks ago. / I've already … / I haven't made a final choice yet. / Things aren't running as smoothly as I'd hoped. / We've hit a problem with …

Tip Refer students to the *Tip* about the word *things* at this stage since it appears in three of these phrases.

3 10▷ Explain to students that they are going to hear the later part of the meeting. Students listen and answer the questions.

Answers

1 It wouldn't help meet the deadlines.
2 Their reputation is at stake.
3 They will look at what they can reschedule.

Watch out! You may have to explain the phrase in 2. *Their reputation is at stake* means that not saying anything about the poor battery life may affect the good opinion that customers have of the company or brand.

4 10▷ Students listen for the phrases to complete the suggestions. You will probably need to play the listening again for students to note the responses. Note that these responses are negative or show reluctance.

Answers

1 a How about finding
   b We could
   c Why don't we wait
   d would be my proposal
   e If you ask me, we should
2 a I don't think that would help us …
   b That's possible, but …
   c That's not an ideal solution.
   d I'm not convinced.
   e I suppose so.

» If students need more practice, go to **Practice file 3** on page 106 of the Student's Book.

5 Students will need some time to study their 'To do' lists and notes before making their call. They are going to ask each other for an update on each item on the list as well as make and respond to suggestions. Encourage them to use as many of the phrases for asking for / giving an update as possible.

Afterwards, ask each pair to report back on what action is still required.

Feedback focus

Make notes as students role-play the situation and give feedback on correct use of the phrases.

ⓘ Refer students to the **Interactive Workbook Email** and **Phrasebank** sections for further study.

Practically speaking

Watch out! Check that students understand the term *catching up* (= getting recent news).

1 11▷ As a lead-in, ask students what they usually 'catch up on' when they haven't seen a friend or colleague for a while. Students then listen and make notes on what is being discussed in each conversation.

Answers

1 free-time activities
2 their jobs (the second speaker has a new job)
3 holidays
4 whether they still work for the same company

2 11▷ Students listen for any key questions and the speakers' answers. It might be helpful to write the questions on the board as students say them in order to refer to them during the activity in **3**.

Answers

1 and **2**

conversation 1: What are you doing at the moment? (I'm learning Mandarin …) / What about you? Are you still playing golf? (Yes, I am. But I don't play as much as I used to.)
conversation 2: How's the new job going? (It's going well, thanks. I'm really enjoying it.) / How are things with you? (Oh, fine.)
conversation 3: Have you been away recently? (I've just come back from a long weekend …) / How about you? (No, I haven't been on holiday for ages.) / Have you booked any holiday? (Not yet. It's difficult to find the time. I'm always so busy.)
conversation 4: Do you still work for the same company? (Yes, and we're really busy.) / Are you still enjoying it? (Yes, definitely. It's always different. And it keeps me on my toes.)

Alternative

In **2**, students are expected to identify quite a lot of phrases. To shorten the task, ask students to listen while looking at the *Useful phrases* on page 134. They can tick the phrases they hear in the listening.

3 Help students prepare for this activity by asking them to organize their ideas in three columns.

Things you do now	Things you have done recently	Things you used to do

When they have two or three ideas in each column, they can begin. They can repeat the activity two or three times with different partners.

Feedback focus

Note that students will need to use the present simple, present continuous, present perfect and past simple in their questions and answers so you could focus on these tenses. Write any mistakes on the board and talk through the problems. This will also provide a useful lead-in to the *Language at work* section which follows.

Language at work

1 As a quick lead-in, ask students to identify the tenses in extracts a–f (present perfect: a, b, d and e; past simple: c and f).

The aim of this activity is to help students analyse the differences in meaning and use of the two forms in extracts a–f.

> **Answers**
> **1** b, d   **2** c, f   **3** a, e   **4** already   **5** yet

2 When deciding which time expressions can be used with each tense, students will find it easier to make complete sentences with the expressions to test their ideas. Also, refer them back to extracts a–f to note the time expressions used. Students could work in pairs to do this activity so that they discuss the differences in meaning.

> **Answers**
> **1** last week, a couple of weeks ago, yesterday
> **2** up to now, so far (this week), since our last meeting, to date, just, over the last few months
> **3** The expressions *today* and *this morning* could work with either. The past simple will refer to a finished action: *We spoke this morning.* We could also use the present perfect if the action has occurred this morning or today and it is still recent: *We've worked on it this morning* (and it is still the morning or very recent).
> *in the last month* could also be used with either. If you are talking on the 30th of the month, you might say *In the last month we've sold 12,000 units*. However, if the month is in the past, we would use the past tense: *2004 was an excellent year, and in the last month we sold 20,000 units.*

3 Students study their *Files* and take turns to ask and answer questions about their progress on the project.

Feedback focus

Give feedback on students' use of the two tenses immediately after this role-play as they will need to use the present perfect or past simple again in the next activity.

4 Students read about the context in the *File* and then decide which items on the 'To do' lists have or haven't been done. When they are ready, they take turns to ask and answer.

Extra activity

To provide some consolidation of the grammar point and some writing practice, ask students to write an email to their colleague giving an update on what has been done on the 'To do' list.

5 Students makes a list of what goals / plans they have or haven't achieved and any details such as why / why not. Note that these goals might be related to personal plans as well as work.

Pre-work learners

Students can think of goals or plans such as deadlines for handing in assignments at college or perhaps taking up a new sport or hobby.

(i) Refer students to the **Interactive Workbook Exercises and Tests** for revision.

Case study

Background

This *Case study* presents a global company which runs investor 'road shows' to update investors on how the company is performing. The topic allows students both to consider how keeping investors informed can build up a relationship of trust and to think about how road shows are organized. The *Task* enables them to practise the language of scheduling, updating and prioritizing within the context of organizing a series of road shows.

Allow a few minutes for students to read the text about Wolters Kluwer and be prepared to answer any questions about vocabulary. Check that they understand basically what Wolters Kluwer does and what a 'road show' is (representatives from the company travel to different cities to give presentations about the company). Ask students if their company gives up-to-date information to its clients and investors and if so, how it does this.

Discussion

1, 2 Discuss these questions in small groups or as a class.

> **Possible answers**
> 1 By sending out regular information, big companies give the impression they are not hiding anything and are being transparent. This in return builds trust.
> 2 The following tasks may be involved: decide suitable dates and destination for each road show, choose and invite investors, book venues for presentations including catering, arrange travel and accommodation.

Task

1 Students can work in groups of three to six. Appoint one student in each group to chair the meeting or 'be in charge' and ask another student to act as secretary to write down any decisions. The group works through each of the stages of the WK guidelines and draws up a list of tasks. This might include, for example, making phone calls, researching names of investors from the Internet or emailing hotels. Once these mini-lists have been written, the group needs to create a schedule over eight weeks. Remember that some tasks will need to be completed before others can begin. Finally, all the tasks can be allocated. Write the name of each person on the schedule so the group knows who is doing what. The meeting can end with the secretary summarizing the key points from his / her notes. It may even be helpful to have these photocopied for everyone.

2 In this stage, students work alone and imagine they have either done or not done the tasks allocated. Students can tick any tasks done and then should think of reasons (or excuses) why two tasks have been delayed.

3 The groups from **1** come back together to hold a meeting. Each student gives an update on what has been done and which two tasks have been delayed. The delays will cause problems for other students so the group needs to make suggestions to resolve any delays. At the end, each group should be able to summarize their revised schedule. Follow this up with any feedback, with particular reference to any problems with the present perfect or past simple.

One-to-one

Read the text on Wolters Kluwer and do the *Discussion* questions. You could work through **1** in the *Task* together and allocate tasks between the two of you. Then each of you works alone and decides which tasks have not been done (as in **2**) before giving an update to each other (as in **3**).

» Unit 3 **Progress test** and **Speaking test**, pages 92–93

4 | New ideas

Unit content

By the end of this unit, students will be able to

- talk about ideas and innovations
- present an idea, product or service
- thank and respond
- talk about present, past and future ability.

Context

Not all your students will necessarily think of themselves as innovators. Many people link the topic 'new ideas and innovation' to those who 'invent'. But while inventions require innovation, all businesses will flourish with staff who are innovative in their thinking.

New ideas and innovation have taken on even greater importance in recent years with the growth in fields such as software development, design and marketing. Companies like Microsoft or Apple have become global giants through their attention to innovation. Steve Jobs, the charismatic CEO of Apple, explains that his company's success with products such as the iconic iPod music player has come about by 'saying no to 1,000 things' (*The Seed of Apple's Innovation*, *Business Week*, 12 October 2004). In other words, innovation requires many ideas before arriving at the best, so companies with a culture of welcoming any new idea, however crazy, are more likely to succeed than those that don't.

The first part of this unit presents language for talking about ideas and innovation before moving on to the language for presenting new ideas, products and services in the context of a formal presentation. This is supported by a language section on talking about ability which will allow students to describe and discuss changes in technology, systems and ways of working. The *Case study* offers students the chance to produce and present their own new product ideas and convince investors of their value.

Starting point

Discuss the first question as a class and establish the difference between 'invention' and 'innovation'. It might be better to allow students to think about and discuss **2** and **3** in pairs before feeding back their comments to the class.

> **Answer**
> 1 'Invention' usually refers to a machine or new system. 'Innovation' refers to both inventions and new ideas or concepts.

Extension / Alternative

If students have trouble thinking of inventions in **2**, write these things on the board and ask students to work in groups of three to put them in order of importance (1 = most, 5 = least).

> *jumbo jet, mobile phones, computers, coca-cola, make-up*

Each group presents their view to the class and argues their case.

Working with words

1 Students will find the answers to 1–3 in the text. The picture in the text, and the one with **6**, will help them understand the concept in question 3. You can point out that sustainable energy tends to use energy produced by clean technologies, e.g. solar power. Question 4 can be discussed as a class. Draw students' attention to the way in which the Ashden Awards encourages people to be innovative.

> **Answers**
> 1 The charity rewards and promotes sustainable energy solutions in the UK and developing countries. It aims to raise international awareness of the benefits of sustainable energy in order to deal with climate change and improve the quality of people's lives. It also aims to encourage more people around the world to find new ways of meeting energy needs and to change the thinking and policy among governments and non-governmental organizations (NGOs).
> 2 It gives cash prizes, publicizes the winners in order to encourage others to follow their example and brings together the winners and main decision-makers of governments and organizations.
> 3 The use of local, renewable energy sources, e.g. solar power, wind power, wave power, hydroelectricity, nuclear power and biofuels.

2 12, 13▷ Students listen and answer the questions.

> **Answers**
> **1** **project 1:** to help villagers build their own biogas systems to provide fuel as an alternative to cutting down trees
> **project 2:** to produce affordable wind turbines to fit on people's houses to generate electricity
> **2** **project 1:** It's reliable and cheap and can be built by local people. The fuel is clean and provides excellent fertilizer. It means trees don't have to be cut down.
> **project 2:** The turbines are small enough to fit on the roof of a building and can produce a significant fraction of household electricity for less money. The turbine is vibration-free and almost silent.

3 Students may need to hear the listening again to help them match the adjectives to the nouns. Afterwards, they decide on other possible combinations.

> **Answers**
> techno_lo_gical _break_through
> key _fea_ture
> _cut_ting-edge tech_no_logy
> _ma_jor ad_van_tage
> revo_lu_tionary i_dea
> _prac_tical so_lu_tion
> po_ten_tial _be_nefit
> _inn_ovative _con_cept
> comm_er_cially-_vi_able propo_si_tion
> state-of-the-_art_ de_sign
>
> **Other combinations**
> There are many possibilities. The most common include: technological design / feature / solution; practical idea / advantage; key concept / benefit / advantage; potential solution / breakthrough; cutting-edge design; innovative design / feature / idea / solution / technology; major feature / benefit / breakthrough; commercially-viable solution; revolutionary concept / technology; state-of-the-art technology.

Pronunciation

Check students can say the collocations in **3**. Drill them and make sure students are stressing the correct syllable (see underlined syllables in *Answers* above).

4 Students work in pairs to create sentences.

Extension / Alternative

Ask students to create five gap-fill sentences for the word combinations in **3**. For example:

> *Our company only uses cutting-edge _____.*

They exchange their sentences with another pair and try to guess the answers.

5 Students can work in pairs to match the phrasal verbs to 1–9.

> **Answers**
> **1** get round
> **2** bring about
> **3** come up with
> **4** take forward
> **5** pay off
> **6** carry out
> **7** bring down
> **8** take up
> **9** set up

6 The two texts are about projects which won Ashden Awards. Students complete them with the correct phrasal verbs.

> **Answers**
> **1** come up with
> **2** get round
> **3** set up
> **4** taken up
> **5** bring about
> **6** take forward
> **7** carrying out
> **8** paid off
> **9** bring down

Dictionary skills

At this level, it is useful to make sure students are aware of the difference between transitive and intransitive verbs and how dictionaries can help. Point out that transitive verbs must be followed by an object, e.g. *come up with **an idea**.* Intransitive verbs don't necessarily need an object, e.g. *the work has paid off.* So in **5**, only *paid off* is intransitive. Ask students to look up these two examples in a good dictionary. The symbols [T] or [I] are shown next to the verb.

➤➤ If students need more practice, go to **Practice file 4** on page 108 of the **Student's Book**.

7 Allow time for students to brainstorm ideas before preparing their talks. The talks could be given to the class or two groups can meet to present their innovations. If students are finding it difficult to think of ideas, they might like to develop one of the following.
   • training and study via distance learning
   • changes to transport for commuting staff / students to help save energy

ⓘ Refer students to the **Interactive Workbook Glossary** for further study.

Business communication skills

1 Discuss these questions as a class. If you need to help start the discussion off, brainstorm different forms of security in the students' place of work, e.g. CCTV, identity badges / cards, alarms.

2 14▷ Allow time for students to read the *Context* and slides before listening. They will probably need to hear the listening twice to make their notes and check them.

> **Answers**
> 1 Overview of the product
> 2 Advantages for your company
> 3 Demo film
> 4 state-of-the-art security
> 5 fingerprint scanning
> 6 intensive R&D
> 7 on the market
> 8 are identified by their fingerprints
> 9 scans their fingerprints
> 10 compares them with a central database

3 14▷ Students listen for key phrases for giving a talk.

> **Answers**
> 1 do in this presentation   4 call the system
>   is basically   5 the result of two years of
> 2 give you a brief overview   6 it's a pretty simple
> 3 'd like to show you   concept

4 15▷ Students listen to the second part of the presentation and answer the question.

> **Answer**
> The main advantages are enhanced security (because no one can copy a fingerprint compared to using a code number) and increased flexibility (because you can control the parts of the building or computer systems that people have access to).

5 15▷ Students listen for the key phrases. You will probably need to play the listening at least twice (or see *Alternative* on page 11). Afterwards, students can compare their phrases with the *Key expressions* list.

> **Answers**
> 1 a There are two main benefits of using … / The biggest potential benefit of … / This means that … / Another advantage is that … / The other major advantage of … is … / And this is another great thing about …
>   b With your current system …, they can … / However, with … they won't be able to … / At the moment, you can only … whereas in the future, you'll be able to … as well
> 2 a So, is everything clear so far?
>   b … now I'd like to move on to …

▶▶ If students need more practice, go to **Practice file 4** on page 108 of the **Student's Book**.

6 Students can work in pairs and take turns to present the slides using the phrases noted in **3** and **5**.

Pronunciation

It may be useful to draw students' attention to how we use pauses in presentations. For example, we often pause after commas, full stops or to separate phrases. This helps the presenter with long sentences and the audience to understand. Illustrate this by writing the following extract from audio 14▷ on the board, with suggested pauses marked with a line (/).

> *What I'd like to do in this presentation is basically three things. / First, / I'll give you a brief overview of the product. / Then / I'll talk about some of the advantages for your company. /*

Students could practise reading the extract aloud with pauses and then think about how to use pauses in their own talks.

Tip Refer students to the phrases for linking ideas. They could practise the language by writing four sentences to contrast ideas or facts about their own product, workplace or place of study. For example: *Although you may have heard the company has had losses recently, we are now back in profit.*

7 If students need suggestions, here are some possible ideas to present.
- any object around the classroom (e.g. stapler, projector)
- a database on the company computer
- security around the (company or school) building

Alternative

Students could use their idea from **7** in *Working with words*. This time, they present the same content but in a more formal presentational style. The benefit of this is that students are familiar with the content so can concentrate on using the new phrases.

Feedback focus

During the presentations, make notes on correct and incorrect use of phrases. As well as feedback on language, you could comment on the quality of students' visual aids, body language and eye contact. You could also ask listening students to comment on one thing they liked about their colleagues' presentation and one thing they would have done differently.

ⓘ Refer students to the **Interactive Workbook Email** and **Phrasebank** sections for further study.

Practically speaking

1 16▷ Students listen and identify what has happened in each situation.

> **Answers**
> 1 Someone has visited a company.
> 2 Someone has copied a document.
> 3 Someone has bought a guest lunch.
> 4 Two people have had a meeting.
> 5 Someone is starting a presentation.
> 6 Someone is allowing someone else to do something first.

2 16▷ You could draw the table frame from *Answers* below on the board for students to copy and categorize the phrases they hear. After they have listened and made notes, students could check their answers in the *Audio script* (as they will look at the script in the next exercise). Note that some of these phrases may be suitable in both a formal or informal context, depending on the situation. However, students will value being given some general guidelines to avoid any kind of inappropriateness.

> **Answers**
>
> | | Formal | Informal |
> |---|---|---|
> | **Thank someone** | Thank you for having me. Thank you very much for lunch. I'd like to thank you for inviting me here today. | Thanks a lot Thanks for your time this morning. Thanks |
> | **Respond** | It's a pleasure. It was good to see you. You're welcome. Thank you for coming. | No problem. That's OK. |

3 Students could underline the follow-up comments. Explain that these phrases add emphasis and will make students sound more fluent.

> **Answers**
> 1 ... it was a really interesting visit. / ... it was good to see you.
> 2 I appreciate it. / ... any time.
> 3 ... it was delicious. / I really enjoyed it.
> 4 ... it was good of you to come in. / ... thanks for your help.
> 5 ... we're glad you could be here.

4 Before starting this activity, you could discuss with the class how formal the eight situations are. For example, the first is obviously less formal than the penultimate one, so the choice of phrase will be affected.

Feedback focus

Your feedback should concentrate on appropriate register for each situation and correct phrases. Don't be afraid to give feedback and ask students to repeat the task if necessary.

Language at work

1 17▷ Students listen and answer the questions.

Watch out! You might need to pre-teach the following before listening.
marina = a place where leisure boats are kept
pilot project = a stage of product development when you test it for the first time
patent = a legal document to allow inventors to sell the idea / product
exclusive contract = a contract allowing one person / company to sell a product

> **Answers**
> 1 It's a specialist Internet service provider that provides wireless Internet access at all the major marinas in the country.
> 2 They can only access it on land or they have to have the right technology.
> 3 They'll be able to access the Internet from their boats for a basic monthly fee.
> 4 They have exclusive contracts in all the major marinas in the country for the next seven years.

2 Note that though some extracts refer to inability (c, i, j), they can still be categorized as present, past or future

> **Answers**
> 1 c, f   2 a, e, h, i   3 b, d, g, j

3 To complete the rules, students will find it useful to look at the words / phrases in the context of the extracts in **2**.

> **Answers**
> 1 can, is / are able to
> 2 be able to
> 3 has / have been able to
> 4 could
> 5 was / were able to, couldn't, wasn't / weren't able to

Tip Refer students to the use of *managed to* here, and explain that it can be used in place of *was able to*.

» If students need more practice, go to **Practice file 4** on page 109 of the **Student's Book**.

Extra activity

Before starting **4**, tell students to close their books. Ask them to make notes about the past, present and future as you read about a recent new technology. Read the example text about mobile phones in **4**. Afterwards, students can open their books to check their notes. This is a helpful lead-in to **4**.

4 Students can work in pairs and take turns to talk about the technologies or work together to prepare mini-talks.

5 Before students have the discussion, it will be helpful for them to think about the past, present and future in the category they choose. For example, for 'vehicles' they could plan their thoughts like this.

Past	Present	Future
• no combustion engine • couldn't travel very far • slow speeds • not much storage space	• travel long distances comfortably • good storage space • radio and CD player	• use biofuels or run on solar power • be 100% non-polluting • will be able to fly

ⓘ Refer students to the **Interactive Workbook Exercises and Tests** for revision.

Case study

Background

This *Case study* presents a situation where two young entrepreneurs are attempting to launch their idea for a building in a bag. The topic allows students to consider how to convince investors and get investment for a new product. The *Task* enables them to use the language of the unit within the context of presenting a new idea to prospective investors.

Allow a few minutes for students to read the text about Concrete Canvas and be prepared to answer any questions about vocabulary. Check that students understand the basic idea behind the innovation. Ask the class: *What does the innovation provide? (shelter in emergency situations) What are the advantages of it? (cheap, easy to use) Who will benefit? (refugees, victims of natural disasters, NGO workers).*

Discussion

1, 2, 3 Discuss these questions as a class.

Possible responses

1 They could borrow money from a variety of sources, e.g. governments or funding bodies for NGOs, wealthy relatives, banks or private investors. The key point to remember is that if someone invests they will want a percentage of any future profits.

2 Potential investors might want to know more about how it will be marketed and distributed. We also don't know the future manufacturing costs and whether, after testing, the idea will work in reality. All of this information will probably be given to investors in the form of a business plan.

Task

You will need to organize this activity quite carefully. The first stage is for all students to prepare the presentation of their new idea. (If you are short of time, this could be assigned for homework prior to the lesson.) Note that the *File* includes suggested ideas, if necessary. Remind students that this presentation or 'pitch' can only last three minutes. Students can either work alone or in teams and give group presentations.

Set up the classroom so that there is an audience and a place for the presenter. It's important that students keep track of what money is invested in their idea and how much they invest. They could keep records in a table like this.

How much was invested in my idea?	How much did I invest (in which idea)?

At the end of all the pitches, students will have to do the mathematics and find out how much they have made. This may take some time and careful checking! Note that it is impossible to be both the winning entrepreneur and winning investor. If you are the winning entrepreneur, this means that other people have invested in you, but the rules say you can't invest in your own idea. That means you have lost all the money you invested in the other losing ideas.

At the end, give feedback on use of phrases for presenting and invite students to comment on why some of their peers were particularly effective at making a 'pitch'.

One-to-one

Your student can read the *Background* and then you can do the *Discussion* questions together. For the *Task*, your student could prepare a pitch of an idea and you give feedback on how convincing their pitch was.

» Unit 4 **Progress test** and **Speaking test**, pages 94–95

5 | Customer service

Unit content

By the end of this unit, students will be able to

- talk about customer service
- deal with customers
- reassure and sympathize
- use direct and indirect questions when dealing with customers.

Context

When we think of customer service, we may presume that 'customers' refers only to the people outside the company. These *external* customers are the people we rely on to buy goods or services. To ensure good customer service, many companies have procedures for staff to follow. They also carry out regular surveys and other means of gathering customer feedback.

However, we can also talk about *internal* customers. Your internal customer could be a colleague in the next office who needs your expertise or someone on the phone in a division based in another country who regularly orders items from your division. These people also require a level of service.

When dealing with customers internationally and in English, it's important to take into account their cultural expectations. For example, the package which is delivered two days late in one country may not bring the storm of protest that you may expect in countries where punctuality is regarded more highly. Linguistically, some nationalities use more indirect forms to sound polite when dealing with customers whereas for others, the over use of 'polite forms' in English can sound exaggerated and insincere.

This unit presents the vocabulary for discussing customer service and then the phrases required for dealing with customers on the phone. Students' attention is drawn to register and how the formality of conversation may change when speaking to an external rather than an internal customer. The grammar of direct and indirect question forms also highlights when it is appropriate to be less or more direct. The *Case study* considers a supplier–customer problem which in part is caused by differences in cultural expectations, and students are able to practise the language of the unit in a series of phone calls.

Starting point

Students could discuss the two questions in small groups before feeding back to the class. Note that students can describe obvious contexts such as buying something in a shop as well as any experiences as internal customers in their companies. With experienced students, discuss how their own companies approach customer service. They could describe any procedures which are normally followed.

Working with words

Extra activity

18▷ This section begins with a listening about a woman who experienced poor customer service. It requires listening for specific information and to infer the woman's views. If your students need extra help with listening, you could write the questions below on the board and students listen for the specific information only. This will help them with the main listening exercise in **1**.

1 *Who and when was the present for? (a friend for Christmas)*
2 *Where was the chocolate shop? (in Bond Street – note that Bond Street is in central London and is famous for its expensive shops)*
3 *Where did the woman work? (South London)*
4 *What time did she arrive at the shop? (5.02 p.m.)*
5 *What time did it close? (5 p.m.)*
6 *Why couldn't she come back the next day? (because of a tube strike)*
7 *How did she offer to pay? (by cash)*
8 *What does the shop do well? (wonderful packaging, a superb product and a great café)*

1 18▷ Students listen and make notes. Reassure them that they won't have to understand everything to answer questions 1–4.

Answers
1 The woman arrived two minutes after closing and couldn't buy the chocolates. The assistants wouldn't open up for her so the problem wasn't resolved.
2 She clearly has a negative view of the shop's customer service.
3 She probably won't use the shop again. ('I do know that if they had tried to help me, I would have been a customer for life.')
4 Students can argue for or against. You could argue that the assistants were probably following procedure and if they had stayed open late for one customer then they would regularly have to stay open for other 'late' customers. On the other hand, their actions lost a customer and created bad word-of-mouth publicity.

2 As students read the comments from the website, they could highlight the main points of each one with a marker. This will help to complete **3**.

3 Working in pairs, students discuss the three questions. Open it up afterwards for discussion as a class.

Answer

The main points of each post are

1 the assistants were probably following the rules but they shouldn't have argued about a couple of minutes; it's harder to gain another new customer than to lose an existing one

2 customers should be aware of the needs of the employees and the shop

3 you should always exceed the expectations of the customer

4 the manager is at fault and needs to train staff properly

5 again, the manager needs to train staff properly to give high-quality service.

4 Students match the adjectives to their definitions.

Answers

1 un<u>ca</u>ring	7 <u>sa</u>tisfied
2 <u>cour</u>teous / dis<u>cour</u>teous	8 high-<u>qua</u>lity
3 a<u>tten</u>tive	9 <u>loy</u>al
4 sub-<u>stan</u>dard	10 re<u>peat</u>
5 e<u>ffi</u>cient	11 dis<u>sa</u>tisfied
6 res<u>pon</u>sive	12 e<u>xis</u>ting

Pronunciation

Read out the words in 1–12 and students mark the word stress (see the underlined syllables in *Answers* above).

5 Students categorize the adjectives in **4**.

Answers

1 uncaring, courteous, discourteous, attentive, sub-standard, efficient, responsive, high-quality

2 satisfied, loyal, repeat, dissatisfied, existing

6 Students can either work on their own or in pairs for this writing activity. One option is to insist on a minimum number of adjectives, e.g. five, in each post. At the end, students could pin their posts on the wall or put them on tables around the classroom. Allow a few minutes for students to walk around and read what other students have written.

7 Students match the two halves of the questions. Focus their attention on the verbs at the end of 1–7 as these will collocate with words in a–g.

Answers

1 f 2 d 3 b 4 g 5 c 6 a 7 e

Extra activity

Ask students which of the questions in 1–7 would give the best idea of how customers feel.

8 Students take turns to ask and answer the questions in **7**.

Pre-work learners

If students can't think of a company they know well, ask them to imagine they run the college or school they are currently studying in. They should answer the questions as if the word *customer(s)* in each case refers to the *student(s)*. For example:

A *How do you measure customer satisfaction and service quality?*

B *Once a term, we ask students to complete a feedback form about their lessons and the whole school …*

» If students need more practice, go to **Practice file 5** on page 110 of the **Student's Book**.

9 Students work in groups to come up with five factors. If you have an overhead projector, the students could write their factors on a transparency and give a short presentation at the end to the class.

10 If you think some students will be unfamiliar with this kind of questionnaire, try to bring in some examples. For example, many hotels have such forms on the reception desk or they can be downloaded from the Internet.

Extension

If students are familiar with each other's companies, and you think it appropriate, they could take turns to use their final questionnaires to interview their peers and get feedback.

ⓘ Refer students to the **Interactive Workbook Glossary** for further study.

Business communication skills

1 If students are unclear about the term *internal customers*, explain that these can be the people you work with. One way for students to define their internal customers is to ask the question: *Who would be affected if I didn't come in to work next week?* Quite often we might treat internal customers less formally (or even seriously) than external customers.

Extension

You could ask these further questions.

- *Do you feel you have to react more quickly to external customers' requests?*
- *Do you take internal customers less seriously?*

Also ask students how they think their language might change when dealing with internal and external customers. With internal customers, the language is likely to be less formal but should still be helpful and service-orientated.

2 19▷ Allow time for students to read the forms. Ask them which forms are for internal customers (1 and 2). To help with the listening, discuss what type of words students think they need to listen for. For example, gap 1 needs students to listen out for the name of a department such as *Human Resources* or *Production*.

> **Answers**
> 1 Sales
> 2 training course
> 3 02/584
> 4 by Friday
> 5 Check the figures and ask Angela to sign it. Fax contract to Training Direct.
> 6 blank screen but hard drive light is on
> 7 Look into the problem and call Johann back.
> 8 AS Consulting
> 9 order arrived out of office hours and left outside building / too much paper and no envelopes
> 10 Check details and call back.

3 19▷ Students listen again for the phrases, which can be compared afterwards with the *Key expressions* list. They will probably need to listen twice while writing.

> **Answers**
> 1 What seems to be the problem? / How can I help you? / What can I do for you today?
> 2 Could you give me ...? / Can/Could you tell me ...? / Could you explain exactly what the problem is?
> 3 Let me get this straight. What you're saying is ... / You mean ... / If I understand you correctly ... / Could I just clarify what you're saying?
> 4 I'll look into it. / What I'll do is ... and see if ... / If you ..., I'll ..., / I'm going to have to look into this. I'll get back to you shortly. / Once I've ..., I'll ... / As soon as I've ..., I'll ...
> 5 by Friday at the latest / in time for the deadline / by lunchtime / as soon as

Alternative

Another way to focus students on key phrases from the listening is to ask them to read the *Key expressions* list on page 33. Then, as they listen, they number the phrases in the order they hear them used in the three conversations, or write the number of the conversation where the phrase is used.

Tip Refer students to the use of *by* and *until* when referring to deadlines.

>> If students need more practice, go to **Practice file 5** on page 110 of the **Student's Book**.

4 Students work in pairs and role-play two different situations. Allow them time to prepare what they will say and remind them to think about which phrases will be useful. Arrange students so they sit looking away from each other, in order to simulate a phone call and the lack of face-to-face contact.

5 This provides further practice with the language but the task is much freer and requires students to create more of their own information.

Feedback focus

You will obviously need to give feedback on use of the phrases from this section in the role-plays in both **4** and **5**. However, also focus on how helpful or polite each person sounded when serving the customer. Note that, even at this level, you may need to give remedial help with some of the language for giving details on times, dates, spellings or numbers. For example, the pronunciation of numbers such as *twentieth* or *fifth* can cause difficulty. Explaining locations or giving directions can also give even upper-intermediate students some problems.

ⓘ Refer students to the **Interactive Workbook Email** and **Phrasebank** sections for further study.

Practically speaking

1 20▷ Students listen and identify what has happened in each situation.

> **Answers**
> 1 The speaker has had a bad day in her new job.
> 2 A client was going to complain about the speaker.
> 3 The speaker has had a long phone call with a difficult customer.
> 4 The speaker has broken an expensive bulb.

2 20▷ Students make a note of the opening question in each conversation.

> **Answers**
> 1 How's the new job going?
> 2 How did the call with that difficult client go?
> 3 What's the matter?
> 4 You seem a bit unhappy.

3 Students choose what they think will be the first speaker's response in each situation.

> **Answers**
> 1 b 2 a 3 b 4 b

4 21▷ Students listen and check their answers.

5 You could suggest the conversation below for 'a difficult interview' as an example of what students are expected to do in this activity. Don't forget to refer them to the *Useful phrases* on page 134.
> A *What's the matter?*
> B *I had an interview today. It went really badly.*
> A *I'm sure you did the best you could.*

Language at work

1 Students match the two sets of questions.

> **Answers**
> a 4 b 5 c 1 d 3 e 2

2 Discuss these two questions as a class. For the first question, note that we often use indirect questions to sound more formal or polite. We also tend to begin conversations with an indirect question and then any subsequent questions may be in the direct form.

Tip Refer students to the *Tip* to compare their ideas.

In response to the second question, you could ask students to begin by underlining the opening phrase for each indirect question in a–e in **1**.
> *Can you tell me …*
> *Could you explain …*
> *Do you know …*
> *Can you tell me if …*
> *Could you let me know …*

Then ask them to study the remainder of the sentence only. Allow time for students to explain the change in their own words and then refer them to the detailed summary of the rules in the *Practice file*.

》 If students need more practice, go to **Practice file 5** on page 111 of the **Student's Book**.

3 Note that transforming questions from direct to indirect notoriously causes students difficulty, so you may wish to give controlled practice with the exercises in the *Practice file* before students attempt to make their own indirect questions.

> **Possible answers**
> 1 Who did you speak to last time? / Can you tell me who you spoke to last time?
> 2 When can I deliver it? / Could you let me know when I can deliver it?
> 3 What exactly is the problem? / Could you explain exactly what the problem is?
> 4 Is the train cancelled? / Do you know if the train is cancelled?
> 5 How long have you had it? / Can you tell me how long you have had it?

Extra activity

For more practice and some fun, ask students to make a note of five direct questions. Then students work in pairs and take turns to say one direct question. Their partner should listen and change it into an indirect question. For example:
> A *Where is our teacher from?*
> B *Can you tell me where our teacher is from?*

4 Students practise making more direct and indirect questions by role-playing situations 1 and 2.

Feedback focus

As well as dealing with any inaccurate questions (listen especially for any indirect questions), address the use of direct or indirect questions in terms of whether the correct form was chosen appropriately and used, for example, politely.

ⓘ Refer students to the **Interactive Workbook Exercises and Tests** for revision.

Case study

Background

This *Case study* presents a customer service situation where students consider whether some issues that arise might be related to different cultural expectations of customer service. The *Task* enables them to practise dealing with customer service problems on the phone and using the language for establishing facts and promising action. Students also have the opportunity to discuss different ways of handling customer service situations.

Allow a few minutes for students to read the text and be prepared to answer any questions about vocabulary.

Discussion

1 Students discuss the three questions in pairs or as a class. There are no obvious responses. CBE Brasilia could have been more efficient with keeping track of the order and could have responded more quickly to the German company. Cultural differences may have affected communication. For example, the German company might have expected prompter action with the expectation that any company should keep detailed records. Extend this part of the discussion by asking students if they have experience of situations where cultural expectations with regard to customer service have had an impact.

2 22▷ Students listen and find out what really happened in this situation, and then discuss the questions.

> **Answers**
> 1 Students may have different views, but since the customer is still doing business with CBE Brasilia their answer is likely to be positive.
> 2 The main lesson would be that the company needs to keep better documentation of orders.
> 3 Suggestions might include that the customer service team has a policy of returning calls more quickly and advising clients on progress of their orders.

Task

1 Students work in pairs and turn to their *Files*. There is a lot of information on the role cards, so allow plenty of time for reading and answering questions about vocabulary. Students have to make two phone calls each. When they receive the call, the action they take should be chosen from options a, b or c.

2 After students have role-played the four calls, they form two groups (A and B) and discuss the reasons for their choices when helping the customer. Then they study the *File* on page 149 to score themselves based on their choices. At the end, students discuss if the explanations are a fair reflection of how they handled the customer (this question / task can easily be omitted if time is short).

Extension

If the topic of customer service is particularly relevant to your students, open up the discussion with these questions after the *Case study*.
  1 *Is it always a good idea to be so flexible and accommodating towards your clients?*
  2 *Is it wise to react immediately to a customer's demand or is it better to give yourself some 'breathing space' to analyse the situation and give a balanced and considered answer?*
  3 *Do you think reacting immediately is often only offering a 'quick fix' for something and the problem will happen again at a later time?*
  4 *Is 'promising the earth' the best option?*

One-to-one

Your student can read the *Background* and then you can do the *Discussion* questions together. You can take on part of the role-play and work through the four calls. Alternatively, assign the role of the person handling the customer to the student each time and then discuss his or her options at the end with reference to the scoring system.

❯❯ Unit 5 **Progress test** and **Speaking test**, pages 96–97

6 | Ethical business

Unit content

By the end of this unit, students will be able to

- talk about ethical business
- explain plans and arrangements
- invite and recommend
- respond to spontaneous invitations
- talk about the future.

Context

Consumers are increasingly affected in their choices by how they perceive the ethical behaviour of companies. More and more of us are asking questions about well-known brand names such as: *Where are the products made? How much are the staff paid? What are their working conditions like? What is the source of the raw materials and are they environmentally-friendly? Is there a huge financial imbalance between the company's profits and its struggling supplier in the developing world?* Being ethical has become a PR issue with consumers, governments and pressure groups all watching businesses carefully for signs of ethical or unethical practices.

In response, many companies have policies on corporate social responsibility (CSR). The central idea of CSR is that corporations should make decisions based not only on financial factors but also on the social and environmental impact of their activities. Company websites generally outline CSR activities, e.g. health and safety policies, projects with the local community and environmental initiatives. The impact on the employee is that they could be asked to become involved in charity work or raise money for a good cause, or concern for the environment may lead to changes in working practices. During the course of this unit, you might want to find out from students if their employers' ethical approach has had an affect on their working lives.

This unit presents vocabulary to enable discussion of ethical issues. The context in *Business communication skills* follows a company wishing to promote its ethical ethos and allows students to practise language for explaining future plans and making invitations / recommendations. In the *Case study*, students plan and present an event to help promote a company and its ethical position.

Starting point

Students discuss the three questions. Ask them to give examples of real companies they have heard about, where possible.

Possible answers

1 Some of the areas may include: paying fair prices for goods (e.g. to workers in developing countries), pollution from factories, using recycled materials, giving staff incentives to share cars to work, sponsoring local charities / events.
2 Many countries have companies which are known for social responsibility. For example, The Body Shop has always promoted itself and its products on the basis of its ethical principles.
3 In recent years, various clothing companies like Gap and Nike were accused of exploiting cheap labour in poor working conditions to produce garments for high-street stores. For some time, they suffered some image problems and have worked hard to counter this by stressing their ethical principles.

Extra activity / Pre-work learners

Ask students to visit the websites for a few companies they are familiar with and to look for information about the company's ethical ethos. For example, most oil companies will offer information on work they are doing to help the environment. Similarly, companies such as The Body Shop have clear ethical positions. This mini-research project will work especially well with pre-work learners. Ask them to report back at the next lesson on what they discovered.

Working with words

1 Students brainstorm the characteristics of an 'ethical business'. Afterwards, write everyone's ideas on the board in preparation for the reading in **2**.

Possible answer

- concerned about its impact on the environment
- pays a fair salary to employees
- charges a fair price
- is ethical in its financial dealings (e.g. with shareholders)
- gives a proportion of its turnover or time to non-profit activities which are beneficial to the local community

Extra activity

Before reading, ask students to write three questions they have about the company. For example: *What product or service do you provide? How many people do you employ? Where do you operate?* Then, when they read, they can see if the text answers their questions.

2 While reading, students can check if any of the ideas on the board from **1** are referred to.

3 Questions 1–4 can be answered by reading the text. Question 5 can be discussed as a class.

Answers
1 They are people who love 'wild and beautiful places' and therefore 'take an active part in the fight to repair the damage that is being done to the health of our planet'.
2 It is committed to protecting the environment. It shows this by donating time, services and at least 1% of sales to environmental groups.
3 They work to reduce pollution, and use recycled polyester and organic cotton.
4 They have stayed true to their principles over the last thirty-plus years.

Extra activity

To introduce the theme of the next activity, which includes a focus on rules and regulations controlling ethical behaviour, ask students if they know of any rules in their country governing issues such as pollution and the environment. Is their company or field of business affected by these rules?

4 Students do the matching and complete the questions.

Answers
1 comply with regulations
2 donate time
3 reduce the impact
4 act responsibly
5 take an active part in
6 stay true to its principles
7 share a strong commitment to

5 Students work in pairs, asking and answering the seven questions. If there is time, they can report back to the class.

6 23▷ Students do not necessarily listen for single words to answer these questions. They will need to interpret the tone of the speakers and make notes on what is said.

Answers
1 The interviewer's style is quite aggressive.
2 The spokesperson's response is calm and he replies to each question with examples of the good work his company is doing.
3 a It is fair and combats discrimination and prejudice within the organization; it improves working conditions and safety; it has schemes for staff education, health and training.
   b It has reduced its methane and hydrocarbon emissions and provides financial support for turtle conservation in Bangladesh.

c It has set up a community project to provide skills training for unemployed youths in Sangu, and health initiatives and other schemes to encourage sustainable livelihoods in Rajasthan.

7 Students can refer to the *Audio script* to read some of the words in context and decide whether they are ethical or unethical.

Answers
1 ethics, responsibility, fairness, generosity, values, credibility
2 bribery, deception, corruption, prejudice, greed, discrimination

Extra activity

Divide the class into two groups. Give the words in 1 to one group and the words in 2 to the other. Students think of an action or a situation to illustrate the meaning of each noun. For example: *bribery – paying money to a government official to get planning permission for a new building*.

8 Students can work in pairs to complete the table.

Answers
deception – deceptive
responsibility – responsible
fairness – fair
generosity – generous
credibility – credible
ethics – ethical
corruption – corrupt
prejudice – prejudiced
greed – greedy
discrimination – discriminatory

Dictionary skills

Students will find it helpful to use dictionaries to complete **8**.

Pronunciation

Check students know where the word stress is in each of the words in **8** (see the underlined syllables in *Answers* above).

Extra activity

Ask students to write five sentences about their own company or a company they know well, using the adjective form of the nouns in **8**. (Note that in classes which are taking place within a company, this may need to be handled sensitively!)

9 Students read about company X and Y in the *File*. X clearly has a positive ethical policy whereas Y requires negative words to describe it.

>> If students need more practice, go to **Practice file 6** on page 112 of the **Student's Book**.

10 Allow plenty of time for students to prepare their presentations. It may even be helpful to have the final version in the following class. When you set up the room for the presentations, ask the speaker(s) to come to the front and position the other students like an audience. Ask the 'audience' students to think of tough questions beforehand to ask at the end of the presentation, similar to those of the interviewer in the listening.

Feedback focus

Give feedback on the use of the vocabulary from this section. You can also comment on the quality of the presentations and how each presenter handled the questions from the audience.

(i) Refer students to the **Interactive Workbook Glossary** for further study.

Business communication skills

1 Students begin by reading the *Context*. You can check their understanding by writing these questions on the board.
   1 *What is Hummingbird Teas? (a company which sells speciality teas)*
   2 *What is its USP? (its ethos)*
   3 *Where does it buy its tea? (from small local farmers)*
   4 *Why does it need Clare? (to raise its profile)*
   5 *Who has been invited to see the operation? (reporters / journalists)*

   24▷ Students listen and make any changes to the notes.

   Answers
   - Trip to China (not South Africa) is confirmed
   - Four days at one tea plantation
   - No opportunities for sightseeing
   - Two dates: February (15th–20th – need bookings by January the 10th) and one in May
   - A lot of road travel and one internal flight

2 24▷ Students listen again and complete the phrases.

   Answers
1 'll email you the final itinerary	4 'll get the opportunity to
2 we're planning to show you	5 we're going to arrange
3 idea is to	

3 25▷ Students listen to the second part of the meeting and answer the two questions.

   Answers
   1 watch the tea being prepared and sample local specialties produced by the cooperative, visit a project to promote schooling in Tibetan language, visit the site of a reforestation scheme, talk to the coordinators of the business in China
   2 stay with the guide who can interpret (because no one speaks English)

4 25▷ Students listen again and complete the phrases.

   Answers
   1 'd like to invite you to
   2 we strongly recommend you stay
   3 you're also welcome to visit
   4 sounds, 'd like to take you up on that
   5 would be a good idea to
   6 is highly recommended
   7 well worth a visit
   8 That's not really what
   9 we'd be delighted to
   10 it's just the kind of thing I need

Tip Refer students to the *Tip* when dealing with the answer for 2.

5 Students can work in pairs to categorize the phrases and then check their answers in the *Key expressions* list.

   Answers
   a 1, 3, 9   **b** 2, 5, 6, 7   **c** 4, 8, 10

Pronunciation

With many of these phrases, a speaker will emphasize certain key words to sound more genuine and polite. Write these phrases from the *Key expressions* list on the board and read them out, stressing the underlined words.
   You're underline welcome to … We'd be delighted to …
   We strongly recommend you … It's highly recommended.
   It's well worth a visit. That would be great.
   That sounds really interesting.
   It's just the kind of thing I need.
   That's not really what I'm looking for.
Alternatively, students can say which word they think is stressed. Then drill the phrases, making sure students stress the words.

>> If students need more practice, go to **Practice file 6** on page 112 of the **Student's Book**.

6 Students work in A / B pairs and use the information to make invitations and recommendations, using the phrases in the *Key expressions* list. For example:

    A *We'd like to invite you to an information day about Hummingbird Teas and fair trade.*

    B *That sounds great! I'd like to take you up on that.*

7 Allow about five minutes for students to prepare their ideas in 1 before working with another partner in 2. If your students are all from different companies, they could do the first task alone. Students who don't work for a company can use the company in the *File*.

Pre-work learners

Students can complete **7** using the company in the *File*. However, they could also imagine their school or college is having an open day for students who are thinking of enrolling next year. They then follow the same procedure as in **7**.

(i) Refer students to the **Interactive Workbook Email** and **Phrasebank** sections for further study.

Practically speaking

1 26▷ Students listen and answer the two questions.

> **Answers**
> 1 and 2
> **invitation 1: 1** have a coffee   **2** P
> **invitation 2: 1** go to the cinema   **2** D
> **invitation 3: 1** go to a pizzeria for lunch   **2** A

2 26▷ Students listen out for the phrases used.

> **Answers**
> **1** How about …? / Do you feel like …? / Would you like to …?
> **2** Why not?
> **3** Maybe. / Can I let you know later?
> **4** Sorry, I'm …

Watch out! For the answers in 1–4, draw attention to the following.

- *How about …?* and *Do you feel like …?* are followed by a verb in the *-ing* form.
- *Why not?* is a peculiar way to accept but basically means 'I can't think of a reason why not'. In translation this may sound rude, but in English it is perfectly acceptable.
- As in 4, we often follow *Sorry* with the present continuous form of the verb to explain why the invitation is being declined.

3 For this activity, ask students to stand and walk around the classroom to make their invitations.

Language at work

1 At upper-intermediate level, this activity should offer a review of future forms. However, if any of the grammar is new for students, follow up with the exercises in the *Practice file*.

> **Answers**
> **1** e (*will* future)   **4** b (*will* future)
> **2** c (*going to* future)   **5** d (present simple)
> **3** a (present continuous)

» If students need more practice, go to **Practice file 6** on page 113 of the **Student's Book**.

2 Make sure students realize they have to choose the incorrect answer (not the correct one). During feedback, ask them to explain why it is incorrect.

> **Answers**
> **1** 'll do (The speaker has already arranged something on Friday. It isn't an instant decision.)
> **2** 's being (We rarely use the verb *to be* in the continuous form and it doesn't refer to an arrangement.)
> **3** is going to arrive (The event isn't intended but is timetabled.)
> **4** 'm letting (The speaker has only just learnt of the news so can't have planned or arranged it.)
> **5** 'll (same explanation as 1)
> **6** meet (This is for timetabled or regular events. If the speaker met Mrs Brasseler every day at 3.30, it would be correct.)
> **7** email (The speaker is making an instant decision and not describing a regular event.)
> **8** is noticing (Greta isn't at work yet. The speaker is making a prediction.)

3 Although the questions are straightforward for this level, students might not respond with the appropriate future form so you will have to monitor carefully. Note that responses to 1, 3 and 8 are likely to use *going to*; 2, 6 and 7 could use present continuous; 4 expects the present simple; *will* is likely to be used in 5 but feasibly will crop up in any of the answers. Note, however, that many students try to overuse *will* and to avoid the other future forms. This is something that can be commented on in feedback afterwards.

4 Students write and explain their important dates.

Feedback focus

Give positive feedback when students are using a range of future forms to explain their dates. If students only use one or two forms, ask them to repeat the activity with wider and more meaningful use of forms.

ⓘ Refer students to the **Interactive Workbook Exercises and Tests** for revision.

Case study

Background

This *Case study* presents two ethical companies. The topic allows students to consider how a company's activities can promote an ethical position. The *Task* enables them to plan events to promote a company's ethical position and to practise giving an informal presentation to explain plans and arrangements.

Allow a few minutes for students to read the company profiles and be prepared to answer any questions about vocabulary. Students could underline key information in the profiles to help with the *Discussion* questions.

Discussion

1, 2 Students can discuss these questions in pairs and compare ideas with the class.

Possible responses
1 Likely customers are people who believe in social and corporate responsibility and will be willing to pay extra for products produced ethically.
2 The companies all have activities to promote their ethical position such as an affiliated charity (Tribes Travel) and Climate Change College (Ben & Jerry's). These projects serve both the function of taking practical action whilst promoting the brand as an ethical business.

Watch out! You might need to explain the following in the two texts.
fair trade = this is both a term and refers to the Fair Trade organization. The concept of fair trade is that businesses pay a fair price to producers especially in developing companies.
affiliated = to be in partnership with. For example, an affiliated charity is one that the company helps sponsor and works with on projects.
climate tickets = an extra charge that can be voluntarily paid for a flight to counter effects of carbon emissions. The money goes towards climate protection projects.

Task

1 Students work in two groups. You may need to allocate a company to each group. Before students start, it might be useful to brainstorm possible ideas for events to inform a wider market about operations and ethical activities. For example:
- sponsoring a charity or fund-raising event
- an open day for journalists and / or key customers to highlight the company's ethical projects
- employees doing something for charity.

Extra activity

If students have more time, e.g. on a pre-work course, they could do some research into the activities of the two companies by visiting their websites.

2 Once students have agreed on a suitable event, they start planning it in more detail. They should consider the following.
- Where and when will it take place?
- Who will be involved?
- What invitations / recommendations will be made?
They should also use their company profile to prepare the first part of the presentation.

3 When students present their companies and plans, encourage other students to ask them questions about their strategies at the end. During the presentations, make sure students use appropriate future forms and give feedback where necessary.

One-to-one

Discuss the two companies together. Then ask the student to prepare a presentation for the next lesson to promote one of the companies or the student can prepare a similar presentation for his / her own company.

Extra activity

If your students need to improve writing skills, ask them to prepare a short report on their plans for the company. Tell them to write the report as if they are a consultant to the company. This will also be a good way to consolidate (and for you to check) their use of future forms.

» Unit 6 **Progress test** and **Speaking test**, pages 98–99

7 | Making decisions

Unit content

By the end of this unit, students will be able to

- talk about personality and decision-making
- participate in a decision-making meeting
- talk about social plans
- talk about countability and quantity.

Context

It is said that the most successful businesspeople are quick to make decisions and slow to change them. On the other hand, Napoleon Hill in his classic guide to motivation and success *Think and Grow Rich* (1937), said that 98% of us end up in our jobs because we are indecisive.

To achieve, businesses must be able to make decisions. This doesn't only mean decisions at a board or strategic level as decision-making is a skill which all employees need. Of course, we all make decisions in different ways. The widely used Myers-Briggs Type Indicator separates us into Thinkers and Feelers. Thinkers approach their final decision by studying the facts and taking time. Feelers base their decision on intuition and their senses. The Myers-Briggs Type Indicator also offers other categories which are presented in the *Working with words* section of this unit. The Indicator is a type of personality test which allows managers to analyse their teams and categorize the decision-making approaches of their staff. For example, someone who is a Thinker may find the approach of a Feeler frustrating. However, at the same time, by combining different types of decision-makers, a manager is able to create a well-balanced team or assess where weaknesses in the decision-making process may occur.

As well as looking at the vocabulary of personality in this unit, students practise the language for giving and responding to arguments and opinions in decision-making meetings. The *Language at work* section reviews and extends students' knowledge of count and non-count nouns, and expressions of quantity. In the *Case Study*, students consider a real company's problem and work together to try to resolve it.

Starting point

Students can briefly discuss the two questions. Responses will highlight students who are Thinkers (those who are guided by facts and need more time) or Feelers (those who follow intuition and work under pressure) in their decision-making.

Working with words

1 Before students read the text, ask them to look at the eight personality types in the question headings (extrovert, introvert, etc.) and guess which type matches to 1–4. They can then read the text and check their guesses.

> **Answers**
> 1 judger   2 thinker   3 extrovert   4 intuitive

2 Students match the adjectives to the statements and can compare answers in pairs.

> **Answers**
> 2 methodical   7 outgoing   12 tactful
> 3 indecisive   8 thoughtful   13 self-contained
> 4 determined   9 creative   14 focused
> 5 instinctive   10 conventional   15 impulsive
> 6 flexible   11 rational   16 pragmatic

Pronunciation

Ask students to find the words with three or four syllables in 1–16 in 2 and categorize them in a table as follows.

●●●	●●●	●●●●	●●●●
flexible	determined	methodical	indecisive
rational	outgoing	conventional	
	creative		
	impulsive		
	pragmatic		

Drill the words as necessary.

3 Students work in pairs and use the adjectives to describe the type of people they like / don't like to work with. Correct any word stress or pronunciation problems on the spot.

4 Students can underline the parts of the text which answer **a** and **b**.

> **Tip** Refer students to the *Tip* for an explanation of *good at* and *good with*.

Answers
Extroverts – good with people / prefer to do lots of things at once
Introverts – prefer to focus on one thing at a time and be behind the scenes
Sensors – good at understanding details and remembering facts and specifics
Intuitives – like to focus on the big picture and future possibilities / prefer to learn new skills
Thinkers – prefer to remain detached
Feelers – good at complimenting
Judgers – like to complete projects
Perceivers – like to be flexible and keep options open / like to start projects / prefer to play now and work later

5 Students now decide which personality type they are most like in each section in the text and write down the first letter for each type (e.g. ESTP). The key in the *File* is a long summary of the different combinations so advise students just to read their own analysis. If they are interested, they can read the rest of the key after the lesson. Ask students to report back on how accurate they think their analysis is.

6 27▷ Students listen and decide which of the personality types applies to each speaker. This is quite challenging as they have to listen and probably will need to refer back to the text to compare the personality types with what they hear. Students could compare their answers in pairs or check in the *Audio script*. For further discussion, ask students to say which speaker they think gives the best advice.

Answers
Speaker 1: Introvert
Speaker 2: Intuitive
Speaker 3: Thinker
Speaker 4: Judger

Extra activity

As a follow-up to the listening and to reuse the vocabulary in this section, ask students to choose one of the personality types and write a short paragraph like the speakers in the listening. They can write about themselves or make up a fictional speaker describing their type. When they have finished, they read out their description to a partner or the class and the listener has to guess which personality type they are describing.

7 If students have difficulty matching or want to check their answers, play the listening again.

Answers
weigh up information
delay my decision
rely on feelings
trust my instincts
consider all the options
have confidence in (my) own judgment
get different perspectives
decide between two things

Extra activity

Other combinations are possible with the words and phrases in **7**, so you could ask students to create some. Encourage them to make full sentences so the new combinations appear in context. For example: *You need to weigh up all the options when making a decision so you can choose the best thing to do.*

> Possible answers:
> *weigh up all the options / two things*
> *delay judgment*
> *get information*
> *trust judgment / feelings / information*
> *consider feelings / information / instincts*
> *have confidence in my instincts / feelings*
> *rely on information / instincts*

8 Students use the phrases in **7** to tell their partner about a recent decision they made. Allow students a minute or so to make notes about the decision. You can also ask them to note the following details.
- How did you arrive at the decision?
- What were the options?
- What affected your final decision?
- Looking back, was it the right decision?

Remind students that it doesn't have to be a decision at work. It might be about how they chose a course at university or even a decision about shopping at the weekend.

>> If students need more practice, go to **Practice file 7** on page 114 of the **Student's Book**.

9 Students work in pairs. They refer back to the information in the text to decide on the personality types for each job. Encourage them to use the vocabulary from **2**, **4** and **7**. For example, they might decide that introverts, intuitives, feelers and judgers would make good website designers because a designer needs to be *creative* and *focused*, would need to *rely on their instincts* and would need to be *good at* thinking of new design ideas, etc.

Feedback focus

Make notes on students' responses in **9** and give feedback after the task. Listen out for correct combinations of verb–noun phrases and drill any problematic pronunciation.

Extra activity

For a more personalized activity, students work in pairs. They think of three friends or colleagues and describe each person's job and their decision-making style. Is it a suitable decision-making style for their job? Why or why not?

ⓘ Refer students to the **Interactive Workbook Glossary** for further study.

Business communication skills

1 Students read the *Context*. Check they understand the basic meaning of *budget deficit* (more money has been spent than was planned). Ask how many people are at the meeting (four in total = three regional managers and one consultant).

Extra activity

Ask students to look at the list of points and discuss if any of these are ever discussed where they work. Has their company done any of the points to help reduce spending?

28▷ Students listen and tick the points discussed.

> **Answer**
> Points 2, 3 and 5 are discussed.

2 28▷ Students listen again and complete the phrases. For 2, point out that *here in black and white* is a commonly used idiom referring to black writing on white paper. It means that the speaker has the facts or proof.

> **Answers**
> 1 if we look at the facts, we'll see that
> 2 Look at, here in black and white
> 3 thing is
> 4 A classic example is
> 5 what you're getting at
> 6 not convinced
> 7 far as I'm concerned
> 8 is right, I think it would be crazy to

Tip Refer students to the *Tip* for more on the idiomatic phrase in sentence 5.

3 Students categorize the phrases. Point out that sentence 8 will fall into two categories (as there are two phrases).

> **Answers**
> a 1, 2, 3, 4
> b 7, 8 (second phrase)
> c 6, 8 (first phrase)
> d 5

4 Students look at Sinead's part in the *Audio script* and focus on the language for leading a meeting.

> **Answers**
> 1 Today, I'd like to establish …
> 2 Jens, could you start us off, please? / Hang on, let's hear what Jens has to say about …
> 3 What's your position on this?
> 4 Can we move on to …? / Let's turn to the next item …
> 5 I don't want to spend too long on this point.
> 6 Let's draw up some action points on what we've discussed so far.

Before students begin free practice with these phrases, it might be helpful for them to complete the *Practice file* exercises.

>> If students need more practice, go to **Practice file 7** on page 114 of the **Student's Book**.

5 Divide the class into small groups.
  1 Ask students to study the agenda item and to add two of their own ideas.
  2 This stage is included to encourage students to use new phrases rather than relying on simpler ones they already know. Note that no one is specifically leading the discussion so students don't need to choose from that list. (If you want them to focus on these phrases as well, you will need to rotate the person leading during the meeting every 3–5 minutes.) You may need to take in small pieces of card or pieces of paper. Alternatively, students could highlight the eight chosen phrases in the *Key expressions* list. As they use each phrase, they can tick it.
  3, 4 As students 'play' their cards, it can become competitive with students wanting to play all their cards first. Other students will need to listen carefully to check phrases are used correctly and you may have to be the final judge in such cases. At this stage, don't give too much feedback to students. The aim here is for students to become familiar with new phrases before using them in a free practice situation in **6**.

6 Students follow the stages for the budget meeting, but if you think students will need help with ideas for stage 1 (e.g. pre-work learners), you can suggest the following.

Your department is Sales. The five suggestions are
  1 increased expense allowances for travel
  2 laptops for everyone in the department

3 company cars
4 bonuses and cash incentives for increased sales
5 a Christmas party.

Also make sure that students take turns to lead the discussion and use the phrases from **4**.

Feedback focus

As well as giving feedback on the use of the phrases, comment on how effectively different students lead the discussion.

ⓘ Refer students to the **Interactive Workbook Email** and **Phrasebank** sections for further study.

Practically speaking

1 As a lead-in, point out that during breaks in meetings, participants often try to avoid talking about business and use the opportunity to make small talk. Ask students what topics / themes they generally talk about in this situation.

29▷ Students listen and establish how certain about plans each speaker is.

> **Answers**
> **a** 4 **b** 1 **c** 5 **d** 2 **e** 3

Watch out! You will probably have to explain the phrase in conversation 2: *We'll probably catch a movie.* In this context *catch* means 'see' a movie.

2 **29▷** Students listen again and identify the phrases.

> **Answers**
> 1 What've you got on …? / What are you up to …? / Are you taking any time off …? / What are you doing …? / Anything nice planned for …?
> 2 Well, I'm supposed to be … / We'll probably … / It depends on … / We're off to … / Nothing special.
> 3 Poor you. / Sounds good. / I see. / Lucky you!

3 It will help if students are standing so they can move around the room and ask different people about their plans.

Language at work

Before starting this section, check that students understand the terminology in **1** and **2**. Some students may have previously seen the terminology *count* and *non-count* nouns rather than the terms *countable* and *uncountable* nouns.

1 Students do the matching task.

> **Answers**
> 1 project, point   3 waste, overtime
> 2 expenses, savings

Dictionary skills

It will be very useful for students to use a dictionary with the next activity. Make sure they know how to identify countable and uncountable nouns in a dictionary with the symbols [C] and [U].

2 Students can work in pairs to do this.

> **Answers**
> **C:** product, colleague, suggestion, fact, journey, proposal, document
> **U:** news, information, travel, accommodation (note that in American English you can have *accommodations* as a plural noun), software, correspondence, money, equipment, insurance, advice
> **C/U:** expenditure (= general spending and can also refer to different areas of spending), paper (= paper in general and 'a paper' given in an academic situation), business (= the whole area of business and individual businesses), experience (= people's experience and different experiences in our lives), time (= time in general and 'remembering times in our lives', for example)

3 To help students group the quantifiers, they could experiment with the quantifiers in their own sentences. They can also check their answers by reading the language summary in the *Practice file.*

> **Answers**
> **first box:** colleague, expenditure, paper, suggestion, business, experience, time, fact, journey, proposal, document
> **second box:** products, colleagues, expenditures, papers, suggestions, businesses, experiences, times, journeys, proposals, documents,
> **third box:** expenditure, paper, information, business, travel, experience, time, accommodation, software, correspondence, equipment, insurance, advice

4 Students complete the sentences.

> **Answers**
> 1 very little   5 any
> 2 fewer   6 enough
> 3 too much   7 too many
> 4 some   8 a

≫ If students need more practice, go to **Practice file 7** on page 115 of the **Student's Book**.

5 Before speaking, students will find it helpful to make lists of differences between each of the situations listed. Give students an example of a comparison if they need help.

*The really nice thing about working for a small family firm is that I know **most** of the people who work there. We have **lots of** contact with the manager so there are **very few** communication problems. On the down side, there's **very little** opportunity for promotion and there's **hardly any** travel …*

6 Again, students should start by making lists of what they need more or less of. If they need ideas, they can comment on things like public transport, traffic, entertainment, shopping, accommodation or restaurants, Internet access at work, office space, etc.

Pre-work learners

Students can consider how to improve their place of study, e.g. its facilities.

Feedback focus

You could encourage students to give peer feedback by listening out for correct use of quantifiers during the activities in **5** and **6**.

ⓘ Refer students to the **Interactive Workbook Exercises and Tests** for revision.

Case study

Background

This *Case study* presents a situation where a new start-up has rapidly taken off. The topic allows students to analyse a company's strengths and weaknesses, and identify its USP. The *Task* enables them to discuss issues relating to an expansion crisis and to practise the language of giving and responding to arguments and opinions in a decision-making meeting.

Allow a few minutes for students to read the text about Cyclepods Ltd and be prepared to answer any questions about vocabulary.

Discussion

1, 2, 3, 4 Students can discuss these questions in pairs and feed back to the class.

Watch out! Check that students understand the term *USP* in **2**. The *Unique Selling Point* (or *Proposition*) refers to the specific feature that differentiates a product from similar products on the market.

Possible responses

1 strengths: the product is environmentally-friendly, it has a space-saving design, it's been sold to eight major organizations, many more orders have been received
weaknesses: the company can't meet demand – no stock, no money to invest in mass production, production is slow, profit margins are low, cannot cover its overheads, has a cash-flow crisis

2 The Cyclepod is very secure. It allows users to lock the bicycle wheels as well as the frame and the vertical position means bicycles are visible to CCTV.

3 The product will appeal to anyone who is environmentally-conscious. Companies will buy this for staff to store their bicycles and therefore it will encourage staff to cycle to work. It might also appeal to universities where many students use bicycles. The product will also appeal to companies who need to be space-efficient.

Task

Students work together in groups of four.
1 Groups need to refer back to the text and summarize the company's strengths and weaknesses, and be clear that cash flow is the route problem facing the company.
2 Each student in the group (or they can work in pairs) spends some time thinking of solutions for the company. Possible solutions could be to borrow money, find investors, improve production, move to another country with cheaper production costs and build up stock.
3–6 Groups follow the instructions and conclude by reading about what really happened to the company. While students are participating in the decision-making meeting, monitor and give feedback on phrases used from the unit.

One-to-one

Your student can read the *Background* and then you can do the *Discussion* questions together. For the *Task*, the student could prepare ideas for resolving the crisis and could discuss these with you, using some of the language of the unit, before comparing with what really happened.

Extra activity

For extra writing practice, students could write a proposal to the owners (James and Natalie) of Cyclepods Ltd. The proposal could list the pros and cons for different ideas and then give a final decision.

»» Unit 7 **Progress test** and **Speaking test**, pages 100–101

8 | Outsourcing

Unit content

By the end of this unit, students will be able to

- talk about outsourcing
- present factual information
- apologize and respond
- distinguish when to use the passive form.

Context

Outsourcing emerged during the eighties as businesses looked at ways to reduce costs and compete in the global economy. Companies assessed which parts of their operations were 'non-core' and gave these to other companies to run and manage. This allowed a company to focus on its 'core competencies'. It also let the company make better use of the emerging opportunities made available by access to a worldwide labour force. This access was also fuelled by the development and boom in telecommunications networks. Consequently, many manufacturing industries are able to move operations overseas – what is referred to as *offshoring*.

The trend has led to the emergence of stronger economies in countries such as Brazil, Russia, India and China, which have embraced the opportunities from outsourcing and offshoring. The fastest growing regions of the world are now Central Europe, the Middle East, Asia/Pacific (excluding Japan) and Latin America.

By definition then, outsourcing and offshoring have resulted in much more communication between people from different countries with different languages and cultural backgrounds. Many of your students may be working for businesses which either outsource or are involved in providing services to another business. So in the first section of the unit, they will have the chance to comment on and discuss the pros and cons of outsourcing. In the *Business communication skills* section, students practise the language of presenting factual information in the context of an outsourcing situation. In the *Case study*, they investigate and present an opportunity to outsource.

Starting point

Make sure students understand the concept of *outsourcing*. It's quite possible that many students will already be familiar with the term and use it in their own language.

Discuss each question as a class. For **3**, you could draw a table on the board to note students' ideas.

Possible answer

+	–
<ul><li>reduces costs</li><li>allows focus on key parts of the business</li><li>can result in lower prices for customers</li><li>makes use of outside knowledge / experience</li></ul>	<ul><li>jobs might be lost</li><li>less control over all operations</li><li>outsourcing overseas might mean exploitation of labour force</li><li>language difficulties / cultural differences</li></ul>

Working with words

1 Students could discuss these questions in groups of three before feeding back ideas to the rest of the class.

Possible responses
1 Countries such as Brazil and Russia will benefit as outsourcing can provide new jobs and income. In some cases, such as India, outsourcing and offshoring have partly been responsible for invigorating the country's economy.
2 It could make the country rely on large foreign corporations who have a great deal of power. It therefore becomes harder, for example, to control the working conditions of employees.

2 Students read the article to compare their ideas and answer the questions.

Answers
1 **opportunities:** earn $60 bn within next five years, large IT market, IT and outsourcing is set to double to 7% of GDP, increased employment including indirect employment
   problems: lack of skilled workers, lack of education / training facilities, poor infrastructure
2 The opportunities appear to be greater. Even where there are problems, it appears that these can be solved with investment.

3 Students find the words to match the definitions and can compare answers in pairs.

Answers
1 sector	6 export growth
2 infrastructure	7 skilled workers
3 core activities	8 business process outsourcing
4 indirect employment	9 expertise
5 training facilities	10 offshore locations

Pronunciation

Provide some practice with vowel sounds /ɔː/ and /əʊ/. Write the following on the board.

core, growth, source, shore, locations, export

Ask students to categorize the words in two groups according to the vowel sound (note that it is the underlined sound in *locations* and *export*). Then ask them to add three more words to each category.

Answers and possible extra words: /ɔː/ *core, source, shore, export, sport, four, law*; /əʊ/: *growth, locations, phone, loan, cope.*

4 **30▷** Before listening, ask students to look at the photos and job titles of the three people speaking. Can they predict what each person might say about outsourcing? Will they be positive or negative about it? Students then listen and answer the questions.

Answers
Paula: 1 It's good for developing countries (emerging economies), but it leads to significant job losses at home.
2 The speaker is fairly positive about the benefits to emerging economies but is negative about the effect on jobs and concerned that the EU (European Union) needs to do more to provide new jobs in home countries.
Christian: 1 It's not only about making savings or gaining a competitive edge – these countries are new markets in themselves. **2** very positive
Chitra: 1 For companies, the workforce is more flexible and productive; there are more well-paid jobs, including jobs for women. **2** very positive

Extra activity

30▷ For further listening practice, write these questions on the board. Students listen and answer.

Speaker 1
1 *Where are jobs in these countries going to?*
the UK (India), France (North Africa), Spain (Latin America), Germany (Central Europe – Poland, Hungary), Scandinavia (Baltic States, India)

Speaker 2
2 *How much lower were labour costs? (70%)*
3 *How much of the IT work is in India? (two-thirds)*
4 *How many potential customers do the new markets have? (hundreds of millions)*

Speaker 3
5 *How many hours a day is productivity? (24/7 – 24 hours a day, seven days a week)*
6 *What is the pay like? (absolutely fantastic)*
7 *How much can you make? (about the same as a junior doctor)*

Extra activity

To help students with the next activity, ask them to look at the *Audio script* and underline any of the verbs in **5** along with noun collocations. For example, Paula says *But it also leads to significant job losses in the home countries.*

5 Students complete the questions with the verbs from the list.

Answers

1 lead to	**4** achieve	**7** get through
2 develop, create	**5** streamline	**8** gain
3 take	**6** free up	**9** improve

6 Students take turns to ask and answer the questions. They should feel free to reply with ideas from the previous reading and listening. They don't necessarily have to come up with new ideas as long as they are using the vocabulary from this section.

▶▶ If students need more practice, go to **Practice file 8** on page 116 of the **Student's Book**.

7 There isn't a definite view on whether this company should outsource, though the opportunities and arguments in favour seem to outweigh those against. However, students should feel free to make up their own minds when preparing to present their ideas.

Feedback focus

During feedback, students can comment on which group had the most convincing arguments. Give positive feedback to any group who used plenty of the words / phrases from this section. You could even note which group used the most (see *Extra activity*).

Extra activity

To add a fun, competitive element to this final task, write all the words below from the unit on the board.

sector infrastructure core activities indirect employment training facilities export growth skilled workers outsourcing expertise offshore locations lead to develop create take achieve streamline free up get through gain improve

While one group presents, the other students count how many of the words / phrases they hear used in the presentation. The group which manages to use the most words is the winner. If you think this will affect the quality of the presentations, then use it as a follow-on activity as a fun way to end the lesson.

ⓘ Refer students to the **Interactive Workbook Glossary** for further study.

Business communication skills

1 31▷ Before listening, check that students have understood what Sanjit's job is and what his responsibilities are (as presented in the *Context*).

Answers
1 10,000 companies already based in the region, buoyant labour market, quality of educational institutions, the number of qualified graduates
2 Sanjit asks rhetorical questions to keep attention and he asks the questions he believes his audience want answering. For example: *What does Bangalore have to offer in business terms? How well qualified is the workforce?* Point out that this is a good way to structure a presentation.

2 31▷ Students listen carefully to identify the phrases used.

Answers
1 Statistics show … / Recent data illustrates …
2 **a** as a result of … **b** due to …

3 32▷ Students listen to the second part of the presentation and answer the questions.

Answers
1 No – Bangalore has a tradition of attracting engineering companies.
2 **a** expected growth in IT services annually
b multinational software and outsourcing companies that have built offices in Bangalore
c number of new offices opened in the city in the first four months of this year
d new staff employed per month
3 Investors will not only obtain a skilled workforce but will also ensure this workforce remains within India.

4 32▷ Students listen again and complete the phrases. Clarify the meaning of the commonly used idiom *food for thought* in sentence 8. It means 'information to consider carefully'.

Answers
1 briefly looked at, let's move on to
2 will notice on this chart
3 I mentioned earlier
4 turn our attention to
5 at this slide, we can see
6 have a look at these figures
7 Subsequently
8 I go today, leave you with some food for thought
9 has resulted in

5 Students categorize the phrases in **4**.

Answers
a 7, 9 **b** 1, 4 **c** 3 **d** 2, 5, 6 **e** 8

Extra activity

Students at this level who have given presentations before will be familiar with the five categories in **5**. Ask them to work in pairs and think of one more phrase for each category. Then ask them to share their ideas with the rest of the class. This both reviews and expands students' range of useful phrases for presenting. Some possible phrases might be as follows.
a *Therefore / Consequently*
b *Let's take a look at / Turning to … now*
c *As I said before / Referring back to what I said earlier*
d *As you can see / This chart shows you*
e *In conclusion / What I'd like to leave you with is*

▶▶ If students need more practice, go to **Practice file 8** on page 116 of the **Student's Book**.

6 Students work in pairs for this activity and can take turns to practise their presentation and use phrases from the *Key expressions* list before presenting to the other pair. With presentations where students work in pairs, it is up to them to decide who will talk about which section.

Allow any students who want to give the whole presentation on their own to do so. In this case, they can rehearse with a partner and then change partner and give a final version.

Students might need help with describing the diagrams in section 3 of the chart. Here are some ideas.
a *Looking at this graph, we can see that as you reduce your costs, more money is available for IT investment.*
b *You will notice on this next chart that the reduction in salary costs was a direct result of outsourcing.*
c *Now have a look at how a knock-on effect of outsourcing has been an increase in shareholder value.*

7 Students may need to research the topics to feel that they can give a credible presentation. If so, set the task at the end of the lesson and begin the next class with the presentations.

Feedback focus

If possible, video the final presentations and set aside time for students to watch and self- or peer-assess the performance.

ⓘ Refer students to the **Interactive Workbook Email** and **Phrasebank** sections for further study.

Practically speaking

1 33 ▷ Students listen and answer the questions.

> **Answers**
> **1** and **2**
> **1** being late – got held up in traffic
> **2** a mix-up with an order – ordering system crashed
> **3** not preparing for a meeting – has been really busy
> **4** finishing the coffee (no reason)
> **5** a mistake – don't know how it happened
> **6** for not answering the phone – speaker wasn't in

2 33 ▷ Students listen again and identify the phrases used.

> **Answers**
> **1** Sorry ... / I do apologize for ... / I'm afraid ... / Sorry about that. / I'm really sorry about ... / I'm sorry that ...
> **2** It doesn't matter. / That's all right. I understand ... / Don't worry about it. / That's OK. / Never mind. / No problem.
> **3** *I do apologize for* is the most formal. *I'm **really** sorry* helps to add emphasis.

Pronunciation

Drill students with these phrases, if necessary, and focus on how they can sound more apologetic by stressing the underlined words in the following phrases.

> I <u>do</u> apologize.   I'm <u>really</u> sorry.

Tip Discuss this with students before the next activity. Look at the *Audio script* together to see the explanations and extra comments the speakers made.

3 Students practise the phrases with the situations provided.

Language at work

1 This opening grammar point should be a review and a quick check of students' understanding.

> **Answers**
> **1** passive – The speaker wishes to emphasize the *thousands of jobs*. The jobs have been outsourced by companies but in this context it is not important which ones.
> **2** active – The focus of the speaker is that the EU companies have done this action.

2 Students answer the first question. If they appear to be finding this analysis new or difficult, ask them to read through the language summary in the *Practice file* and complete the exercises before moving on to **3**.

> **Answers**
> **1** The agent in this sentence is not known or not important.
> **2** *Who* expects (the agent) is not important. The information might have come from economists but this is irrelevant to the main aim of the speaker. The passive here is also used for distancing the source from the information (so if the economists' predictions are wrong they are not held directly accountable).
> **3** Again, it is unimportant to know who built the offices. The emphasis is on the effect rather than the agent.
> **4** Here, the passive is being used to focus on what is happening in the job market but it is important to know who did the action so the speaker includes *by + person.*

Discuss the second question regarding how students use the passive form in their own language. It is worth noting that English tends to use passive structures more than many other languages because of its indirectness.

3 Students can work in pairs to do this.

> **Answers**
> **1** This sounds better in the passive because we are not interested in *who*, but the fact that it is stored somewhere: *A lot of our sensitive information is stored in secure remote sites.*
> **2** The speaker is interested in *who* so the active form is appropriate.
> **3** The speaker can't believe that no one knows where Jason is, so the active form is natural.
> **4** We know that workers produce cars, so here we need to use the passive: *The new Mini will be manufactured at BMW's factory in Oxford.*
> **5** Again, the person or agent in this sentence is not important to the listener so the passive should be used: *The road has been closed for repairs for two weeks.*
> **6** The first clause sounds natural in the active, but the second clause doesn't need to refer to who is doing the action: *You can't use the lift today because it is being serviced.*

4 Explain that the structure *It* + passive form is often used to be impersonal and more formal.

> **Answers**
> **1** It is said that Bangalore's very nice ...
> **2** It is known that Indian software engineers are ...
> **3** It is thought that property there is ...
> **4** It is believed that Microsoft is interested in ...
> **5** It is expected that outsourcing to China will increase ...

5 Students make their own sentences using *It* + passive form. Write the forms from **4** on the board to help them.

> *It is said … It is known … It is thought …*
> *It is believed … It is expected …*

If students struggle with ideas, suggest they make sentences about news in their own company or college, or about the current news on TV.

6 The passive can be used to hide the name of a person. It is often used with bad news or where a mistake has been made.

> **Answers**
> **1** The decision has been made …
> **2** the photocopier hasn't been fixed
> **3** The package was sent (from the post room) yesterday …
> **4** they are being made
> **5** your complaint will be dealt with

>> If students need more practice, go to **Practice file 8** on page 117 of the **Student's Book**.

7 After students have described the new law to their partner, ask them to tell the rest of the class (if there's time).

Extra activity

The student who is listening to their partner could pretend to be a journalist and write up details of the law as described in **7**. The article would require students to make use of the passive form.

Feedback focus

Give feedback on both the active and the passive. The danger is that students will try to overuse the passive. Remind them that in the majority of cases, the active is the better option as it is more direct and clear.

i Refer students to the **Interactive Workbook Exercises and Tests** for revision.

Case study

Background

This *Case study* presents a situation where a company outsources the development of a software solution. The topic allows students to consider the advantages of outsourcing for the company and the issues involved in choosing an outsourcing provider. The *Task* enables them to practise the language of the unit within the context of a persuasive presentation to senior management.

Allow a few minutes for students to read the text about Epam and be prepared to answer any questions about vocabulary.

Discussion

1, 2 Discuss these questions as a class.

> **Possible responses**
> **1** The main advantage is that Colgate-Palmolive's sales force became more efficient and effective. This led to improved staff morale and gave greater productivity.
> **2** Factors to consider are whether the provider is located in a stable country, lower costs, guaranteed expertise in areas like IT and language skills, practical issues such as time difference.

Task

Students work in groups of three. This is a straightforward activity. They need to assess the facts about Russia as an outsourcing location and Epam as a provider, and create a presentation. They will need to use the phrases from the *Business communication skills* section. An obvious three-part structure to follow would be as follows (you could write this on the board).

> **1** *Provide an overview of Epam.*
> **2** *Give background and the advantages of outsourcing to a Russian provider.*
> **3** *Present the work done with Colgate-Palmolive.*

Suggest that students create slides similar to the information in the chart in **6** on page 51. After each presentation, you and / or other students in the class can comment on the following.

- range of ideas in the presentation
- quality of visual aids
- use of phrases from this unit
- how persuasive the arguments were

At the end of all the presentations, students could vote on which was the most persuasive.

One-to-one

Your student can read the *Background* and then you can do the *Discussion* questions together. Ask the student to prepare the presentation for the next lesson.

>> Unit 8 **Progress test** and **Speaking test**, pages 102–103

9 | Employees

Unit content

By the end of this unit, students will be able to
- talk about changing jobs
- talk about ways of keeping staff
- negotiate solutions
- make and respond to quick requests
- use first and second conditionals for negotiating solutions.

Context

The days when employees were seen as disposable and replaceable have ended in many businesses. Employees are the company's most important resource. With more staff needing to be employed and possibly trained for highly-skilled positions, it is expensive for companies to lose staff. At the same time, with many countries introducing measures to encourage greater fluidity within the labour market, companies are more willing to hire on a freelance basis and more employees are keen to sell their expertise to the highest bidders.

Companies must therefore work harder to retain good staff. They might use benefits and incentives, as a good wage or salary might not be enough to keep an employee. Companies will need to offer yearly appraisals to plan a strategy of professional development with members of staff to ensure they feel they have career ambitions which can be met within the limits of the company.

In the first section of this unit, students will discuss some of the issues arising from these points – the major one for a company being how to retain staff and avoid high staff turnover. The communication skill of negotiating is normally considered to be about buying and selling, but the context in this unit – an internal situation where managers need to redeploy existing staff – highlights students' need for negotiating skills in all areas of business. To support the language of negotiating, students review and practise first and second conditionals before negotiating an attractive repatriation package with Human Resources in the *Case study*.

Starting point

Students discuss these questions. Encourage them to give examples from their own experience of different jobs. Ask them why they like their current job and what the benefits are.

Pre-work learners

Ask students to draw up a list of what they would like to receive from their first job other than a good salary.

Working with words

1 34▷ Students listen and answer the questions. You could write students' answers on the board in the form of a table (see *Answers* below). Note that for question 2, the speakers don't say directly what they've learnt but we can guess from the comments.

Answers

1

	Tyler	Fabia	Karl
a	worked on the production line at an automobile factory / now an IT consultant	worked for multinational insurance company / set up own recruitment agency	was production manager for Ericsson / now a hospital administrator for a charity
b	made redundant	not much opportunity for advancement, not valued by management	restless, needed a new challenge and change of direction and didn't like the corporate culture or rules and red tape
c	went on courses to retrain	opted for self-employment	came across the charity which was looking for an administrator
d	relocation, unemployment or early retirement	make a sideways move within the company	apply for a temporary secondment in the UK

2 Possible answers
Tyler: You are never too old to learn new skills.
Fabia: People don't only work for money. What job we choose is affected by personal reasons or the desire for more personal and professional growth.
Karl: You can transfer many skills to a totally different job. Sometimes it's worth having a lower salary in return for improved quality of life.

2 Students turn to the *Audio script* and find the phrases in bold before explaining the difference in meaning.

> **Answers**
> 1 Taking early retirement is voluntary. Being made redundant is not.
> 2 Temporary secondment is a short-term transfer to another position, department or organization. Relocation is more permanent and is the transfer of a home or business to another place, town, etc.
> 3 Being laid off is the action of the company to employees (because there isn't enough work). Unemployment (having no job to go to) is the result.
> 4 A sideways move means the person may be in a different part of the company or have a different job but there is no progress or development. A change of direction will bring new opportunities.
> 5 Transferable skills are already existing and can be used in another job. Updating your skills means learning new skills.
> 6 The 'glass ceiling' refers to the limit in a company you can reach in terms of advancement. In other words you can see higher positions above you but you will never be able to move into these for reasons such as gender. Opportunity for advancement means you have a chance to move up the company.
> 7 Corporate culture refers to the beliefs of the company or the way things are done at the company. These things are not necessarily formally written. Rules and red tape are formal and may be demanded by government law.
> 8 Training is a formal situation where a 'trainer' works with employees. Personal development refers to broader ways of learning and developing, for example being assigned new responsibilities, reading a trade journal or attending a conference will all help the employee 'develop'.

3 Allow students enough time to prepare their questions. An alternative way to set this up is for students to work in pairs to create eight questions and then work with another pair in a group of four to ask their questions.

Extra activity

Before students do **4**, discuss how students think large retail companies can reduce staff turnover. (Possible ideas: increase salaries, offer more benefits such as pension policies, promote internally rather than bring in new staff to fill posts, give more responsibility, provide training and opportunities for professional development, give plenty of praise and recognize success.)

4 Students read the interview and answer the questions.

> **Answers**
> 1 **Possible answer:** Ian's main message is that high staff turnover is expensive and your workforce is your most important resource.
> 2 They invest in internal development programmes, redeploy or promote staff into vacancies where possible (offer job mobility) and celebrate success.

Watch out! When discussing question 3, note that the content may be sensitive. Students might not be forthcoming with comments on how to improve staff retention where they work – especially if the class is taking place within the company or if a manager is in the class. You could lead into this question by asking what techniques the students' companies already use for staff retention. Note also that staff do not always welcome extra training or redeployment so students should not feel obliged to be positive about Tesco's approach.

5 Students do the matching task and can compare answers in pairs.

> **Answers**
> 2 key vacancy   8 redeploy
> 3 invest in   9 staff turnover
> 4 resourcing   10 staff development
> 5 appoint   11 get on
> 6 job mobility   12 ability
> 7 promote

Extra activity

For extra speaking practice with the new vocabulary, put students in A / B pairs. Tell A to ask the three questions in the interview. B closes the book and pretends to be Ian Dickson responding to the journalist's questions. B tries to remember what Dickson says in the interview and to use as many of the twelve words as possible. Afterwards, they change roles and repeat the activity.

6 Students can compile a numbered list or bullet points. Write the following example on the board to give them an idea of what is required or let them try to complete it.
> *Policy on retaining staff*
> *This company recognizes the importance of **staff development** and tries to make use of everyone's **abilities** …*

>> If students need more practice, go to **Practice file 9** on page 118 of the **Student's Book**.

7 Students discuss the three statements. To help students prepare their ideas and opinions, you could draw this table on the board for them to copy.

	Arguments for	Arguments against	Examples from the group
Statement 1			
Statement 2			
Statement 3			

As students discuss each statement, they can complete the table with the pros and cons. This will help to ensure a balanced discussion before students come to a final opinion to present to the class at the end. In the third column, students can make notes on any relevant examples given from the group. (Note that this column could be left out with pre-work learners.)

ⓘ Refer students to the **Interactive Workbook Glossary** for further study.

Business communication skills

1 Before starting the listening, ask students to read the *Context* and briefly comment on what thoughts Dermot and Johanna might have before the meeting starts. The likelihood is that both will be keen to avoid losing any good members of their existing staff to the new team. For this reason, there may be a conflict of interests at the meeting.

35▷ Students will need to have read the three proposals before listening.

Answers
1 Johanna
2 Dermot
3 Johanna
They agree on Dermot's proposal (2).

2 35▷ Students match the phrases, then listen and check. They can also find the phrases in the *Key expressions* list and make a note of the functional use of each phrase.

Answers
1 c   2 b   3 a   4 f   5 e   6 g   7 d

Tip Refer students to the *Tip*. It is a useful phrase when putting forward a proposal.

3 36▷ Students listen to the negotiation and correct the notes.

Answers
- Three people to be transferred …
- Brett can't be expected to do the trainees' work.
- Timo won't join the new team (Sabrina will go instead).
Deadline from HR = before Friday
Students might also decide to add the following to the notes.
- Lena and Marlon will also go from Johanna's team.
- Jamie and Pascale will also go from Dermot's team.

4 36▷ Students listen carefully to complete the phrases in the sentences. To check answers, students could refer to the *Key Expressions* list and also make a note of the functional use of the phrases as in **2**.

Answers
1 just summarize
2 could offer, I'd expect
3 guaranteed, 'd let you have
4 'll be happy for, provided you
5 Unless we get, won't be
6 a quick recap
7 can live with

» If students need more practice, go to **Practice file 9** on page 118 of the **Student's Book**.

Extra activity

The next two activities provide negotiation contexts for practising the language. Students will also need to digest much of the context. If you feel they need greater controlled practice of the new phrases – especially the bargaining phrases – write the following negotiation situations on the board for students to role-play in A / B pairs.

- *You both work on reception. A wants to do some shopping at lunchtime so needs an extra half an hour. Negotiate with B for him / her to work longer today and answer the phones.*
- *You both share one TV. B wants to watch soccer this evening (for 90 minutes) but A's favourite programme is on for 30 minutes on the other channel during the second half of the match. Negotiate a solution.*

Give feedback on the use of the phrases only. As these are quite short and fun, some pairs could perform their negotiation for the rest of the class.

5 This is a controlled practice and gives students the opportunity to discuss how the negotiation could proceed and what phrases to use before doing the negotiation. Students read the situation. To begin with, they could study the headings in 1 and check they know the phrases to use with each stage. Then, in pairs, they structure how the negotiation could proceed. They will need to think about the negotiating position of both the employer and employee and what they might ask for at each stage of the negotiation. Unlike other role-plays, this activity lets students add more of their own ideas and demands. Once they are happy with their structure, they can decide which role to take and carry out the negotiation. Afterwards, ask students to say what they received in the negotiation. Find out which employee and employer got the best deal.

Another way to set this up is to put all the employees together in one group and all the employers in another group so they can discuss together what they would like to achieve in the negotiation. Then students pair up and negotiate.

6 Students work in groups of four. Each pair turns to their *File* to read and prepare for a negotiation between managers and their employees who are thinking of leaving to join a competitor with better working conditions. Managers have to negotiate a series of incentives to retain the employees. Allow enough time for preparation beforehand as well as time at the end for pairs to report their results to the class.

Feedback focus

In either **5** or **6**, elicit from students what they think makes a successful or effective negotiation. For example:
- both sides are satisfied with the deal
- different options are looked at
- both sides bargain and give some things away.

Students can also comment if they did these things in their negotiations.

(i) Refer students to the **Interactive Workbook Email** and **Phrasebank** sections for further study.

Practically speaking

1 37▷ As a lead-in, ask students what things they might need to request from colleagues in a typical working day, e.g. the telephone number of a client, help with a difficult report, etc. Then ask students to listen and identify what help is requested in the six conversations.

> **Answers**
> The first speaker wants the other person to
> 1 answer a survey
> 2 help with a computer
> 3 check an email
> 4 help with the photocopier
> 5 look at some figures
> 6 help with the holiday roster.
> Speaker 2 agrees to help in 1, 4, 5, 6 (though not immediately).

Watch out! In 6, *roster* means timetable or schedule.

2 37▷ Students listen for the responses and replies.

> **Answers**
> 1 Yeah, sure.
> 2 Sorry, I'm a bit busy right now. (Oh, well, never mind.)
> 3 Sorry, I'm just on my way to a client's. (OK, it's not that urgent.)
> 4 Give me two minutes and I'll be right with you.
> 5 Certainly. Take a seat.
> 6 Sorry, no time! … I'll look at it later. (OK.)

3 Students categorize the requests in **2**. Note that some of the requests are neutral and will be appropriate in most situations.

> **Suggested answers**
> **M:** 3, 4, 5　　**L:** 1, 2, 6

4 Student practise the phrases with the situations provided. Which phrases they use will be determined by the formality of the situation.

Language at work

1 Students read the extracts and answer the questions.

> **Answers**
> 1 real possibility – a, c　　less realistic / imaginary – b, d
> 2 a and c = first conditional　　b and d = second conditional
> 3 first conditional = *If* + present simple, *will* + verb
>   second conditional = *If* + past simple, *would* + verb
> 4 The use of *might* and *could* adds lack of certainty or possibility to the meaning.

Students at this level should find this a useful review. If the class seems weak in this language area, it would be worth working through the controlled exercises in the *Practice file* before moving on to **2**.

>> If students need more practice, go to **Practice file 9** on page 119 of the **Student's Book**.

2 Students take turns to be A or B. A begins the sentences (*I'm) thinking of* … and B reacts with both a first and second conditional. The first conditional will show that B thinks the idea is realistic or possible whereas the second conditional will indicate A's statement isn't very realistic.

3 Students have already come across these alternatives to the word *if* in the phrases from the previous section.

> **Answers**
> 1 Unless　　2 provided　　3 Supposing　　4 in case

>> If students need more practice, go to **Practice file 9** on page 119 of the **Student's Book**.

4 Note that in sentences 2, 4 and 5, students are offered two options to make sentences with. In 5, the phrase *as long as* meaning 'on condition that' is given.

> **Possible answers**
> 1 you pay in cash.
> 2 (unless) you pay extra / (in case) there's a delay.
> 3 would you be interested then?
> 4 (Unless …) you won't be eligible for the special offer / (Provided that …) we can give you a lower price.
> 5 (in case) you have any problems / (as long as) you use this number.
> 6 would you be able to do mine next month?

5 Students study the situation between the manager and the employee in the *File*. They use conditionals to weigh up the different options and outcomes. Once they have worked through all the items and prepared arguments, they role-play the situation. Afterwards, pairs can comment on and compare the final agreement.

Tip Refer students to the *Tip* on how the two conditionals are used in a negotiation before they begin **5**.

Feedback focus

Listen for and make comments on use of conditionals and the linking words. Note that in speech it is often unrealistic and unnatural to use a full two-clause conditional sentence. Students will tend to use parts of the conditional.

ⓘ Refer students to the **Interactive Workbook Exercises and Tests** for revision.

Case study

Background

This *Case study* presents a company which advises and supports clients on relocation and repatriation packages. It includes an audio interview with a representative of the company, who describes repatriation problems. The topic allows students to consider the difficulties employees can face when returning home after relocation overseas. The *Task* enables them to negotiate a repatriation package and practise the negotiating language in the unit.

38▷ Allow time for students to read about GMAC and then make notes on the listening. Be prepared to answer any questions about vocabulary.

Alternative

If your students need more guided listening, write the following questions on the board to answer while listening.

> 1 *When do employees get remuneration packages? (when they work overseas)*
> 2 *What do companies need to consider about these people? (what their requirements are when they return home)*
> 3 *What did the Indian employees suffer when they returned from Scandinavia? (reverse culture shock)*
> 4 *What did the company give them? (a compensation package)*
> 5 *Are all repatriation packages the same? (no – they're made case-by-case)*
> 6 *In the example, what did the employees receive? (a salary higher than normal, finance for private education for their children, support for spouse to find work, interest-free loans for a house / living expenses)*

Discussion

1, 2, 3 Students can build on ideas from the *Background* for questions 1 and 2, before giving their own personal reactions to question 3.

> **Possible responses**
> 1 **advantages:** to develop valued staff, to gain know-how, to provide a good incentive
> **disadvantages:** reverse culture shock, potentially lose good staff to overseas companies, need to offer expensive incentives on return
> 2 money and finance, education, infrastructure, less opportunities, overall standard of living

Task

1 Students read the information. Check any vocabulary.

2 Allow students plenty of time to study their *Files* and to do preparation tasks 1–3. If necessary, put two As and two Bs together to help each other work through the details. Then put them into A / B pairs for the negotiation. Make sure they understand the points system before they begin. For feedback, you might wish to concentrate on *if* clauses and use of conditionals that should occur during negotiations.

One-to-one

The *Case study* can be worked through as presented though you will need to take the role of A or B in the negotiation. It may be helpful to record this for feedback afterwards.

≫ Unit 9 **Progress test** and **Speaking test**, pages 104–105

10 | New business

Unit content

By the end of this unit, students will be able to

- talk about starting up a new business
- ask about work and life
- ask a favour
- avoid saying 'no' directly
- talk about activities and results using the present perfect simple and continuous.

Context

Many people, possibly including some of your students, would like to start their own new business. Perhaps they have a good business idea and they are attracted to the idea of working alone. Their motivation might be to make more money by running their own company and therefore improve their lifestyle. However, very few of these people will ever get past the thinking stage and of those that do, the vast majority of businesses close down within their first year of trading.

Lack of planning is one key reason why new businesses fail. A good idea is not enough. Writing a business plan will help prepare for all aspects of the business from marketing to financing. This document is also needed if a future entrepreneur is to attract any kind of investment from banks or business angels (investors).

You also have to convince such people that you can do something the competition is unable to. Very few new business ideas are completely new and there's always someone else doing something similar or a company which will copy your idea very quickly once it's launched. In addition, competition for new business is increasingly coming from overseas as companies can 'go global' much more quickly nowadays through selling overseas via websites.

In this unit, students begin by hearing interviews with successful owners of business start-ups who mention some of the issues above. In the *Business communication skills* section, students practise the language for asking about work and life along with the tricky skill of asking a favour and politely saying 'no'. They will then need these skills to complete the *Case study* where they start up a new division in a company with help and 'favours' from other divisions.

Starting point

Discuss these questions as a class. Even students with no experience of business start-ups should be able to guess at answers for **1** and **2**.

Possible answers
1 to be your own boss, to make money, a new challenge, to be more motivated by work, having a good idea
2 initial finance, compensating for lack of expertise and skills in certain areas, competition, getting good advice and help
3 Currently, online selling / retail seems to be a successful area to move into whatever part of the world you come from. However, answers may vary according to the students' country.

Working with words

1 39▷ Students listen and make notes in the table. It will probably be necessary to play the listening twice, so let students compare their notes in between each listening.

Answers

	James Murray Wells	Jurga Zilinskiene
Nature of business	sells glasses and contact lenses online at a low price	runs one of the top translation companies in the UK
Sources of finance	his father	her own money (profit from previous ventures)
Biggest problem	getting the manufacturers to work with him (because they didn't want to damage their relationships with big retailers)	lack of financial backing limited speed of expansion
Advice	You need a sound business plan and to see a gap in the market.	Be prepared to take risks and be self disciplined. 'Do your homework'* and have a clear effective business model.

* This is a common phrase in business meaning 'do your research'.

2 Students may find it helpful to read the *Audio script* to see the nouns and noun phrases in context before doing the matching task.

Answers
1 venture capitalist
2 stake
3 return on investment
4 gap in the market
5 business plan
6 network of contacts
7 business angel
8 financial backing
9 start-up capital
10 turnover
11 loan
12 business model

3 Students complete the text and can compare answers in pairs.

Answers
1	gap in the market	8	stake
2	start-up capital	9	return on investment
3	loan	10	network of contacts
4	business model	11	financial backing
5	business plan	12	turnover

6 / 7 business angel / venture capitalist

4 40▷ Students listen to the extracts and identify the adjectives.

Answers
1	important	5	brilliant
2	generous	6	different
3	helpful	7	perfect
4	difficult	8	excellent

Tip Before students attempt the next part of the activity, ask them to read the *Tip* on gradable and ungradable adjectives.

Many students will work out when to use a gradable or ungradable adjective according to whether it 'sounds right'. They can test the three adverbs in **a** and **b** by using them with adjectives *good* and *perfect*. For example, *extremely good* (✓) and *extremely perfect* (✗).

Answers
a gradable
b ungradable
c The adverb *really* can be used with either.

5 Students decide which of the adjectives are gradable and which are ungradable, and think of others to add (shown in brackets in *Answers*).

Answers
gradable: kind, nice, expensive, risky, complex, profitable, high (good, rich, famous)
ungradable: terrible, fantastic, impossible, outrageous, useless, ridiculous, wonderful (incredible, amazing, awful)

Pronunciation

Note that we often stress these types of adverbs in sentences to add emphasis. For example:
> That's **extremely** kind of you!
> It's a **really** profitable business.

To practise, write these two example sentences on the board and drill them with the stress. In the next activity (**6**), encourage students to stress the adverb in their responses.

6 Students think of ways to responds to the situations. You could organize this so that, in pairs, one student reads statements 1–6. The other student keeps the book closed and listens and responds.

Suggested answers
1 That's totally outrageous!
2 It can be extremely risky.
3 That's absolutely fantastic!
4 That must be really worrying for you.
5 That's completely impossible.
6 That's incredibly high.

» If students need more practice, go to **Practice file 10** on page 120 of the **Student's Book**.

7 Students read the two business ideas (or think of their own). For question 1, encourage students to respond with an adverb + adjective combination. Groups could make notes on their discussion for each question and feed back to the rest of the class afterwards.

Possible answers
2 They might need help with finance and start-up capital. As well as approaching business angels or investors, they might be able to get funding from local councils / government departments who are keen to sponsor initiatives for reducing congestion.
3 Previous schemes to encourage road users and commuters to give up their own private transport have not been wholly successful. People prefer the independence and comfort of cars. The PIN number cars may offer the users comfort but the scooters are likely to attract only a niche market in the same way that some people take collapsible bicycles to work. In addition to this, people will also only ride scooters in good weather.

Feedback focus

Comment on the use of the vocabulary from **2** as well as the use of adverbs + adjectives. Make sure students stress the adverbs so their intonation doesn't sound too flat.

ⓘ Refer students to the **Interactive Workbook Glossary** for further study.

Business communication skills

1 To discuss this lead-in question, students don't necessarily have to mention someone they met in a work-related or business situation. It could be an old school friend or distant relative they hadn't seen for years.

2 41▷ You might need to play the listening twice for students to complete the entire table. Tell them that the background noises will help them identify the situation in conversation 3.

> **Answers**
> **conversation 1:** A phone call at work / Ex-work colleagues / Had a promotion / New local member of staff
> **conversation 2:** At an airport / College friends / Works in car industry / Business contacts
> **conversation 3:** In a coffee shop / Business acquaintances / Business has lost customers / Contacts in Internet insurance business

3 Students may find it helpful to listen again to answer this. Also ask them to make a note of any phrases which tell them if the conversation is more or less formal. For example: *What are you doing here?* (less formal in conversation 2) and *Thank you for finding the time to meet* (more formal in conversation 3).

> **Answers**
> **a** 3 **b** 1 **c** 2

4 Students can do this in pairs.

> **Answers**
> **1** h **2** e **3** f **4** a **5** g **6** c **7** b **8** d

5 41▷ Students listen to the first conversation again and check their answers.

6 Students categorize the phrases. They can check their answers in the *Key expressions* list.

> **Answers**
> **a** 1h, 2e, 5g **b** 3f, 4a **c** 6c **d** 7b **e** 8d

7 Students identify the phrases in the *Audio script* and compare the phrases used in all three conversations.

> **Tip** Refer students to the uses of *anyway*.

> **Answers**
> **conversation 2:**
> **a** What are you doing here. / When was the last we saw each other?
> **b** What about you? / What have you been up to? / Are you still working in …?
> **c** By the way, could you do me a favour?
> **d** Could you put me in touch with …?
> **e** Let's chat about that over dinner.

> **conversation 3:**
> **a** Good morning … Thank you for finding the time to meet. / It's been a long time since we've been in contact.
> **b** How's life treating you? / How's business with you? / What's been happening?
> **c** And with that in mind, maybe I could ask you for a favour.
> **d** We are looking for … and I wondered if ….
> **e** It sounds an interesting proposal. / Send me the details. / I can't promise anything, though.

Extra activity

Now that students have focused on the phrases, they will need plenty of practice using the language. In **8**, they will have two conversations. However, for more controlled practice, ask students to work in pairs and look back at the table in **2**. There are two extra pieces of information which are unused in each column. Students can combine one piece of information from each column to write a short dialogue between two people. For example, the conversation might take place in a taxi queue between a customer and a supplier, one of whom has recently married a French woman. The supplier is looking for venture capital to start up on his own. Students write their A / B conversations using phrases from the section and perform their dialogues to the class or to other pairs of students.

>> If students need more practice, go to **Practice file 10** on page 120 of the **Student's Book**.

8 Students use the flow chart to have the two conversations. Tell them to agree whether the conversations will be more formal or not.

Feedback focus

Give feedback on use of the phrases, but also focus on register and the level of formality. Make sure that students aren't mixing phrases with different formality or meaning. For example, if A begins by saying *Thank you for finding the time to meet me*, it will sound strange for B to reply with a phrase like *I haven't seen you for ages!*

9 This is a fun way to end this section. Students write true events but also create untrue information. They both attempt to guess what is true / untrue at the end of the conversation.

ⓘ Refer students to the **Interactive Workbook Email** and **Phrasebank** sections for further study.

Practically speaking

Watch out! Note that the issue of avoiding saying 'no' is both a question of someone's personality and perhaps of their national or business culture. For example, we can feel uncomfortable saying 'no' to a friend or colleague. And for some nationalities, saying 'no' immediately is considered impolite.

1 Allow time for pairs to discuss these questions and then discuss as a class. With mixed-nationality classes, explore the idea that some cultures will avoid saying 'no' more than others. Do your students have any experience of this?

Watch out! You might need to explain the meaning of *on-call shift* in 3a. This refers to an aspect of a job where someone can be called upon to do some work at any time of day. For example, a doctor may have to answer the phone at night in case of an emergency.

2 Students take turns to respond to the four situations. Make sure that no one says 'no'!

Language at work

1 Students match the extracts to the situations and identify the tenses.

> **Answers**
> 1 c (present perfect simple)
> 2 b (present perfect continuous)
> 3 a (present perfect simple)

2 Students refer to the extracts to answer the questions.

> **Answers**
> 1 temporary (present perfect continuous)
> 2 permanent (present perfect simple)

3 When discussing this language point, it might be helpful to draw the following timelines on the board.

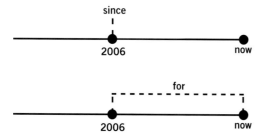

> **Answer**
> *for* is used to describe an amount of time and *since* is used to refer to a point in time.

4 Students can do this in pairs.

> **Answers**
> 1 I've worked out a final price – b (It is finished and the speaker has made final conclusions.)
>   I've been working out a final price – a (This is unfinished.)
> 2 I've been calling Mrs Fischer – a (The situation is unfinished. Presumably the speaker has to keep calling.)
>   I've called Mrs Fischer – b (The speaker won't call again because he/she has left a message.)
> 3 I've worked with Karen – b (This is permanent.)
>   I've been working with Karen – a (This is temporary.)
> 4 We've been hiring – b (This emphasizes the activity.)
>   We've hired – a (This emphasizes the result.)

5 Students take turns to ask questions using the present perfect simple or continuous. The student answering will use the simple form if the task has / hasn't been done but the continuous form if it is ongoing.

6 Allow about five minutes for students to prepare a list of activities to refer to.

Pre-work learners

Students could draw up a list of current activities taking place in their place of study. They could also describe activities of a company they know well or perhaps one they've read about in the newspaper or on the Internet. If necessary, they could research this before the next lesson.

Feedback focus

Any feedback should concentrate on the correct use of form and use of the two tenses.

ⓘ Refer students to the **Interactive Workbook Exercises and Tests** for revision.

Case study

Background

This *Case study* presents a situation where a Japanese IT graduate set up a bagel shop in Tokyo, thus successfully introducing a business idea from another culture into her own. The topic enables students to consider the issues involved in introducing products from other cultures as well as the importance of making the most of any help / expertise that is on offer when setting up a new venture. The *Task* enables them to practise the language for asking and responding to favours within the context of setting up a new company division.

42▷ Allow a few minutes for students to read the text and be prepared to answer any questions about vocabulary. Students then listen to the interview with Miho.

Extra activity

You will probably want to check students' understanding after they have read and listened. You could ask them to summarize Miho's business. Alternatively, write these questions on the board and ask them to find the answers in the reading or listening.

1 *What did Miho graduate in? (IT)*
2 *Why was the idea risky? (Bagels aren't well known in Japan and she didn't 'bow to Japanese tastes'.)*
3 *How did she get the necessary experience? (working for free in a New York bagel shop)*
4 *How did she get the start-up capital? (working on an IT project and with a loan from her parents)*

Discussion

1, 2, 3 Discuss these questions as a class.

Possible responses
1 Eastern food has become popular in the West such as noodles and sushi. Pizza and pasta have also become exports around the world. Students may have more specific examples from their own countries.
2 Businesses will need to decide whether to keep the product in its original form or to adapt it for other cultural tastes or assumptions. Some of their marketing may need to educate a culture in the uses of a product. They will also need to consider perceptions of a culture and associations with the product. For example, products made in Norway often have the Norwegian flag on their packaging because this is associated with quality in many countries. Alternatively, when two countries disagree politically, one country may discourage consumers from buying another culture's products.
3 One of Miho's skills was developing contacts. She initially stayed in New York with friends. Then she developed a crucial relationship with Mrs Wilpon in New York. She persuaded a contact to work on the IT database in order to make money. She borrowed money from her parents. The moral of her story is that contacts and 'favours' are two of the key factors in starting a new business.

Task

Students work in groups of four and read their *Files*. Make sure they make special note of which favours they must avoid doing. When taking turns to ask each other a favour, it will be helpful if the group stands in order to move from one person to the next. Suggest to students that they could begin each conversation by asking about work and life before changing the direction of the conversation to ask a favour.

You could comment on politeness during the activity and use of correct formality.

Alternative

This can also be a whole-class activity. Allocate a *File* to each member of the class (it doesn't matter if more than one student is Student A, etc.). Encourage the whole class to get up and mingle. Students ask for one favour and then move on to another student. Students should listen to the request from their colleague and simply agree to or refuse the favour, depending on what they think about it. They can draw on the language from *Practically speaking* when refusing favours. As the rules state, they must say 'yes' to at least two favours.

One-to-one

Your student can read the *Background* and then you can do the *Discussion* questions together. The *Task* isn't designed for one-to-one. If your student needs more practice with asking favours, turn to *Files* for Student A and B and take turns to ask each other the favours listed.

» Unit 10 **Progress test** and **Speaking test**, pages 106–107

11 | Communications

Unit content

By the end of this unit, students will be able to
- talk about communications
- explain procedures
- practise language for taking part in a teleconference
- deal with situations on the phone
- talk about obligation and prohibition.

Context

The topic of *Communications* refers both to the technology of communication and the importance of person-to-person communication in business.

The technology of communication has probably had the greatest impact both on the way business is done and what type of businesses have emerged. Firstly, it's hard to imagine our world without a mobile phone or Internet-based communication. Secondly, the boom in companies offering communications-related products seems unstoppable.

Most of your students will have noted the changes that telecommunication has brought to their working lives. It means the learning of new procedures and the need to be able to explain complex procedures. It also presents a new way of communicating with people in other countries.

In many ways we are at an early stage of this digital age. People can communicate by phone and have started to interact with machines, for example using the Internet as a resource. The future stage will be machines communicating with machines and making decisions (this is one of the issues students look at in this unit). At the same time, such forms of communication remain accessible to a relatively small portion of the world's population – it's estimated that well over half the world's population has never even seen a telephone.

In this unit, students discuss ways of communicating using technology and the implications for business and organizations. Students are also encouraged to consider what aids better communication within groups or teams of people. The *Business communication skills* section allows practice of the language for explaining procedures as well as useful phrases for teleconferencing. In the *Case study*, students are given a communication problem to solve.

Starting point

Students can discuss these questions as a class. Some issues which may come up are that telecommunication has improved our lives and given people the chance to keep in contact wherever they are in the world; but on the other hand, for many people, it has meant they are never out of contact, e.g. from their place of work. With regard to **2**, the majority of your students will probably rank their mobile phones highly as a piece of technology they cannot live without.

Working with words

1 43▷ Students may need to listen twice to make comprehensive notes on the three questions.

> **Answers**
> 1 Communications will become more integrated with other systems and allow us to collaborate with colleagues anywhere in the world.
> 2 using machines to communicate with people, interacting with machines, machines talking to other machines
> 3 Communications systems need to spread more fairly to those people who don't have access.

2 Students could check their answers in the *Audio script*.

> **Answers**
> 1 e 2 g 3 b 4 a 5 d 6 h 7 i 8 f 9 c

3 Students complete the questions and can compare answers in pairs.

> **Answers**
> 1 be involved in   4 interact with   7 connect to
> 2 collaborate with   5 have access to   8 subscribe to
> 3 integrate with   6 have an impact on 9 focus on

4 Students take turns to ask and answer the questions. At the end, ask each pair to report back on their answers to two of the questions.

5 Students need to skim the two texts to understand the general meaning. Reassure students that they will have a chance to read the texts in more detail later and check any unknown vocabulary.

> **Answer**
> 1 Africa calling – mobile phones are used for payment
> 2 Mercy ships – a microscope and satellite communication

6 Students read the texts again. Check any difficult vocabulary before they answer the questions.

> **Answers**
> 1 It allows volunteers to analyse blood and tissue samples and on-board operations can be carried out.
> 2 Mobile phones allow people to pay without access to a bank or the use of a cheque or credit card.

7 Students build the words and complete the table.

Dictionary skills / Pronunciation

Students will find it helpful to refer to dictionaries for checking their answers to **7**. Also encourage them to check which syllable is stressed in each word.

Answers

Verb	Personal noun	Noun	Adjective
analyse	analyst	analysis	analytical
volunteer	volunteer		voluntary
innovate	innovator	innovation	innovative
consult	consultant	consultation	consultative
economize	economist	economy	economical
develop	developer	development	developmental
connect		connection	connected
transfer		transfer	transferable
participate	participant	participation	participative

Extra activity

Ask students to underline the suffixes in columns 2–4 of the table. This will help them to notice the common endings for each type of word form. For example:

Personal nouns: *-or, -eer, -ant, -er*
Nouns: *-ion / tion, ment*
Adjective: *-ive / tive, -al, -ary, -able*

» If students need more practice, go to **Practice file 11** on page 122 of the **Student's Book**.

8 You could begin by brainstorming and writing on the board all the types of communications technology students can think of. This will provide a useful springboard for the groups to discuss what has changed.

Pre-work learners

Students can discuss the changes that communications technology has brought about in life in general, such as in the home and in entertainment.

ⓘ Refer students to the **Interactive Workbook Glossary** for further study.

Business communication skills

1 As a lead-in, ask students to suggest all the different ways companies can recruit new staff (e.g. newspaper adverts, through contacts, job agencies). Either elicit or suggest the concept of websites designed to match employers with new staff.

Check that students understand the *Context*. Ask them to summarize the main details, i.e. Job Seeker links employers and potential employees via the Internet and they are now offering services in Romania and Austria. The teleconference is to tell the people working for Job Seeker in these countries how to deal with key account customers.

Watch out! A *teleconference* is when more than two people speak on the phone. This is useful for meetings where people are in different locations.
Key account customers are those customers which bring a company the majority of its business. Some companies will appoint *key account managers* whose job is specifically to maintain and develop business with these people.

44▷ Play the listening for students to find the four answers to the queries.

Answers
1 once a quarter / every three months
2 a special price for three job postings, one-month resumé access and logos on job ads
3 It is based on the approximate number of postings the client will make in one month.
4 Yes – Jimmy will email the information.

2 Students categorize the phrases.

Answers
a 1, 3, 6   **b** 2, 4   **c** 5

Extra activity

Ask students to underline the key parts of phrases 1–6 in **2** (and you can write them on the board). They can use these in the next task.

You must …
It's a good idea to …
You need to (make sure) …
What's useful is to …
What happens is …
It's essential to …

3 Students talk through the instructions for teleconferencing. They should decide which are necessary and which are recommended for a successful teleconference and use the appropriate phrases in **2**.

4 44▷ Teleconferencing is a relatively new form of communication and students who use this at work will find the phrases identified here useful for the medium.

Play the listening again and students note their answers. Note that in question 2, students should also listen out for the use of intonation. After Angelika has replied to Jimmy's 'Are you with me', Jimmy checks Mirela has also understood by using her name (*Mirela?*). Here he needs to use rising intonation. It only makes sense as a form of checking understanding when the intonation is correct.

> **Answers**
> 1 What exactly do you mean by ...? / So you're saying ...?
> 2 Are you with me? – OK ... Yes, I've got that. / OK. I'm with you.
>   Is that clear? – Yeah, that's clear.
> 3 Can we speed up a little ...?
> 4 In both cases there is a bad connection. The speaker is too quiet in the first case and cannot be heard in the second:
>   **Mirela** Jimmy, you're very faint.
>   **Angelika** Hello? ... I can't hear Mirela!

Tip Refer students to the additional useful teleconference language in the *Tip*.

» If students need more practice, go to **Practice file 11** on page 122 of the **Student's Book**.

5 This activity provides controlled practice of phrases used in a teleconference.

> **Answers**
> 1 Could you slow down a bit? We're having problems following you.
> 2 What exactly do you mean by ...? / Can you run through that again?
> 3 You're breaking up. / You're very faint.
> 4 Can we speed up a little ...?
> 5 Is that clear? / Are you with me?

6 Allow time for students to work alone and make a list of stages for their chosen procedure. You might need to provide some other ideas for procedures such as using a new coffee machine, using the photocopier at work or asking for time off. Remind students to think about which stages of the procedure are essential and which are recommended. With large classes, students can present to each other in groups of four or five.

Feedback focus

As well as commenting on the use of phrases by the presenting students, note and monitor how the listening students ask for clarification during the presentation.

Alternative / Extra activity

You can either do the following suggested activity as an alternative to **6** or repeat the discussion in **6** but in the following context. Put students into groups of three or four. They are going to simulate a teleconference. If you have teleconference facilities available, that is perfect. If not, put the groups into circles but with their backs facing inwards so they can't see anyone else. Explain that during the teleconference, students take turns to explain their procedure in **6** while the other students listen and take notes. Listening students should also ask for clarification where necessary and use the teleconferencing phrases from **4**.

ⓘ Refer students to the **Interactive Workbook Email** and **Phrasebank** sections for further study.

Practically speaking

1 As a lead-in, ask students to describe any difficult situations they have had on the phone. These might be difficulties with people but also technical difficulties with a mobile phone, for example.

Watch out! Note that some of your students might be more familiar with the American English *cellphone* meaning *mobile phone* (British English).

45▷ Students listen and answer the questions.

> **Answers**
> **conversation 1:**
> 1 There's a bad line between two (mobile) phones.
> 2 One speaker will call back on the landline in five minutes.
> **conversation 2:**
> 1 One speaker is about to get on a plane (so will have to switch the mobile off).
> 2 The other speaker will call back in two hours.
> **conversation 3:**
> 1 Beatriz wants to speak but the other person is on another call.
> 2 The other person will call back in a few minutes.

2 45▷ Students try to match the statements and responses before they listen again and check.

> **Answers**
> 1 b 2 c 3 d 4 a

3 Students categorize the statements.

4 For each situation, students need to be clear that there will be a problem with communication or it isn't a good time to call. It might be helpful to talk through the situations and elicit some of the phrases which will be helpful. For example:

1 The person answering is on holiday so might say it's a bad time to call.
2 The line might be bad because the call is from a remote place.
3 The person is in the middle of watching a film and the phone call will disturb other viewers.
4 There will be a lot of noise from the sporting event so it will be difficult to hear.

Language at work

1 Students match the extracts to the meanings 1–4.

Answers
1 b **2** d **3** a **4** c

2 Students can discuss this in pairs.

Answers
a *don't have to* – needn't, don't need to
b *must* – have to
c *should* – ought to
d *can't* – mustn't, aren't allowed to

3 The aim of this activity is to draw students' attention to past forms of modal verbs. For example, it reminds students that *must* has no past form.

Answers
1 have to, must, have got to
2 needn't, don't need to, hasn't got to
3 are allowed to, mustn't, can't

>> If students need more practice, go to **Practice file 11** on page 123 of the **Student's Book**.

4 When asking questions, students will need to decide which of the two question forms is more appropriate. The most likely question forms are as follows.
Do you have to pay for phone calls?
Do you have to work at weekends?
Do you have to sign in and out of the office?

Can you take holiday at any time?
Do you have to record use of the office photocopier?
Do you have to carry an identity card?
Can you work at home?
Can you take time off in lieu for working overtime?

When answering these questions, encourage students to vary the use of modals in their answers. For example:
A Do you have to pay for phone calls?
B Yes, we've got to pay for personal calls. But if there's an emergency, we can use the office phone and needn't pay for the call.

5 Remind students to use the past modals in **3**: *had to, didn't have to, could(n't), was(n't) / were(n't) allowed to.* Then the pairs choose two (or more) problems to talk about. For example:
I forgot an appointment with a really important client so I had to telephone and apologize.
I ran out of money on holiday and I couldn't get any from the local bank so I had to borrow some from …

6 Allow 5–10 minutes for students to draw up and prioritize their list of guidelines. Note that many of the modals used in the presentation will be those used when something is obligatory, not possible or not allowed.

Feedback focus

Monitor for correct use of modals. Even at this level, you may hear students confuse the form (e.g. *must ~~to~~ do something*) or use modals for the wrong function.

ⓘ Refer students to the **Interactive Workbook Exercises and Tests** for revision.

Case study

Background

This *Case study* presents a situation where a company has had to develop a new internal communication procedure related to dealing with client queries and problems. The topic enables students to consider what communication problems a company might face following rapid expansion internationally and how these might be dealt with. The *Discussion* includes an audio interview with a representative of the company who describes the new procedures developed to deal with communication from clients. The *Task* enables students to develop and explain a procedure for dealing with queries from clients operating check-in systems at airports.

Allow a few minutes for students to read the text and be prepared to answer any questions about vocabulary. Ask the following to check understanding of the situation.

1 *Why has the company introduced a shift system? (because of the time difference between FWZ's working hours and those of customers in the US and Asia)*
2 *How does the team communicate with each other about client queries and problems? (by email)*

Discussion

1, 2 Discuss these first two questions as a class.

Possible responses
1 When a company grows, there is a greater possibility that information is not given to everyone or client enquiries can get lost or not be dealt with.
2 Problems that may occur:
- calls are made when no one is in the office
- calls are at inconvenient times
- misunderstandings about when emails have been sent
- expectations that a problem will be followed up on, but the working day may not have begun
- teleconferences arranged for a time but the time difference has been forgotten about.

3 46▷ Play the interview with Robert Turner and ask students to discuss the two questions. Students may have used software where they work that is similar to that mentioned in the listening. If they haven't, they may be able to give examples of online communication which avoids the need for speaking to a person. For example, tracking a package with a courier firm where you have a code number and the website updates you on its progress.

Possible responses
1 The current prioritizing system used at FWZ still relies on people and therefore is open to human error if a person from one shift doesn't pass the information on to another shift. The new software will help though it's important to note that these kinds of systems still rely on people putting in the right information about the status.
2 As Turner says in the interview, this kind of software allows a customer to check on status at any time of day, so it doesn't matter where you are calling from or if there is a big time difference. Customers also avoid the frustration of waiting to speak to or hear from a person.

Extra activity

46▷ If you feel students need more guidance with their listening, write these questions on the board to answer as they listen.

1 *What is the long-term measure to improve the communication procedure? (to buy some help-desk software)*
2 *What is the short-term measure? (to have a 'man of the day' who checks and prioritizes emails)*
3 *Which three types of emails are prioritized? (those connected to the auto warning system, those which the client has flagged as high priority and 'show-stoppers')*
4 *How does Robert find out what has been done? (by talking to the 'man of the day')*
5 *How will the new software help? (It tracks the progress and status of the query.)*

Task

1 Students work in groups of four. The *File* outlines a very similar situation to the one at FWZ, with different shifts and no guarantee that the customer can always speak to the same person. Students will have to come up with a solution.

2 The groups may need 20–25 minutes to discuss each point listed and agree on answers.

3 The groups present and make notes on each other's procedures. Encourage listening groups to ask questions and get clarification using phrases from the *Key expressions* list on page 69.

4 The class can vote on the best procedure or even draw up a perfect procedure taking the best ideas from each group. Follow this up with feedback on language used for explaining procedures.

One-to-one

Your student can read the *Background* and then you can do the *Discussion* questions together. The *Task* can be carried out between you and the student. Alternatively, ask the student to study the *File* for homework and prepare a short presentation for your next lesson in which he / she suggests a procedure. While listening, you can ask for clarification.

➤➤ Unit 11 **Progress test** and **Speaking test**, pages 108–109

12 | Change

Unit content

By the end of this unit, students will be able to

- talk about change
- present future plans
- be negative diplomatically
- use future continuous and future perfect to talk about plans and changes
- talk about probability.

Context

The importance of change in business is symbolized by the fact that we have the concept of 'change management', and 'change managers' who help organizations cope with change. You can even take courses in handling change.

Change affects us all, but it has become a key factor in business because companies recognize that once they have become successful they must be prepared to change to remain competitive. In addition, the digital age has forced change at a much faster pace. Companies who do not keep up will suffer.

Once a business recognizes the need for change, there is the question of how to implement it. Classic mistakes include things being decided by upper management with little regard to how the rest of the workforce may react. Worse still is when change comes in the form of a faceless memo, sent to all departments, demanding change but with no suggestion of how to bring it about or how it will be supported over time. Without real support from staff and good management of new systems, change will not occur. In fact, change which is implemented badly may cause even more damage or ill-feeling than if things had been left unchanged.

In this unit, students consider the challenge of change for organizations and staff reactions to change. Most of your students will have experience of what it's like to cope with new systems and processes, either as the person trying to introduce change or the employee trying to cope with it. The *Business communication skills* and *Language at work* sections help students to present and talk about future plans and changes. In the *Case study*, students decide on and present possible changes to help a company operate more efficiently.

Starting point

If students don't work for a company or don't think they have much experience of dealing with change, go straight to **3**. Students could work in groups before feeding back ideas.

Extra activity

As part of answering question 3, you could ask students to initially discuss why employees might be negative about the three changes.

Possible answers for 3
a new system of working hours: will help employees make work fit around home life, will make things run more efficiently, will provide more opportunities for paid overtime
using English only in meetings: will speed up meetings with people from different countries and save time
a camera monitor system: will make everyone feel more secure, will protect employees as much as managers from false accusations of not doing work

---

Working with words

1 Students read the first paragraph only.

Answers
1 The most critical part of organizational change is the initial stage when it's first announced. That's when people consider how it affects them personally and they consider the pros and cons.
2 enthusiastic support, apathy, rejection

2 Students read the rest of the article and can work in pairs to discuss the behaviour of the three groups of employees.

Answers
1 These employees will be positive and work towards making the changes happen. They may help management convince other employees.
2 These employees will have questions and need lots of convincing. They will be open to arguments from both sides.
3 These employees will be negative and resist the change. They could work against the changes if they are brought in or respond by doing very little work.

Alternative

To vary the reading task in **2**, put students into groups of three. Each student in the group reads one of the paragraphs about the three types of employees (the supporters, the ambivalent and the opponents). Then students close their books and each student in the group describes the type of employee they read about.

3 Students do the matching task and can compare answers in pairs.

> **Answers**
> 1 resist   4 accept
> 2 react   5 oppose
> 3 affect   6 adapt

Pronunciation

Tell students that all six verbs have the same stress pattern and ask them what it is (the main stress is on the second syllable on each verb).

4 Students discuss their answers in pairs and try to use words from **3**. For example:

> *I tend to react positively to change and accept it as a necessary part of work. I like to know how it will affect me personally but it's the same for everyone so in general I'd say I'm a supporter.*

Any students not working can discuss how they react to change generally.

Extra activity

Tell students to look back at the three situations in *Starting point*. Ask them to imagine these changes are about to happen where they work. Which of the three groups will they put themselves in for each situation? For example, they might be a supporter for a new system of working hours but an opponent of the idea to have a camera monitor system.

5 47▷ Before students listen, find out if their companies have a policy of using English only in meetings. What are the reasons for this? Do they think it's a good idea? Then students listen and decide on a group for each speaker.

> **Answer**
> **Speaker 1:** The opponents
> **Speaker 2:** The ambivalent
> **Speaker 3:** The supporters

6 Students do the matching task.

> **Answers**
> 1 g 2 f 3 d 4 e 5 h 6 b 7 a 8 c

7 Students make sentences with the phrasal verbs in **6**. If possible, they can make sentences about their job or changes at work.

Pre-work learners

Students could talk about change at their place of study or in their life in general. For example: *My new course is working out well, I've run into a few problems with the new timetable … .*

8 Students can do this in pairs.

> **Answers**
> 1 worried, nervous, ambivalent, anxious, apprehensive
> 2 resistant, hostile, critical, resentful, against
> 3 committed, in favour, enthusiastic, keen, positive, optimistic

9 Students can work in the same pairs to match the prepositions to the words / phrases in **8**.

Dictionary skills / Pronunciation

Students will find it helpful to check the words in **8** in a good dictionary, as this will indicate which prepositions generally follow them. Also, use this opportunity for students to study the dictionary notes on pronunciation and check they can say the words correctly.

> **Answers**
> **about:** concerned, worried, nervous, ambivalent, anxious, enthusiastic, positive, apprehensive, optimistic
> **of:** in favour, critical, resentful
> **on:** keen
> **to:** antagonistic, receptive, resistant, committed, ambivalent, hostile
> **towards:** antagonistic, ambivalent, hostile
> **no preposition:** against

10 Make sure students use the words / phrases + prepositions, if possible, during their discussion.

Extra activity

One way to encourage students to use the vocabulary is to write each word on a small piece of paper. Each group gets a set and deals out the pieces of paper so each member of the group has an equal amount of different words. When a member of the group speaks, they have to use a word in their hand. They then put that piece of paper down. The groups discuss until everyone has put all their words down.

>> If students need more practice, go to **Practice file 12** on page 124 of the **Student's Book**.

11 Students need to think of a change and then discuss each part of the experience. If students can't think of a change at work, they can talk about changes at home. For example:

- a marriage in the family
- a change of plan (e.g. someone in your family plans to change a job or a course they are doing)
- decorating the house (e.g. reactions to new colour or decor).

ⓘ Refer students to the **Interactive Workbook Glossary** for further study.

Business communication skills

1 This discussion acts a lead-in to the section.

Watch out! Note that students' answers to these questions will depend on the culture of their company and their country. In some cultures, it is the norm that management makes all decisions and employees have little opportunity to comment. If you are teaching a group from a company, it is possible that some of your students may feel quite critical of the company's current decision-making processes. Be aware that these issues may need to be handled sensitively.

2 48▷ Tell students they are going to listen to a presentation by Rachel and Imran. Ask them to read the *Context* and find out what the presentation is about and who these people are. (The presentation is about proposed changes suggested by business consultants to make FGR more efficient. Rachel and Imran are department leaders.) Once you have concept checked the context, students listen and complete the notes.

> **Answers**
> 1 Through 'natural wastage'*.
> 2 Through departmental meetings and updates on the Intranet.
> 3 By the end of the month.
> 4 Most employees are free on Friday afternoons and the forum will mean staying at work longer.
> 5 Yes, if management sees real results after the changes are made.
> *natural wastage* = reducing the workforce by not replacing employees who leave through retirement or resignation

3 48▷ Students listen again and categorize the phrases.

> **Answers**
> **a** 4, 5, 6 **b** 3, 9 **c** 1, 2, 7 **d** 8, 10

4 Students identify the phrases for 1 and 2.

Tip Note that in the presentation, Imran uses the phrase *Let's digress for a moment* … . Refer students to the *Tip* for more on this use of *Let's*.

> **Answers**
> 1 I'd like to pass the next point over to …
> 2 Let's digress for a moment and look at this in more detail …

» If students need more practice, go to **Practice file 12** on page 124 of the **Student's Book**.

5 Before students work in pairs, allow them a few minutes to find suitable phrases from the *Key expressions* list and think of how to structure their sentences. Some students may want to write the sentences first. This is fine as long as you ask them to cover them up when speaking with their partner.

6, 7 Students can choose a topic that relates to their job or make up the situation entirely. Students could work in pairs on the presentation with each of them giving half. Remind them to use the phrase *I'd like to pass the next point over to* … halfway through in order to let their partner carry on.

During the presentations, the listening students tick the phrases used and could ask questions at the end about the changes.

Feedback focus

While students listen and tick phrases, ask them also to listen out for any phrases which are incorrect. Encourage peer feedback afterwards.

Extra activity

Put students into groups of four. One student gives their presentation from **7**. The listening students are all given a role from the article in *Working with words* on page 72 (supporter, ambivalent, opponent). The presenter speaks and then takes questions and reactions at the end. The listening students play their roles and react accordingly. After five minutes, stop the activity and everyone changes roles so there is a new presenter and each listener responds in a new way. By the end, everyone has presented and been a different kind of listener. The role-play will be fun but also will let students see / feel what it's like to respond in different ways to change. Discuss students' reactions to the activity afterwards.

ⓘ Refer students to the **Interactive Workbook Email** and **Phrasebank** sections for further study.

Practically speaking

1 As a lead-in, ask students to read the rubric about negative feelings and responding diplomatically. Ask them if they think this is true for them. Do they say what they think or are they always diplomatic? Does their culture encourage a direct response or one that is diplomatic or neutral?

49▷ Students listen out for what idea / proposal is being discussed in each conversation.

2 **49▷** Students listen again and identify the phrases used in conversations 1–5.

3 Students make use of the phrases noted in **2** to respond to the situations.

Extension

Set up the five situations in **3** as role-plays. Students work in pairs and take turns to be the manager trying to implement the idea and the employee who responds. The students can discuss the idea further and come to agreement. For example:

A We're thinking of introducing a car-sharing policy and reducing the number of car parking spaces.

B I have some reservations about it. For example, what happens if I don't live near anyone else or my colleague needs to work late but I want to go home on time?

Language at work

1 This expects students to know the names of these tenses. It may be that students at this level are familiar with the constructions, but have not come across the terms. You may wish to illustrate the tenses and their uses on the board with these timelines.

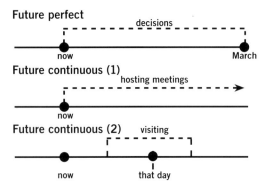

Future perfect

Future continuous (1)

Future continuous (2)

If you think students need more controlled practice with the future continuous and perfect, go to exercise 1 in the *Practice file* before continuing this section.

» If students need more practice, go to **Practice file 12** on page 125 of the **Student's Book**.

2 The aim here is for students to produce sentences containing the future continuous and future perfect. For example:
1 *They'll be clearing the ground over the next six months.*
2 *They'll have completed the project by this time next year.*

3 **50▷** Students listen to identify what is being discussed in each extract.

4 Students find the phrases and write the percentages.

» If students need more practice, go to **Practice file 12** on page 125 of the **Student's Book**.

5 Students discuss 1 and 2, using the phrases in **4** and the correct tenses.

6, 7 Allow students 3–4 minutes in pairs to make predictions about working life. Then they join another pair to compare their predictions and to comment on their likelihood.

ⓘ Refer students to the **Interactive Workbook Exercises and Tests** for revision.

Case study

Background

This *Case study* presents a situation where a company is trying to remain competitive. The topic allows students to consider ways of making a company efficient and more competitive whilst coping with the changes that this may require. The *Task* enables students to decide on a programme of changes for the company and concludes with a presentation using the language for explaining future events and making predictions.

Allow a few minutes for students to read the text about Medstin and be prepared to answer any questions about vocabulary.

Discussion

1, 2 Students can discuss these questions in pairs before discussing as a class.

> **Possible responses**
> 1 The company could move more of its operation to parts of the world where labour and production is cheaper. (Note that this follows on from issues raised in Unit 8 on outsourcing and offshoring.)
> 2 Medstin might respond with lay-offs and redundancies, closure of certain plants and offices, cuts in salaries, renewal of machinery and technology and flattening of management structures.

Task

1 Students work in groups of three. The answers to **2** in *Discussion* should help them come up with ideas for answering questions 1–3. It may help students if you suggest looking at the case of the least profitable sales and manufacturing offices. Work through suggestions and reactions to the problems with the Mannheim office. Then encourage them to work through the rest of the locations and the staff issues.

> **Possible answers**
> **Mannheim Sales office**
> **suggestion:** increase sales targets for sales staff
> **reaction:** unhappy about more work and not comparative remuneration
>
> **Los Angeles**
> **suggestion:** relocate
> **reaction:** job losses / inconvenient site that's difficult to reach

> **Oslo – Norway**
> **suggestion:** close office
> **reaction:** job losses / fear that this will be a trend throughout company
>
> **Old manufacturing technology slows down production**
> **suggestion:** invest in hi-tech equipment – may need to reduce workforce
> **reaction:** job losses / retraining / too old for retraining
>
> **Highly hierarchical structure**
> **suggestion:** restructure – flat matrix structure
> **reaction:** change of colleagues / maybe change of job description, responsibilities
>
> **Trend for open-plan offices**
> **suggestion:** reorganize office space
> **reaction:** concern about upheaval, change of colleagues, breakdown of communication
>
> **12-hour shifts in manufacturing plant**
> **suggestion:** 10-hour shifts
> **reaction:** hostility – lose 2 hours of pay
>
> **Flexitime in office is unmonitored**
> **suggestion:** log-in on computer monitors work times
> **reaction:** concern about lack of trust within company
>
> **Office staff lunch hours**
> **suggestion:** introduce new policy of working hours including breaks
> **reaction:** likely to be hostile
>
> **Computer system downtime**
> **suggestion:** invest in new system
> **reaction:** mixed – it will assist work and make the job easier but it will need more training and possibly more time 'wasted'

2, 3 You might want students to prepare the presentation at home and present it the following day or at the next lesson. Remind them to include phrases for handing over to the other people in the group during their presentations. During monitoring and feedback, pay special attention to use of future forms and probability phrases.

One-to-one

Your student can read the *Background* and then you can do the *Discussion* questions together plus questions 1–3 in the first part of the *Task*. The student can prepare the presentation for the next lesson.

>> Unit 12 **Progress test** and **Speaking test**, pages 110–111

13 | Facts and figures

Unit content

By the end of this unit, students will be able to

- talk about numbers and trends
- ask for / explain factual and numerical information
- talk about news at work
- report back.

Context

It is often said that people suffer from information overload in the 21st century and that the Internet is responsible for a great deal of this. Its ability to provide facts and figures at the click of a mouse has meant that we can find out virtually anything straightaway. Consumers can research prices and specifications of products. Students use it for educational research. For others, access to facts and figures has simply become an addiction with many people searching for 'trivia' or facts which do not necessarily have any relevance or importance in life but are easy to come by and enjoyable.

Facts and figures are, however, relevant and necessary for people working in business. They present them, exchange them and interpret them. In this unit, students work with facts and figures in the context of the Internet. They consider the Internet as a 'killer technology' and look at how it has replaced previous forms of technology, with special focus on e-commerce uses. For example, most businesses now use the Internet as part of their strategy including advertising. The *Business communication skills* section focuses on how advertising has evolved on the Internet. Students will have experience of this either as a consumer or as part of a company which is making use of the Internet. In the *Case study*, students look at the facts and figures behind a series of successful websites and decide which one will be most successful as a place to advertise a new product.

Starting point

This is a light introduction to the topic. Ask students to circle their preferred answer or to suggest another. Then discuss views as a class or working in groups. Make sure students give reasons for their answers. Also use this as an opportunity to assess or help students with saying figures. For example, students may need help with the fractions in 4 (*half, third, quarter, fifth*) and some may not have come across the use of *-s* after the decade (*1890s = eighteen nineties*).

Working with words

1 Discuss the pictures as a class and ask students to speculate why they might be described as 'killer technologies'. Then students search the text to find out why they are called 'killer'.

> **Answer**
> Each technology took over from another and destroyed or superseded it. For example, the petrol engine quickly replaced what came before it in the 19th century.

Watch out! You may need to pre-teach or deal with the following terms and abbreviations from the text during the reading tasks.
transistor = a small device that controls the flow of electricity inside a piece of electronic equipment
chip = a silicon chip which contains invisible transistors
nm = a nanometre (or one billionth of a metre)
kbps = kilobits per second (a *bit* is the smallest unit of information on a machine)

Extra activity

To introduce the text and give students practice with listening for numbers, tell them to close their books. Read the text aloud and students write down any numbers or figures they hear. Afterwards, they check their answers by searching for them in the text on page 78.

2 Students read the text again and answer the question about the five statements.

> **Answers**
> Statements 1 and 2 are made or implied in the text:
> 1 'When the steamship was introduced, it was known for blowing up.'
> 2 'The petrol engine proved to be by far the most important technology of the early 20th century ...'
> Statements 3, 4 and 5 are not made or implied:
> 3 The production of transistors has grown very fast since 1955.
> 4 The transistor was indirectly responsible for television not mass tourism.
> 5 Internet speeds have increased substantially.

3 Make sure students can say the numbers as well as find what they refer to in the text.

Answers
1 number of transistors produced in the world – ten to the power of eighteen (i.e. ten followed by 18 zeros)
2 kilobits per second connection on broadband – twenty-eight point eight
3 the first year that car ownership began growing by 50% each year – nineteen ten
4 between 2000 and this year, Internet usage grew by 206.2% – two thousand and seven
5 the average price of a transistor in 1975 – one tenth
6 a century – twentieth
7 growth in Internet usage (see 4) – two hundred and six point two per cent
8 a century – twenty-first
9 the size of silicon chips in 1974 – five thousand
10 people using Internet – three hundred and twenty-two million

Pronunciation

Students often have pronunciation problems with the /θ/ phoneme at the end of numbers such as *one tenth* and *twentieth*. In other contexts, problems with the phoneme wouldn't necessarily affect understanding but with figures it can. So you might want to focus on and drill the sound where necessary.

Extra activity

Ask students to discuss in what ways the Internet is a killer technology. What technologies is it replacing and how do they think it is changing society? For example, it is replacing traditional libraries, TV and the way we listen to music. We are also able to telephone and conference call via the Internet. Society has become more dependent on it and expects instant information.

4 Point out that we rarely use exact figures but talk about them approximately. The language here is useful for that.

Answers
1 fractionally
2 just over
3 substantially
4 slightly less than
5 approximately
6 somewhere in the region of

5 Students work through questions 1–5. Make sure they are using the words / phrases in **4**.

Watch out! The listening in **6** includes some Internet-related vocabulary which students might want to know.
downloads = music which is delivered as a sound file via the Internet
filesharing = making files available to other users via the Internet

P2P = *peer-to-peer* and refers to users storing files on their own computer and giving them to other users

In audio **51**▷, the music producer mentions that filesharing and P2P are problems for music retailers because people can download music and then share it with other users for free so a large amount of revenue is lost in this way.

6 **51**▷ Before listening, ask students to suggest a couple of reasons why they think the Internet has affected the music industry (e.g. music downloads and people copying and sharing music). Play the listening twice, if necessary, so that students have time to listen and make notes.

Answers
1 growing rapidly – accounted for 45% of singles sold last year
2 have dropped slightly
3 haven't crashed like they have in the UK
4 a threat to big music retailers
5 an opportunity for making your own single and getting heard

7 Students can do this in pairs.

Answers
fast / big fall – crash, a significant drop
slow / small fall – drop slightly
no change – stay the same
slow / small rise – grow gradually
fast / big rise – rise substantially, grow rapidly

Extra activity

Students look back at the text in **1** and underline examples of other words and phrases used to express rises and falls. The text includes: *grew, extremely fast growth, has fallen steadily, have shrunk, continuing to fall, have increased substantially, growth in, reached.*

8 Students can work with the same partner to decide where to put these phrases.

Answers
fast / big fall – plummets, a substantial drop
slow / small fall – a slight fall
no change – levels off
fast / big rise – shoots up, a significant increase, a noticeable rise, rockets

Tip Refer students to the *Tip* about the use of *by* and *from … to* when talking about trends.

Extra activity

The phrases in **7** and **8** include various word forms, combinations of word forms and examples of verbs that can be made into nouns. Ask students to categorize the phrases in their notebooks, like this (examples are shown in brackets).

verb + adverb (*grow gradually, rise substantially*)
adjective + noun (*a significant drop, a noticeable rise*)
phrasal verb (*shoot up, level off*)
verb / noun (*grow / growth, rise / rise*)

Afterwards, drill some of the combinations and ask students to mark word stress on the longer adverbs and adjectives, e.g. *sub<u>stan</u>tially, sig<u>nif</u>icant*.

>> If students need more practice, go to **Practice file 13** on page 126 of the **Student's Book**.

9 Students uses the phrases in **7** and **8** to talk about the cost of living in their country.

Feedback focus

Make sure students are using the phrases appropriately and can pronounce the long adverbs and adjectives.

10 Students follow the instructions in the *File* and begin by noting down the key facts and figures. These can be approximate if necessary. When they are ready, students can give their talks in small groups or to the class.

Alternative

You could ask students to look up a company on the Internet and research the figures required for the talk in **10** ready for the next lesson. Most company websites will give the information needed.

ⓘ Refer students to the **Interactive Workbook Glossary** for further study.

Business communication skills

1 Discuss these questions as a class. Ask students to give examples of the most common types.

Watch out! The listening in **2** includes some vocabulary which some students might want to know more about.
blogs = short for *web logs* which are webpages written by individuals either about their own lives or a topic or issue they are interested in. Some blogs attract many visitors.
podcasts = files (often audio) delivered to users via subscription (often free)

RSS feeds = files containing short amounts of information sent to users to encourage them to visit a much larger site, e.g. a news organization can send a user breaking news
user-generated media = media like blogs, podcasts, RSS feeds which are created by independent online users

In advertising terms, many companies have recognized that these kinds of media provide a much more direct and effective way to reach target audiences.

2 When students have read the *Context*, ask: *Why would online advertising be particularly effective for SurAuto.com?* The answer is probably that it targets younger drivers who will often use the Internet.

52▷ Play the listening and students make notes on what the figures refer to.

Answers
1 age of the target market
2 growth in advertising spending on blogs and podcasts
3 the proportion spent on blog advertising
4 the projected expenditure on blog advertising in four years
5 the annual growth rate of podcast advertising

3, 4 52▷ Students match the two halves of the phrases and then listen and check.

Tip When checking answers for number 2, you can refer to the *Tip*.

Answers
1 e 2 i 3 a 4 g 5 c 6 d 7 h 8 j 9 b 10 f

5 Students categorize the phrases.

Answers
a 1e, 3a, 6d, 7h
b 2i, 4g, 5c, 8j
c 9b, 10f

>> If students need more practice, go to **Practice file 13** on page 126 of the **Student's Book**.

6 This is an information-gap activity where students have to report and ask for information on blog advertising. Students will practise saying figures and should also be trying to use the phrases from the section. Note that the *Comments* column in the table suggests conclusions and provides information to interpret the facts and figures given. At the end, students compare their tables to check the information is correct.

Feedback focus

Monitor for use of the phrases, but also work on any individual problems with saying particular numbers or figures.

ⓘ Refer students to the **Interactive Workbook Email** and **Phrasebank** sections for further study.

Practically speaking

1 As a lead-in, ask students to say what type of news people talk about where they work. What is the latest news at their company (or place of study)?

53▷ Students then listen and identify the topic of each conversation.

> **Answers**
> 1 conversation 3
> 2 conversation 2
> 3 conversation 1

2 53▷ Before you start, check students understand the word *rumour* (a piece of news passed from person to person that may or not be true).

> **Answers**
> **introduce news:** 4, 8, 10
> **repeat news:** 1, 3, 5, 7, 9
> **respond to news:** 2, 6

3 If students have problems thinking of news, write the following prompts on the board for ideas to use with the phrases.
- *job losses at your foreign subsidiary*
- *colleague crashed the company car*
- *colleague forgot his / her passport when going on an important business trip*
- *two colleagues are getting married – no one knew they were a couple*
- *project manager in trouble – miscalculated costs and is already in the red*
- *company is relocating to new, state-of-the-art office building*

Pre-work learners / Variation

Students can think of news where they study. Students could also make up one of the pieces of news. The other student has to guess which piece of news is true and which is made up.

Language at work

1 As a lead-in, ask students in what situations at work reported speech is useful, e.g. updating on progress, after a meeting or conference, reporting back on a trip.

The activity reviews reported speech. Students discuss how to report 1–5. Note that there isn't a correct choice between *say* and *tell* as long as students remember that a pronoun must follow *tell*.

> **Possible answers**
> 1 My manager told me to contact Helen immediately if I had any problems. / My manager said to contact Helen immediately if I had any problems.
> 2 My manager asked me if it was OK to come back a little later.
> 3 My manager asked me if I knew when Jan was getting back.
> 4 My manager asked me if I'd seen Mr Smith.
> 5 My manager told me he always feels a bit nervous when he gets on a plane. / My manager says he always feels a bit nervous when he gets on a plane.

Extra activity

Students could check their understanding of reported speech by referring to the language summary in the *Practice file*. However, you can review the general rules by asking these questions about 1–5.
1 *What happens to the verb in reported speech? (It goes back a tense. For example, present simple becomes the past simple.)*
2 *Why doesn't this happen in 5? (If the information is still true, the verb stays the same. In 5, the manager hasn't stopped feeling nervous – it's a state.)*
3 *What word can we use to report Yes / No questions? (if)*

2 Note that students are able to vary their choice of pronouns for each speaker in 1–7.

> **Suggested answers**
> 2 She encouraged me to apply for the promotion.
> 3 I apologized for not finishing the report yet.
> 4 I denied responsibility for the mistake.
> 5 He refused to do her shift on Friday.
> 6 He offered to reduce the price by €200.
> 7 She agreed to look at the terms and conditions again.

➤➤ If students need more practice, go to **Practice file 13** on page 127 of the **Student's Book**.

3 54▷ The reason for Student A and B making notes on what was said in different parts of a meeting is so that they can report back to each other. This will generate reported speech.

4 Allow students a few minutes to think about and make notes on their chosen situations. Ask them to use appropriate reporting verbs when reporting the situation to their partner.

Feedback focus

As well as giving feedback on reported speech, you could give the listening student the task of noting and giving peer feedback to the speaker where he / she thinks there is a mistake with the reporting verbs and tenses.

ⓘ Refer students to the **Interactive Workbook Exercises and Tests** for revision.

Case study

Background

This *Case study* presents a 'middleman' company that has decided to exploit the rapid growth in the ringtone industry and set up its own direct-selling venture. The topic allows students to consider how the Internet can be used as an advertising platform. The *Task* enables them to analyse facts and figures in the context of a decision-making meeting where they can use the language of the unit.

Allow a few minutes for students to read the text and be prepared to answer any questions about vocabulary.

Discussion

1, 2, 3 Discuss these questions as a class.

Task

Students work in groups of three and turn to the relevant *File*.

1 Allow students enough time to read their information and make notes.
2–4 Students take turns to present the information to the rest of their group, who take notes. As they present, they will need to interpret the facts from the three websites in terms of how much traffic they receive and the type of market using them. Encourage students to ask for interpretation of the information where necessary.
5 Once the groups have all the facts, they discuss the sites with these questions. At the end, each group can report back to the rest of the class on their conclusions. You could encourage them to use reported speech at this stage and make this the focus of part of your final feedback.

One-to-one

Your student can read the *Background* and then you can do the *Discussion* questions together. In the *Task*, ask your student to report back from the *Files* for Student A and B. You can play the part of Student C and give your information. Then discuss together which website is the most suitable.

》 Unit 13 **Progress test** and **Speaking test**, pages 112–113

14 | Culture

Unit content

By the end of this unit, students will be able to

- talk about cultural differences
- narrate past events
- give explanations
- talk about films, TV and books
- talk about past events using past continuous, past simple and past perfect.

Context

In business, an awareness of the beliefs and values of cultures can be a crucial factor in the effectiveness of communication between two people from different countries. Even though two people may be speaking the same language, how that language (verbal and body) is used or interpreted can mean the difference between good or poor relationships.

The writer Geert Hofstede has researched and written about the behaviour of many cultures, and this unit includes a reading based on his work. Hofstede says that cultures have certain traits which, if we are aware of them, can help us to anticipate any possible difficulties. For example, someone from Malaysia will expect plenty of clear direction and control from management. However, someone from Denmark may expect much more freedom and involvement in the decision-making process. If two people from each of these cultures were expected to work together, there could be predictable consequences. For example, a Danish manager might choose to give an employee plenty of space for individual choice but the Malaysian employee might interpret this to mean that the manager was not offering leadership or doing his or her job properly. For more on this topic, you or your students might wish to read more about Hofstede at his excellent website http://www.geert-hofstede.com which includes a country-by-country analysis of culture.

In this unit, students discuss different cultural beliefs and values. They practise the language of narrating past events and review the relevant past tense grammar. In the *Case study*, they are faced with a situation which requires a good level of intercultural awareness to solve it.

Starting point

As you discuss these two questions, encourage students who regularly do business or work with people from different cultures to give real examples from their experience of cultural differences. For **2**, if students have little experience of visiting other countries, they can comment on how foreign visitors to their country behave.

Watch out! As you begin this lesson, it's important to note that discussion of culture and how other nationalities behave can be a very sensitive topic. Inevitably, the topic lends itself to generalizations and one criticism of teaching 'cultural differences' is that we are prone to stereotyping the behaviour of different nationalities. Throughout this unit, steer conversations away from what might be interpreted as stereotyping or even prejudice.

> **Answers**
> 1 The expression means that when you are in another country, you should behave like the people who live there. This might include eating the same food, wearing similar clothes and respecting local customs.
> 2 Answers will vary depending on the experience and attitude of your students.

Working with words

1 Students could begin by brainstorming in small groups and then feed back to the class. Write everyone's ideas on the board.

> **Possible answers**
> how they greet people (shaking hands, bowing)
> which gestures might be considered rude (showing the sole of your shoe in Arab countries)
> some typical food dishes
> their attitude to time (Do they like to be punctual or are they relaxed about time?)
> whether small talk is important for relationship building (or if they like to get down to business quickly)
> which topics you don't discuss (such as politics, sex, religion)
> their view of work versus life (Is work more important than free time?)

Once you have listed these on the board, students read the text and see if they are referred to (directly or indirectly).

2 Students read again and identify the cultures.

> **Answers**
> 1 collectivist (Korea, Colombia) and feminine (Sweden and Finland)
> 2 hierarchical (Malaysia, Indonesia) and cautious (Greece and Portugal)
> 3 risk-taking (Jamaica and Singapore)

Extra activity

Ask students if they have met anyone from the cultures listed in **2**. Do they think the people (or companies) in question display these characteristics?

3 Students might need to read the text again in detail to draw conclusions about their own culture.

4 Students can do this in pairs.

Answers

1	formal	6	liberal
2	hierarchical	7	collectivist
3	egalitarian	8	strict
4	cautious	9	accepting
5	open	10	individualistic

Pronunciation

Read out the words in 1–10 and students underline the stressed syllables (see *Answers* above).

5 Note that the adjectives could be seen as positive or negative depending on your cultural viewpoint. For example, someone from the US may see traits such as *individualistic* as positive whereas someone from Japan might take a more negative view. Typically, for a European student, you would expect that terms like *open* and *liberal* would be positive.

Ask students to consider both views for each adjective. For example, with *hierarchical*, the positive interpretation could be that a clear structure ensures that everyone knows where they stand and can aspire to climb the ladder; however, from a negative viewpoint, it could reinforce class differences and lead to low self-esteem in people at the bottom.

Variation

Students begin by working alone and categorize the adjectives into positive or negative. Then afterwards, they can compare their thoughts with a partner or in small groups. They should discuss the reasons for their difference in interpretation. For in-work students, ask them to comment on how they think their company culture would view the adjectives. For example, does the company encourage individualism or collectivism or both?

6 55▷ Students listen and answer the questions.

Answers

1 The first speaker stresses the importance of researching the local culture you're doing business with. The speaker's boss sold computers in the Middle East. He was familiar with the local culture and their way of doing business. He was competing against a US company with a better and cheaper product. However, the American representative did not do business in the way people were used to. So he lost the contract.

2 The second speaker is describing a course in understanding the culture of the place participants are going to work in. People learn about the political system, the social structure, basic cultural norms, taboo subjects, significant cultural differences between home and host country, and work culture.

Alternative

55▷ To help weaker students, you might want to give them a more focused listening task. Write these questions on the board for them to answer.

Speaker 1

1 *What, according to the speaker, is essential for business success? (to be informed about the culture and be tolerant)*

2 *What main advantage did his boss have over the competitor? (He had been there for a few years and was familiar with the country.)*

3 *In what way was the American both good and bad at his job? (He had a better product at a better price – and could give presentations – but he didn't understand the need for long relationship building in the Middle East.)*

Speaker 2

4 *What kind of companies and industries do participants come from? (telecom, engineering, computers, banking)*

5 *What does the company hope is the outcome of their courses? (Participants will be more sensitive and their colleagues from other cultures will have more respect for them).*

7 Students complete the sentences and can compare answers in pairs.

Answers

1	sensitive	5	respectful
2	adjust	6	informed
3	familiar	7	used
4	aware	8	tolerant

Dictionary skills

To complete **7**, it would be helpful for students to realize that all eight words are typically followed by a particular preposition, e.g. *sensitive to*, *familiar* **with**. A good dictionary will contain this information. Show students this if they are unaware of the feature and let them check their answers in **7** using a dictionary.

8 Students make five questions about cross-cultural understanding. Below are some suggested questions, so you could write the first two on the board as examples.

> *Are you aware of different ways in which cultures can greet each other?*
>
> *Do you think it's important to be sensitive to foreign visitors' eating requirements?*
>
> *Are you very familiar with one particular culture?*
>
> *Is it important to be especially respectful of older people in your culture?*
>
> *Would you describe your country as tolerant of different cultures?*
>
> *Are people in your country informed or trained about other cultures they deal with?*
>
> *Do you find it easy to adjust to a new country?*
>
> *Are you used to dealing with people from other countries?*

In pairs, students ask and answer their questions. Alternatively, students can work in pairs to prepare their questions and then ask and answer with another pair.

>> If students need more practice, go to **Practice file 14** on page 128 of the **Student's Book**.

9 Students will need 10–15 minutes to prepare their list of ideas for each item. Encourage them to mention the key cultural factors in the article and explain how they might affect behaviour. Afterwards, they can either present their ideas to the whole class or to another pair.

Feedback focus

Give positive feedback on any use of vocabulary used from this section.

Extra activity

As a follow-up, which can be done in class or for homework, students write a short leaflet for colleagues who come on six-month secondments from overseas to work in their company. It should cover similar information to that in **9**.

(i) Refer students to the **Interactive Workbook Glossary** for further study.

Business communication skills

1 Before you start, ask students to read the *Context* to find out what 'critical incidents' are. Also mention that critical incidents are often used on training courses in intercultural awareness. Course participants are given a critical incident to discuss in groups.

Watch out! You might be interested to read *Intercultural Business Communication* by Robert Gibson (2002, Oxford University Press). It contains a number of these critical incidents for intercultural training purposes.

56▷ Before you play the listening, check understanding of the term *loss of face* in situation 5 (= to lose other people's respect).

Answers
conversation 1: 3, 5   **conversation 2:** 2, 3

Extra activity

Ask students if they have come across similar incidents where issues of seniority, asking questions or loss of face have been critical factors.

2 56▷ Students listen again and complete the sentences.

Answers
1	time went by	6	but then
2	That was when	7	So that was
3	that's	8	So what
4	it wasn't until	9	in the end
5	due to	10	It came about because of

3 Students categorize sentences 1–10 in **2**.

Answers
a 1, 2, 4, 6, 7, 9   **b** 5, 10   **c** 3, 8

Tip Also refer to the *Tip* when you are checking answers for category b.

Extra activity

In category c, there are two examples of how a listener can encourage the speaker. Showing you are listening like this is an important communication skill. Ask students to study the *Audio script* and find more examples of these kinds of phrases. They will include: *Yeah … / Oh? / Go on … / What had you done?/ I see. / So you mean …? / What happened? / And …?* Note that students have already focused on this feature in **4** on page 15 of Unit 2.

» If students need more practice, go to **Practice file 14** on page 128 of the Student's Book.

4 Students need to read the culture tip first as this will help them understand the cultural faux pas in the pictures. Then students study the pictures and prepare a narrative of the critical incident. They need to combine phrases from the *Key expressions* list and the prompts below each picture.

Extension

Students change partners and take turns telling the story to each other. The listening student must use phrases to show they are listening (see previous *Extra activity*).

5 After students have both discussed a situation, ask some students to volunteer to tell their story of an incident to the rest of the class.

Feedback focus

Comment on correct or incorrect use of phrases and how students structured their stories.

ⓘ Refer students to the **Interactive Workbook Email** and **Phrasebank** sections for further study.

Practically speaking

1 As a lead-in, ask students to think of their coffee break today. Find out what topic(s) they discussed.

57▷ Students listen and identify the topics of conversation in the extracts.

Answers
1 a book 2 TV 3 a film

2 Students can do this in pairs.

Answers
1 (It's) a blockbuster. / (It's) a box office hit. / ... a star-studded cast ... / (You'll be) on the edge of your seat.
2 I'm completely hooked on it. / I can't miss an episode. / I tend to channel-hop. / I just like to unwind in front of ...
3 It's a real page-turner. / I couldn't put it down. / I've just finished ... / It's very well written.
4 I don't get / have much time to ... / There's a ... twist at the end. / I'd definitely recommend it. / It's set in ... / It's about ... / What I really can't stand is ...

3 57▷ Students listen again and check. Note that some phrases don't appear in every conversation but could go in category 4.

4 Students talk about a film, TV programme or book using the phrases in **2**. Encourage the listening students to ask questions about it.

Language at work

1 As a lead-in, ask students to close their books and write the following words randomly around the board.

American billionaire Christmas flat tyre flowers wife mortgage

Tell students that these words come from a real story. Students work in pairs and try to predict what happens in the story using the words. After a couple of minutes, ask for suggestions before students finally read the story on page 88.

Note that in this activity, students will be tempted to simply order the events in the order they appear in the story itself. However, the idea is that the events are numbered as they really happened so, for example, with *e The chauffeur left the tool kit behind*, this is listed later in the article but in reality was the first event because of the use of the past perfect in the story.

Answers
a 6 b 3 c 2 d 4 e 1 f 8 g 5 h 9 i 7

2 Students begin by underlining the verbs.

Answers
was driving, was raining, was, were leaving, had, pulled, opened, realized, had left, was standing, (was) wondering, saw, stopped, changed, was leaving, wound, asked, was, could, said, might like, arrived, was, had been paid

As students answer 1–4, ask them to give an example from the story.

1 the past continuous (... *an American billionaire **was driving** down the motorway in New Jersey.*)
2 the past simple (... *the car **had** a flat tyre*)
3 The past continuous is used for actions in progress. The past simple is used to interrupt these actions. (*While he **was standing** there in the rain, **wondering** what to do, another motorist **saw** him and **stopped**.*)
4 the past perfect (... *he realized that he **had left** the tool kit behind.*)

» If students need more practice, go to **Practice file 14** on page 129 of the **Student's Book**.

3 Students complete the sentences with the correct tenses.

Answers

1 was snowing, slept	4 was staying, decided
2 was talking, sent	5 was leaving, gave
3 had forgotten, apologized	6 had lost, wore

4 Allow students a few minutes to prepare their stories. If none of the situations listed relate to them, they can use their own ideas. They might find it helpful to list the events and then think about how they could give background information with the past continuous or how they could show one event happening before another with the past perfect. Feedback afterwards should only focus on use of these past tenses.

Extra activity

Your students might find it useful to write their stories and this will also allow you to assess their ability to produce narrative tenses correctly.

(i) Refer students to the **Interactive Workbook Exercises and Tests** for revision.

Case study

Background

This *Case study* deals directly with cross-cultural issues. It presents a situation one company faced when providing a new IT software system for a company from another culture. The topic allows students to consider some of the difficulties which may arise when companies from different cultures do business together. The *Task* enables students to investigate the reasons for an intercultural communication problem whilst practising the language of the unit.

Allow a few minutes for students to read the text and be prepared to answer any questions about vocabulary. Ask one student to briefly summarize the situation.

Discussion

1, 2 Discuss these two questions as a class.

Possible responses

1 Problems might include: incompatibility with current hardware, that the software doesn't do all necessary operations, inability of staff to use it properly (need for training).

2 There is obviously a communication problem. It could be that the Malaysian bank doesn't understand the system. Refer students back to the earlier reading in this unit which outlined that Malaysian work systems tend to be very hierarchical and employees tend not to take so much responsibility. In audio 56▷ students also heard about avoidance of 'loss of face' which may also be an issue here.

Task

Students work in groups of four and turn to their *Files*.

1 Students begin by working alone with their piece of information and making notes on it. Make sure they have considered (the cultural) reasons for the problem.

2 While reporting back to their groups, check that students are narrating the information using their notes and not reading the information directly from their *Files*! The other listening students should all be making notes under the two headings.

3 During this stage, students need to read the detailed summary of Malaysian cultural information in the *File*. This should clarify a number of issues and reasons, and help them come to some conclusions.

4 Each group plans and gives a verbal report about the situation. Encourage groups to come up with possible suggestions and solutions for PCR. This report can be given to the whole class or you could put two groups together to report to each other for comparison. Final feedback can include remedial work on past tenses and use of key phrases.

Extra activity

If your students need practice with writing, ask them to write a report on the situation. Tell them to present the report with the following headings.

- Introduction and aim of the report
- Findings
- Conclusions
- Recommendations

One-to-one

Complete the *Background* and *Discussion* sections in class but then for stages 1–3 of the *Task*, ask your student to read all four *Files* and make notes on the situation. This could be set for homework. Finally, the student reports back to you as in stage 4.

» Unit 14 **Progress test** and **Speaking test**, pages 114–115

15 | Performance

Unit content

By the end of this unit, students will be able to

- talk about staff appraisals
- discuss and evaluate performance
- make people feel relaxed
- talk about hypothetical past events using third and mixed conditionals
- point out alternative courses of action using *could have* and *should have*.

Context

There are a number of steps a company must take to understand if it is performing well. Firstly, it has to create standards by which performance is measured. Then it must measure performance using the criteria in order to analyse or evaluate the results. Either the standards are met or they are not and action may be required.

For many companies, the criteria for assessing performance will be based on financial information. Typically, the amount of profit made in a year is indicative of whether a company is performing well. However, financial results do not tell the whole story and could be misleading. We can also measure performance in other areas such as the performance of staff. This kind of information can be crucial to long-term success though may be somewhat harder to evaluate objectively or meaningfully.

Such is the importance of performance in modern business thinking, that it has given rise to its own concept. 'Performance management' is about managing staff so that they know what is expected of them. Staff are trained in the skills that will help them to deliver and the company must create a culture of openness where staff feel free to discuss and contribute to individual and team aims and objectives.

In this unit, students begin by considering performance in terms of staff and the process of staff appraisals. They practise the language for discussing and evaluating performance supported by a language section on third / mixed conditionals and past modals. In the *Case study*, they read about two companies currently experiencing setbacks. They assess the companies' strengths and weaknesses before suggesting ways to improve performance.

Starting point

1 Discuss this as a class. Alternatively, divide the class into three groups and assign 1, 2 or 3 to each group. Each group brainstorms a list of criteria and then reports back. Write any ideas on the board.

> **Possible answers**
> 1 This is usually based on financial information such as turnover, and profit and loss. It could also consider figures relating to productivity or speed at which raw materials are turned into the finished product.
> 2 A project is often assessed on budget (over or under), effective use of resources and if it is completed on time.
> 3 Employees are measured by criteria which are often subjective such as how well the employee works with other members of a team. However, in some jobs such as sales which are results driven, it is easier to assess performance by the number of units sold. Similarly, staff can also be measured in terms of timekeeping and attendance.

2, 3 It will be helpful for students to refer back to the ideas on the board from **1** for this.

> **Answers**
> 2 There is no wrong or right answer to this.
> 3 Any criteria which involve figures or analysis of financial results will be easier to measure.

4 For students who work, ask how performance is measured. Extend the discussion by asking if they think the system of measurement gives a fair or meaningful measurement. What might they change about it?

Pre-work learners

Students can talk about how their performance is measured or assessed at their place of study.

Working with words

1 Before reading, check that students understand the concept of staff appraisal. If any of them have experience of appraisals, either leading or taking one, ask for a brief description of what happens.

> **Answers**
> 1 E 2 G 3 A 4 C 5 F 6 B 7 D

Extra activity

If you know your students use appraisals in their companies, ask how similar the approach described in the article is to the system where they work. The article also describes how appraisals went from being quite informal to being formal. Ask students how formal they would say their system of appraisal is.

2 Students read again to answer the questions.

> **Answers**
> 1 The three aims are given in paragraph A. They were to
> - make sure that employees' contributions fitted the goals of the business
> - have the chance to recognize good performance
> - address any issues for the employee.
> 2 The completed appraisal form is discussed as well as future performance objectives and any views / issues that employees have. 'Constructive two-way feedback' is preferred.
> 3 They use a scoring system where the manager and employee rate each objective on a scale of one to four and compare their results.

3 Students can do this in pairs.

> **Answers**
> monitor performance
> conduct an appraisal
> agree objectives
> address issues
> give constructive feedback
> rate objectives on a scale
> express views

4 Students match the phrases they made in **3** to the definitions.

> **Answers**
> 1 conduct an appraisal
> 2 express views
> 3 address issues
> 4 give constructive feedback
> 5 rate objectives on a scale
> 6 monitor performance
> 7 agree objectives

Pronunciation

Ask students to pick out any words with three syllables and underline the stressed syllable.

> Answers: *appraisal, constructive, objectives, monitor, performance.*

5 To help students with this task, write an example question on the board.

> *How do you **agree** performance **objectives** with your manager?*

Students could report back on their findings to another pair or the whole class.

6 58▷ It may be helpful to clarify the meaning of *top-down appraisal* before focusing on 360° feedback. The appraisal described in the reading is top-down and basically means that a manager talks to the employee about how he or she is doing. Following this, before listening, ask students if they have heard of or can guess what 360° feedback refers to.

> **Answers**
> 1 360° is a development tool. Employees assess themselves using a form and several other people – manager, colleagues, anyone they work closely with – also give feedback using the same form. This gives a more complete picture of how someone is doing.
> 2 job skills, abilities, attitudes and behaviour
> 3 It has to be completely confidential and suitable counselling should be available when you go through the feedback results.

Watch out! You may need to clarify 'suitable counselling', e.g. someone trained to handle giving feedback sensitively and constructively.

7 Draw students' attention to the fact that they are making noun + noun phrases with these words.

> **Answers**
> 1 appraisal   3 criteria   5 judgement
> 2 tool   4 rating   6 management

8 Students need to refer back to the information in audio 58▷ to answer some of these questions. They will need to summarize key points in some of their answers so they might need to listen again before they ask and answer the questions in pairs.

9 Students can do this in pairs. When they make sentences with the phrasal verbs, it might be helpful for them to think of an appraisal process where they work. For example: *You end up with a clear idea of your targets.*

> **Answers**
> 1 end up with   4 hand out
> 2 came over   5 go through
> 3 moved on   6 carry on

Alternative

58▷ With a very strong class, you could play the listening and students listen out for the phrasal verbs.

Pre-work learners

Students could use the phrasal verbs in the context of receiving exam results, an end-of-term report or feedback from their teacher. For example: *The teacher hands out the exam paper. Afterwards, we go through the answers together.*

>> If students need more practice, go to **Practice file 15** on page 130 of the **Student's Book**.

10 Students can work in pairs. It might be useful to work through an example with the class first. For example:

> Doctor
>
> Job skills: knowledge of science / medicine and how the body works, diagnostic and surgery skills
>
> Other abilities: able to respond to patients' questions, put them at ease and discuss their concerns
>
> The usefulness of top-down feedback for a doctor is that you can: monitor the performance of technical skills to check the person is doing the job adequately; rate objectives on a scale to see how well they're doing; agree objectives for improvement / development; address any issues of concern, e.g. long hours.
>
> The usefulness of 360° feedback is that you can carry out peer rating (by other doctors, nurses, lab staff). It could also be a development tool for 'people' skills.

During the discussion, prompt students with vocabulary from the section. Students could make a list and tick a word / phrase every time they manage to use it.

ⓘ Refer students to the **Interactive Workbook Glossary** for further study.

Business communication skills

1 59▷ Ask students to summarize the company's appraisal philosophy in the *Context* before listening. Then they listen and complete the table.

Answers

	Appraisee feedback	Appraiser comments	Action to be taken
Positive achievements	1 helping to produce the in-house magazine	1 demonstrated great prioritizing skills, even with tight deadlines 2 move to new office went very smoothly	
Areas for improvement / development	1 to improve chances of working with international colleagues 2 no other areas need improving on	1 sign up for a language course 2 need to focus on gaining more qualifications	1/2 language course and management course to be put on lists of goals for coming year

Areas of concern	1 too much work with magazine project 2 found it difficult to delegate 3 would have been better to take the old rota to the new location	1 shouldn't have been expected to take on so much 2 – 3 the call centre rota – there has been negative feedback	1 let them know if it happens again 2 – 3 arrange a meeting to discuss it next week
Resources required	1 training on the new program 2 some new software	1 A to check the budget 2 T to put request in email	

2, 3 59▷ Students work in pairs to decide who said the phrases, then listen again and check.

Answers
1 A 2 T 3 A 4 A 5 T 6 A 7 A 8 T
9 T 10 T

Tip With sentence 6 in **2**, refer students to the *Tip*. Note that it isn't enough to add emphasis by simply including the word in a sentence. It also has to be stressed. It may be helpful to drill students with the three sentences given and make sure they stress the words in bold (*really, certainly, must*).

4 Students categorize the phrases in **2**.

Answers
a 4, 7   b 1, 3   c 2   d 6, 8   e 5   f 9, 10

▶▶ If students need more practice, go to **Practice file 15** on page 130 of the **Student's Book**.

5 Using the information in their *Files*, students role-play two appraisals in which they play the part of appraisee and appraiser. Allow students enough time to read their information and to think about possible phrases to use from the *Key expressions* list. Then ask them to carry out the appraisals according to the instructions.

Feedback focus

Monitor for correct use of the phrases in the *Key expressions* list. You might also want to lead a discussion afterwards about what makes a good appraisal. Ask them to comment on the skills of their partner in the role of the appraiser as it's a particularly difficult task. For example, was their partner tactful and made them feel motivated?

Extra activity

Ask students to consider their own job over the past year. Write the following points on the board and ask students to think of two examples for each of them (the information they give doesn't have to be true).

1 *something you've enjoyed or think has worked well*
2 *something you haven't enjoyed or think hasn't worked so well*
3 *something where you've needed more time / resources*
4 *something you would like to achieve / do in the next year at work*

When students have prepared their examples, they work in pairs and take turns to interview each other about their performance at work. For example:

A *Are there any areas you've particularly enjoyed or thought have worked well?*
B *Well, I enjoyed going to the conference in Milan in March …*

(i) Refer students to the **Interactive Workbook Email** and **Phrasebank** sections for further study.

Practically speaking

1 As a lead-in, ask students why it's important to be able to make employees feel relaxed. For example:
   • If people are relaxed, they will do their job better.
   • In an appraisal, people will speak more honestly if they are relaxed.

60▷ Students listen to the three conversations to identify how the first speaker tries to make the second speaker feel more relaxed.

Answers
1 offers a seat and a drink
2 offers help with coat / bag and discusses the journey / traffic
3 discusses journey / weather

2 60▷ Students listen and tick the phrases on the list on page 135.

Answers
Please take a seat. / Can I get you something to drink? / A cup of tea would be nice. / Let me take your coat. / You can leave your bag over there. / Did you have any trouble finding us? / No, not at all. / The traffic was terrible. / I hope you managed to avoid the roadworks. / You've driven over from … today? / What was the weather like when you left? / Much worse than this.

Extension

Ask students to suggest other themes / topics which might be appropriate for making people feel relaxed. For example: talking about their country, the place they work, a colleague both people know. You could also brainstorm phrases for these themes / topics.

3 Students role-play two difficult situations in which they need to make the other person feel relaxed. Afterwards, if there's time, ask some of the pairs to perform one of the situations for the rest of the class.

Language at work

1 Once students have answered 1–4, they could check their answers by reading the language summary in the *Practice file.*

Answers
1 imagined past action and imagined past result – b
   imagined past action and imagined present result – a
2 a = mixed conditional
   b = third conditional
3 third conditional = *If* + past perfect, *would have* + past participle
   mixed conditional = *If* + past perfect, *would* + present infinitive
4 *could have* or *might have* are also possible in the result clause. They both add lack of certainty or possibility to the meaning.

⟫ If students need more practice, go to **Practice file 15** on page 131 of the **Student's Book**.

2 Make sure students are using the conditionals and give feedback on any problems at the end.

Possible answers
1 If I had waited to get authorization for the car, I would have been late for the meeting. If I'd been late for the meeting, we might have lost the contract. If we had lost the contract, the company wouldn't be expanding now.
2 If we hadn't used our regular supplier, we would have got a discount. But if we had used the new supplier, he might not have delivered on time. And if he hadn't delivered on time, we wouldn't have enough paper for the current mailshot.

Extra activity

If you feel students need more practice with the target structures in **2**, write this scenario on the board for them to discuss in a similar way.

> *Your company invested heavily in a small company in South America. The South American company went bankrupt. Your company lost a substantial amount of money. Present result: your company is scaling back and making people redundant.*

3 Discuss the answers to these two questions as a class.

> **Answers**
> 1 pointing out what someone has done wrong – b
>   pointing out what it was possible for someone to do – a
> 2 *could have* can be replaced by *might have*
>   *should have* can be replaced by *ought to have*

>> If students need more practice, go to **Practice file 15** on page 131 of the **Student's Book**.

4 There are various ways to respond to the situations so encourage students to suggest more than one way.

> **Possible answers**
> 1 You should have found out more about the company.
> 2 You could have let me know!
> 3 You should have checked with me.
> 4 You should have told me about the change.
> 5 You could have lost your job over that.
> 6 You should have been more polite in the letter.

5 Allow students a few minutes to think of examples for some of the topics first. This is the first opportunity for students to use third and mixed conditionals more freely, so expect to correct verb forms used by students during the conversations.

(i) Refer students to the **Interactive Workbook Exercises and Tests** for revision.

Case study

Background

This *Case study* presents two companies that have had business success with good products but have also faced setbacks. The topic allows students to consider the strengths of the companies and to identify the main challenge each one faces. The *Task* enables students to evaluate the performance of one of the companies and to consider how it can improve on its current situation.

Students use the language of the unit to present their evaluation and advice.

Allow a few minutes for students to read the texts and be prepared to answer any questions about vocabulary.

Discussion

1, 2 Students look at the texts again and can make notes to answer these questions before feeding back.

> **Possible responses**
> **Maximuscle**
> 1 The strengths are: the owner's credibility from his book, capital from book used to finance company, strong brand with reputation for quality, very successful trade and Internet sales.
> 2 The challenges have included: promoting the brand, bad PR from athletes.
> **Innocent Drinks**
> 1 The strengths are: the owners' enthusiasm, they have funding from a business angel, the product is fresh and has good packaging.
> 2 The challenges are: convincing people about the product, that the product is expensive and has a short shelf life, distributors are not interested.

Task

Students work in two groups. They can choose their company but make sure that each company is represented.

1 Write these guidelines on the board to help students respond comprehensively to this stage of the *Task*.
  Make sure you
  * *evaluate and comment on the company's successes and failures / strengths and weaknesses*
  * *prepare recommendations and advice on how the company could improve on its current situation*
  * *suggest possible resources necessary or time frames the company should work towards.*
2 Each group gives their final presentation to the rest of the class. Encourage students to ask questions at the end. Give feedback at this stage on the quality of the ideas and compliment use of phrases from the unit.
3 Students find out what the two companies did in the *File*.

One-to-one

Complete the *Background* and *Discussion* with the student in class and then ask the student to prepare a presentation on one of the companies for the next lesson.

>> Unit 15 **Progress test** and **Speaking test**, pages 116–117

16 | Career breaks

Unit content

By the end of this unit, students will be able to

- talk about taking a career break
- present a personal case
- talk about taking time off
- choose between *-ing* form and infinitive.

Context

The 'career break' is a relatively modern concept and not necessarily one that will be familiar to students from all parts of the world. There are also different levels of career break. For example, someone might take a break for personal or family reasons, such as to have children, before returning to the same (or a similar job) some months or years later. However, the notion of 'gap years' for professional people has also become acceptable in some businesses. After working a number of years, a person can request extended time off or a 'sabbatical'. This could be to travel round parts of the world or to take an extended holiday. In fact, some research now suggests that companies offering career breaks are able to recruit and keep good staff. It is estimated that 1 in 5 UK companies have career break policies. This trend has been aided by the increase in companies which specialize in arranging gap years.

Many professionals also make use of their skills during a career break and do voluntary work for an organization such as an NGO in the developing world. The advantage of this is that they are actively enhancing their CV and future employers are more likely to look favourably on this kind of career break experience.

This unit begins by looking at examples of career breaks where people travelled or were involved in overseas projects. Students consider the pros and cons of taking such a break before presenting their own idea for a personal break. In the *Business communications skills* section, they practise the language for presenting a case in the context of convincing others about a break from work. In the *Case study*, they look at a volunteer programme and consider whether they might be suitable for such a placement.

Starting point

1 Traditionally, the idea of a 'gap year' was that someone took a year to travel or take a break from studying between school and university. It has become the norm in places such as North America, Europe and Australia. Not all your students will be familiar with the concept.

2 Again, the idea of a career break is not common to all countries. You will also need students to define what they consider is a career break. For example, would they count maternity leave as a 'career break'?

3 You could brainstorm ideas for this as a class.

Possible response

For the employee, the career break will be expensive and the person will need to anticipate reduced (or no) earnings and therefore a change in their spending. They may also find that they miss the routine life more than they expected. Ideally, the employee will take the break and return to the same employer. However, this means the employer needs someone to temporarily replace the person and possibly pay for retraining.

Pre-work learners

If you are teaching students in a college, it is possible that some of them will have taken gap years after school. Ask them to briefly tell the class the kind of gap year it was and what they think the benefits were.

Working with words

1 As a fun lead-in, offering further speaking practice, put students into groups of three. Each student in the group chooses to be one of the three people on page 96 (Freya, Roberto or Jenny). Students have two minutes to read and memorize the information about their character. Then they close their books. Each student briefly summarizes who they are and what they have done. The two listening students make notes about this person. When everyone has spoken, students read all three profiles on page 96 and check how comprehensive and correct their notes were.

Set a time limit of about three minutes for students to read the texts and answer 1–5. Avoid dealing with too much unknown vocabulary at this stage. Tell students to underline the parts of the text which helped them answer and ask them to say when you check answers.

Answers

1 Roberto and Jenny (south-east Asia and Bangladesh), Roberto and Freya (Australia)
2 Roberto and Jenny (both employers 'kept the job open')
3 Freya and Roberto (make sure you've got good career experience before you leave / take it after you've worked for five years)
4 Freya and Jenny (voluntary work in Australia / worked with local communities to improve education and health care)
5 Freya and Jenny (it has given me a new perspective / it broadened my outlook)

2 Students discuss the question in pairs and then can report back to the rest of the class.

3 Students find the pairs of words with similar meanings.

> **Answers**
> perspective / outlook
> hesitating / feeling uncertain
> piece of advice / tip
> put off / postponed
> appreciate / feel grateful for
> voluntary organization / charity

Pronunciation

Ask students to identify words in **3** with
- three syllables (*perspective*, *voluntary*, *charity*)
- four syllables (*hesitating*, *appreciate*)
- five syllables (*organization*).

They should also mark the word stress. Note that students might query the pronunciation of *voluntary* /vɒləntri/ on the final syllable. It looks like it should be two syllables not one.

4 Note that in some cases, both synonyms can be used. However, in sentence 2, *recharged* would sound slightly odd as we tend to use it as a metaphor with the word *batteries*.

> **Answers**
> 1 voluntary organization / charity
> 2 revitalized
> 3 put off / postpone
> 4 perspective / outlook
> 5 appreciate / feel grateful for
> 6 piece of advice / tip

5 Students ask each other the questions in **4**. At the end, ask each pair to report back on their answers to two of the questions.

6 61▷ Before listening, ask students to read the questions and to suggest what they think the term *flexiwork* might refer to. (*Flexiwork* means the practice of being able to work when you want to, e.g. working intensively for three months and then taking a break for three months. It isn't the same as being freelance because you keep a contract with the company.)

> **Answers**
> 1 because the industry was having a bit of a downturn
> 2 because a lot of their work is project-based and consultants work for different lengths of time on projects
> 3 cost savings, improves staff retention rate, a chance for staff to broaden horizons, a way to attract new staff
> 4 The employee learns new skills which the company also benefits from. He or she also has renewed motivation.

7 Students can underline the correct words in the questionnaire.

> **Answers**
> 1 off
> 2 soft
> 3 renewed
> 4 broaden
> 5 development
> 6 policy
> 7 retention

8 Students respond to the questionnaire in **7** in relation to their working situation.

Pre-work learners

Students answer questions 1–4 only, as these will apply to most people.

» If students need more practice, go to **Practice file 16** on page 132 of the **Student's Book**.

9 Students can do this alone or in pairs. The presentations can be given in small groups or to the whole class. It's probably useful to set a time limit of two minutes. Explain that they only have this amount of time to convince the other people listening. When everyone has given a presentation, the class could vote on which was the most convincing.

Feedback focus

Give extra positive feedback to any student who managed to use lots of the vocabulary from this section.

Pre-work learners

As a variation to **9**, tell students that they plan to take a gap year when they finish their current studies. They need to convince their parents and they will also need to borrow some money from them. Students prepare their ideas, remembering they will need to talk about the benefits and financial arrangements. Finally, students can give their presentations to the class. Or you could set up a role-play situation where one student plays the part of the parent who must be convinced by the other student.

ⓘ Refer students to the **Interactive Workbook Glossary** for further study.

Business communication skills

1 As a lead-in, ask students to suggest situations in which they might need to present a personal case. For example: at a job interview, when they have been criticized for something (by a customer), to suggest a new innovation or idea.

62▷ Students need to study the *Context*, which is a profile of Lena, and the notes giving possible reasons for a career break. Before they listen, discuss which of the reasons listed are likely to convince an employer. For example, *I'm feeling burnt out!* might be true but may not be so convincing. When checking answers, note that Lena does mention advertising opportunities but these relate to her company sponsoring her exhibition afterwards, not her trip.

> **Answers**
> I've been a loyal employee.
> I'll be more motivated after the trip.
> I'll gain experience I can bring to the company.
> It's a lifelong ambition of mine.

2 62▷ If time is short, students could match 1–9 to the correct phrases in the *Key expressions* list instead.

> **Answers**
> 1 It's been a long-term goal of mine to …
> 2 I've been inspired by …
> 3 It's a once-in-a-lifetime opportunity.
> 4 It's a win-win situation.
> 5 … the experience I'd gain would be invaluable for …
> 6 I understand your misgivings …
> 7 … this is a chance I can't afford to miss.
> 8 That's hardly fair. I've never refused to …
> 9 I'd really appreciate it if you could speak to HR …

Tip With sentence 5, refer students to the *Tip* about *valuable* and *invaluable*.

3 Students categorize the phrases they underlined in **2**.

> **Answers**
> a 1, 9   d 3, 7
> b 4, 5   e 6, 8
> c 2

» If students need more practice, go to **Practice file 16** on page 132 of the **Student's Book**.

4 Students work in pairs and follow the instructions given. As they prepare their arguments, monitor each pair and check they have followed the structure for presenting their case. Also remind them to make use of the phrases from the *Key expressions* list at each stage. Note that this is meant as controlled practice and students talk through their case and arguments with another pair – they don't have to actually present the case. However, you could ask them to go on and role-play the situation instead of doing the freer practice in **5** and **6**.

Feedback focus

Comment on each pair's use of phrases and also ask students to say which students' arguments were particularly convincing and why. What strategies did they use?

5, 6 This offers freer practice with the language in this section. Allow students enough time to prepare their case before they present to a partner.

Feedback focus

If you feel that after the first situation, students still need more practice with the language, then ask them to choose another situation and repeat the task.

(i) Refer students to the **Interactive Workbook Email** and **Phrasebank** sections for further study.

Practically speaking

1 As a lead-in, ask each student to say what they did last weekend and write activities on the board. Find out if this is typical of how they spend their time off from work. This will help set the scene for the section and the activity in **3**.

63▷ Students listen and identify what each speaker did during their time off.

> **Answers**
> 1 did DIY jobs
> 2 went on a spa break
> 3 visited family and played golf

Watch out! *DIY* means 'Do-It-Yourself' and refers to decorating and doing jobs to your house. The DIY business in places like the UK has grown hugely in recent decades. However, it is not a typical free-time activity in all countries so may need to be explained.

2 Students can do this in pairs.

> **Answers**
> 1 A   2 T   3 E   4 E   5 E   6 T   7 A   8 E   9 T   10 A

Watch out! You may need to clarify the phrasal verbs in 6, 7 and 8.
take (day) off = to have a free day from work
catch up on = to do something which needs doing
switch off = to relax and stop thinking about work

3 It will help if students stand for this activity so they can easily move from one person to the next. Students can refer back to the ideas for free time on the board (see lead-in idea in **1**) if they want to invent information.

Language at work

Dictionary skills

Throughout this section, students will find it useful to make use of good dictionaries. Make them aware that if they look up a verb like *want* or *enjoy*, it will tell them if the verb that follows is in the *-ing* or the infinitive form. It will also show common verb patterns following words like *easy* and *worth*.

1 Students answer the questions about the extracts.

> **Answers**
> **1** a **2** d **3** b **4** e **5** c **6** f

2 Students categorize the verbs.

> **Tip** Note that the verb *like* is commonly followed by *-ing* but it can actually go in either category. Refer students to the explanation in the *Tip*. There is also more information on verbs connected with likes and dislikes in the language summary in the *Practice file*.

> **Answers**
> **infinitive:** want, would like, fail, decide, refuse, seem, it's very difficult, manage, arrange, can't afford, plan, it's easy
> ***-ing* form:** like (see *Tip*), there's no point, enjoy, look forward to, miss, it's not worth, risk, finish

>> If students need more practice, go to **Practice file 16** on page 133 of the **Student's Book**.

3 Students work alone to fill in the survey form. Monitor closely at this stage and deal with any errors individually. If you feel that students may find the idea of commenting on their own company a little sensitive, tell them to make up their answers or to choose an imaginary company.

Pre-work learners

As an alternative to commenting on a company, students could comment on their courses or place of study.

4 As students compare their answers, remind them to peer-correct or to discuss any instances where they are unsure whether to use the *-ing* form or infinitive.

5 Students read the instructions in the *File*. They are going to role-play a conversation between an employee (Student A) who wants to take a career break and the employer (Student B). Student B needs to form questions using the *-ing* form or infinitive so may need a minute or so to prepare. Student A should use correct forms when responding. Afterwards, students can repeat the activity with a new partner and change their role to employer or employee.

Feedback focus

Give feedback on any problems with the target verbs.

(i) Refer students to the **Interactive Workbook Exercises and Tests** for revision.

Case study

Background

This *Case study* presents a company which is involved in a volunteer programme to help poor communities manage their resources. The company allows some of its employees to take a career break to work on the programme. Students have the opportunity to listen to one of the company's workers describing their experience on the programme. The topic allows students to consider how both employees and companies can benefit from taking part in such programmes. The *Task* enables students to use the language of the unit to present a personal case for working on a similar volunteer project.

Allow a few minutes for students to read the text about Accenture and be prepared to answer any questions about vocabulary.

Discussion

1, 2 Discuss these questions as a class.

> **Possible responses**
> **1** Employees would develop management and leadership skills in difficult or new types of conditions. They would also experience working with new cultures.
> **2** Companies would benefit from the new skills their employees acquired. This type of project would provide very positive publicity for the business. It would also develop knowledge of potentially new markets.

Extra activity

64▷ In **3**, students listen to a consultant who worked on the programme. With students who need more help with listening, write these questions on the board. Play the listening and students note down one- or two-word answers only.

1 *Where was the consultant based? (Manila)*
2 *Which nationalities does he mention? (British and Swedish)*
3 *What did he do? (strengthened SPARK / worked with documentation)*
4 *What did he find most enjoyable? (different experience / immediate results)*
5 *What does he think are becoming important for Western business? (developing countries)*
6 *Would he recommend the experience? (yes)*

3 64▷ Students listen and compare their ideas in **1** and **2**.

Answers

The experience gained: new skills, more confident, knows he can achieve things on his own, making decisions, knowledge and cultural awareness.
The benefits for the company: the consultant believes his new skills will benefit the company though he doesn't say exactly how. He also refers to the knowledge and cultural awareness that he's developed which will be of benefit to the company in the future.

Task

Check students understand the context before you start.

1 As students read the extract, it may be useful for them to underline key information to help with the next stages. They should underline
   • the subjects they need teachers for (English, literacy, numeracy, computer skills, bookkeeping, basic accountancy)
   • the administrative roles required (coordinate centres, back office administration, find resources).
2 For a basic example of an employee profile, students can look back at the information about Lena in the *Context* on page 98. However, they will also need to include reasons for going and why the company should support them.
3 It is suggested that students give their presentations in pairs, but with smaller classes and more time, these could be given by individual students. Remind students to make use of the phrases in the *Key expressions* list on page 99 while presenting.

4 After students have presented their cases, the most convincing presentation is chosen in a decision-making meeting. The phrases in the *Business communication skills* section in Unit 7 will be useful to refer back to here.

Feedback can be given on both the presentations in 3 and the meetings in 4.

One-to-one

Your student can read the *Background* and then you can do the *Discussion* questions together. For the *Task*, let the student develop and present their own profile for a place on the volunteer programme.

>> Unit 16 **Progress test** and **Speaking test**, pages 118–119

Working with words

Complete these sentences with words from the list.

> innovation   rapport   tradition   principles
> reputation   professionalism   extravagance

1 Our famous _____ with customers is built on good quality and a fair price.

2 I don't think he has any _____. As long as it makes money, he'll sell it.

3 Ongoing staff training is crucial in order to maintain a high level of _____.

4 Buying this brand new car was an _____, but it's good to spoil yourself sometimes.

5 The company needs some fresh ideas and real _____ to bring it into the 21st century.

6 I'm sad he's going. We had a good _____ and relationship, so I liked doing business with him.

7 If we stretch the brand to appeal to a younger market, we might lose the customers who like _____ and have always chosen our products.

Replace the words in bold with words from the list.

> expensive   complex   positive   suspicious
> practical   over confident   wary

8 Why are you **cautious** _____ about employing her?

9 I like the **functional** _____ design. There's nothing too showy about it.

10 The second candidate seemed a little too **arrogant** _____ for working in a team.

11 Feedback on our latest line has been **favourable** _____ from nearly all our markets.

12 I'm a little **mistrustful** _____ of this applicant. He's only 20 but says he's been a CEO!

13 Buying that subsidiary could turn out to be rather a **costly** _____ mistake.

14 That was a rather **complicated** _____ explanation. Can you say it in simple English?

Business communication skills

There is one incorrect word in each phrase. Underline it and write the correct word at the end. See the example.

My name's Peter Dill and I work <u>to</u> BNI.   *for*

15 I have given your name by a colleague of mine.

16 Hello, I call about the email I sent you.

17 I wanted to see if you are still interested of my proposal.

18 I suggest we meeting to discuss things further.

19 Can you tell me how I go to your office?

Complete this conversation with phrases a–e. Write the letters in the spaces.

a Whatever's best for you.
b I'll email you a map with directions.
c Let's say, provisionally,
d See you next week.
e Is it best by taxi or public transport?

A When would you like to meet?
B **20**___ Wednesday at 2.00.
A Fine. **21**___
B Can you tell me how I get to your office? **22**___
A Public transport. There are trams to the centre every five minutes. **23**___
B Great, thanks. **24**___

Language at work

Complete these sentences with the present simple or present continuous form of the verbs in brackets.

25 We _____ (currently / update) our website.

26 The bus _____ (leave) every half hour.

27 Online ordering _____ (become) more and more popular with many of our clients.

28 Let's talk again when I _____ (get) back.

29 The department _____ (work) harder than normal because two people are off this week.

30 Yes, I _____ (remember) you told me.

Result _____ / 30 marks

Speaking test

Role cards

Copy this page and cut out the role cards for the students. Students should do both role-plays. Then use the *Speaking test results* forms to evaluate each student's performance. You can then cut out the results and give them to the students.

Cut along this line

Student A

1 You work for a company which translates documents.
   - Make a follow-up call to your partner, who you met at a conference.
   - Explain that you are visiting his / her city next week.
   - Arrange to meet.
   - Ask about directions to his / her office.
   - End the call appropriately.

2 You work for a company which needs its website redesigning.
   - Answer a call from someone who designs websites.
   - Arrange to meet.
   - Give advice on the best way to travel to your office.

Student B

1 You work for a company which is interested in finding a translation service.
   - Answer a call from someone you met at a conference.
   - Arrange to meet.
   - Promise to email directions.

2 You work for a company which designs websites. A colleague gave you your partner's details.
   - Make a follow-up call about designing his / her company's website.
   - Explain that you are visiting his / her city next month.
   - Arrange to meet.
   - Ask what the easiest way is to the office. (taxi? public transport?)
   - End the call appropriately.

Cut along this line

Speaking test results

Use these forms to evaluate the students.

Cut along this line

Student A

Can the student ...	Didn't do this (0 points)	Yes, but with some mistakes (1 point)	Yes, did this very well (2 points)
introduce himself / herself and start the call?			
give reason for calling?			
arrange to meet?			
discuss travel arrangements / directions?			
end the call appropriately?			

Result _____ / 10 marks

Student B

Can the student ...	Didn't do this (0 points)	Yes, but with some mistakes (1 point)	Yes, did this very well (2 points)
introduce himself / herself and start the call?			
give reason for calling?			
arrange to meet?			
discuss travel arrangements / directions?			
end the call appropriately?			

Result _____ / 10 marks

Cut along this line

Working with words

Complete these sentences with words from the list.

> rewards   schemes   recognition   motivate
> performance   achievement   morale

1 One way to _____ staff is to simply give them praise.

2 Winning this contract is my biggest _____ so far.

3 I don't feel I get any _____ for the work I do. No one ever says how well I've done.

4 Maybe you'd boost staff _____ by holding some team meetings and offering some incentives.

5 We need to improve the overall _____ of this department – we're quite inefficient at some things.

6 The company offers a number of incentive _____. For example, we give bonuses to effective employees.

7 Getting staff to work harder isn't all about money. There are a number of non-cash _____ we can use.

Complete the missing words in these sentences.

8 I think all our staff feel v_____ and appreciated. That's why they stay working here.

9 The best benefit of my job is the company c_____. It saves me a lot of money on travel.

10 Giving positive f_____ and saying things like 'Well done' and 'Good work' can be simple but effective.

11 My company pays 30% of my private pension p_____.

12 I have a low salary but I receive some perks and benefits like private medical i_____.

Business communication skills

Match 13–20 to a response in a–h.

13 You don't mind if I go and get myself a coffee? ___

14 I'm afraid I've been a bit unwell recently. ___

15 Hi, I don't think we've met. My name's Gertrude. ___

16 Is this your first conference? ___

17 Apparently, there's over 3,000 people here! ___

18 I did my degree at Boston University. ___

19 I've heard the speaker has cancelled. Is that true? ___

20 Sorry, I don't have time to chat at the moment. ___

a Oh, I'm so sorry to hear that.

b That's amazing!

c What a coincidence! So did I!

d Actually, I've been to a few, but not this particular one.

e That's OK. Call me tomorrow.

f Hello. I'm Frank.

g Apparently, yes.

h No, not at all. Catch you later.

Language at work

Put these words in the right order to make questions and write them in the conversation.

21 spent you China much time in have

22 you who told

23 Jem do know you

24 that Randall and Sons was with

25 India you from aren't you're

26 did she where from come

A So, 21_____?

B No, only a few weeks. Before that I was in India.

A Yes, I heard.

B Really? 22_____?

A Your colleague Jemima.

B 23_____?

A Yes, we both began with the same company.

B Amazing! 24_____?

A It was. Anyway, 25_____?

B That's right. My father was Indian and met my mother.

A 26_____?

B Ireland.

Complete the question tags.

27 It's Anthea, _____ it?

28 The speaker wasn't very interesting, _____ he?

29 You haven't been here before, _____ you?

30 Everyone liked the entertainment, _____ they?

Result _____ / 30 marks

Speaking test

Role cards

Copy this page and cut out the role cards for the students. Students should do both role-plays. Then use the *Speaking test results* forms to evaluate each student's performance. You can then cut out the results and give them to the students.

Cut along this line

Student A

1 You are at a conference.
   - Start a conversation with your partner.
   - Ask some questions and keep the conversation going.
   - Find out who he / she works for.
   - Ask if he / she knows Michael Roberts (he works for your company now).
   - End the conversation politely after three minutes.

2 You are at your company's annual sales convention.
   - An old colleague from the Madrid office comes over.
   - You are very tired from the flight and don't feel like talking. Talk to your colleague in order to be polite.
   - You work in the Milan office.
   - You know Michela Richards. You were in the same sales office in Hong Kong.

Student B

1 You are at a conference.
   - You are very tired from the flight and don't feel like talking. Talk to the other person in order to be polite.
   - You work for BS Construction.
   - This is your first time at this conference.
   - You know Michael Roberts. You went to the same university.

2 You are at your company's annual sales convention.
   - You see an old colleague from your Madrid office and start a conversation.
   - Ask some questions and keep the conversation going.
   - Find out which office he / she works in now.
   - Find out if he / she knows Michela Richards. You now work with her in Berlin.
   - End the conversation politely after three minutes.

Cut along this line

Speaking test results

Use these forms to evaluate the students.

Cut along this line

Student A

Can the student ...	Didn't do this (0 points)	Yes, but with some mistakes (1 point)	Yes, did this very well (2 points)
start the conversation?			
keep the conversation going?			
show interest?			
ask questions?			
exit the conversation politely?			

Result _____ / 10 marks

Student B

Can the student ...	Didn't do this (0 points)	Yes, but with some mistakes (1 point)	Yes, did this very well (2 points)
start the conversation?			
keep the conversation going?			
show interest?			
ask questions?			
exit the conversation politely?			

Result _____ / 10 marks

Cut along this line

Working with words

Choose the correct answer from the words in *italics*.

1 Everything's going according to plan and we're even *ahead of / behind* schedule.

2 I've looked at these figures and you're *over / within* budget. How do you plan to solve that problem?

3 Your *lack of / upfront* planning shouldn't result in a later breakdown of the project.

4 To avoid delays, we mustn't *miss / make* the deadline.

5 I've run *out of / into some* money. Can you lend me some?

6 How *unrealistic / accurate* is your forecast for the budget? Can you check it again to make sure it's right?

7 Spending in your department seems to be completely *under / out of* control! What can you do to cut costs?

Match 8–13 to a–f.

8 Resolve any … ____

9 I'd like to check your … ____

10 Let's set … ____

11 I'm having trouble keeping … ____

12 Try to stay … ____

13 I'd say everything is running … ____

a a launch date for the new brand.
b conflicts as soon as possible.
c very smoothly since he took over.
d on track, please – we don't need delays.
e progress on the project.
f track of where you are this week.

Business communication skills

Complete this conversation with phrases from the list.

| How about   How far   How's the   What you're |
| How are   What do   Why don't |

A Hi. ¹⁴_____ things?
B OK, thanks.
A ¹⁵_____ launch coming along?

B Everything's gone well. No major problems.
A ¹⁶_____ are you with the final design?
B Well, we've hit a slight problem with the colour.
A ¹⁷_____ you mean exactly?
B Two of the focus groups don't like the range of colours.
A Which ones in particular?
B They say the green is too light, the white looks like the main competitor's and the pink isn't bright enough.
A ¹⁸_____ saying is they don't like any of them?
B They all like the blue one.
A ¹⁹_____ changing them?
B That's not an ideal solution. It would put our schedules back. We'd have to postpone the launch.
A ²⁰_____ we launch the blue one and say it will be available in other colours at a later date?
B I'm not convinced. It wouldn't be good for our reputation.

Language at work

Complete this conversation with the present perfect or past simple form of the verbs in brackets.

A So what are you doing at the moment?
B I ²¹_____ (change) companies since I saw you last. I'm with Anateck now.
A Really? I ²²_____ (not / know) that!
B Do you still work for the same company?
A Yes, and we're really busy. We ²³_____ (just / win) a new contract. So not much time for golf! What about you? Are you still playing?
B Yes. Actually, we ²⁴_____ (have) a holiday in Dubai last week so I ²⁵_____ (play) there. ²⁶_____ (you / book) a holiday this year?
A No, not yet. Dubai sounds nice.

Choose the correct option a–c to complete each sentence.

27 _____ there haven't been any real difficulties.
   a Up to now   b Yesterday   c A couple of weeks ago

28 We received all the offers by the end _____.
   a in the last month   b of last week   c to date

29 They haven't made their final decision _____.
   a already   b just   c yet

30 He booked the hotel two months _____.
   a already   b ago   c so far

Result _____ / 30 marks

Speaking test

Role cards

Copy this page and cut out the role cards for the students. Students should do both role-plays. Then use the *Speaking test results* forms to evaluate each student's performance. You can then cut out the results and give them to the students.

Cut along this line

Student A

1 You gave your PA this 'To do' list.

  - Book my flight to Warsaw for Monday evening.
  - Book a hotel near to the centre.
  - Arrange a meeting with Carole on Tuesday.
  - Confirm the venue for the presentation to ATI.

  • Call your PA for an update on each item.
  • Clarify any problems.
  • Make a suggestion for the first problem.
  • Make a suggestion for the second problem.

2 Your manager calls for an update on this 'To do' list. Two items are done (✓) but two are not (✗). The reasons are in *italics*.

  - Book caterers for launch party on 18th. (✓)
  - Book room at gallery. (✗) *This room is booked that night.*
  - Invite journalists from all national newspapers. (✓)
  - Contact printers to confirm press information for journalists. (✗) *Printers say they were told to print for 28th not 18th, so information won't be ready.*

  • Your partner calls for an update.

Student B

1 Your manager calls for an update on this 'To do' list. Two items are done (✓) but two are not (✗). The reasons are in *italics*.

  - Book my flight to Warsaw for Monday evening. (✓)
  - Book a hotel near to the centre. (✗) *They are all full.*
  - Arrange a meeting with Carole on Tuesday. (✗) *Carole is away until Friday.*
  - Confirm the venue for the presentation to ATI. (✓)

  • Your partner calls for an update.

2 You gave this 'To do' list to your PA.

  - Book caterers for launch party on 18th.
  - Book reception rooms at gallery.
  - Invite journalists from all national newspapers.
  - Contact printers to confirm press information for journalists.

  • Call your PA for an update on each item.
  • Clarify any problems.
  • Make a suggestion for the first problem.
  • Make a suggestion for the second problem.

Cut along this line

Speaking test results

Use these forms to evaluate the students.

Cut along this line

Student A

Can the student ...	Didn't do this (0 points)	Yes, but with some mistakes (1 point)	Yes, did this very well (2 points)
start and end the call appropriately?			
ask for an update?			
clarify a problem?			
make a first suggestion?			
make a second suggestion?			

Result _____ / 10 marks

Student B

Can the student ...	Didn't do this (0 points)	Yes, but with some mistakes (1 point)	Yes, did this very well (2 points)
start and end the call appropriately?			
ask for an update?			
clarify a problem?			
make a first suggestion?			
make a second suggestion?			

Result _____ / 10 marks

Cut along this line

Working with words

Choose the correct answer from the words in *italics*.

1 Nanotechnology is one of the great technological *advantages / breakthroughs* of the last few years.

2 Don't bother me with theory! I need some *key / practical* solutions to this problem.

3 We use *cutting-edge / key* technology in all our phones. No one else uses anything quite as modern.

4 One potential *benefit / concept* is that it could help refugees around the world.

5 A *major / revolutionary* advantage of using fingerprints is that they are nearly impossible to copy.

6 Apple always uses *viable / state-of-the-art* design which makes its products so distinctive.

7 I'm not convinced this is a commercially-viable *proposition / potential* and so I can't invest in it.

Complete these sentences with words from the list.

off round up out down up with about

8 How did you come up _____ such a good idea?

9 Can we get _____ the problem of high start-up costs?

10 The company was set _____ in 1996.

11 My staff have taken _____ the challenge and are working on ways to reduce delays.

12 I think my idea will bring _____ real improvements for people in underdeveloped countries.

13 We're carrying _____ research on the new systems.

14 Our hard work has paid _____. Results are good!

15 We're over budget. Can we bring _____ travel costs?

Business communication skills

Choose the correct option a–c to complete each sentence.

16 First, I'll _____ you a brief overview of the product.
   a do   **b** give   **c** tell

17 After that I'd like to _____ you some results.
   a show   **b** say   **c** look

18 There are two main benefits _____ using this system.
   a by   **b** about   **c** of

19 This _____ that you won't need an identity card.
   a results   **b** means   **c** causes

20 At the moment, you have to remember a code, _____ in the future you won't.
   a whereas   **b** although   **c** in comparison

21 Now I'd like to _____ on to the next point.
   a look   **b** turn   **c** move

22 Finally, I'll answer questions. Does that _____ OK?
   a hear   **b** listen   **c** sound

23 **A** I'd like to thank you for inviting me here today.
   B We're _____ you could be here.
   a pleasure   **b** glad   **c** appreciate

24 **A** After you.   **B** _____
   a You're welcome.   **b** Thanks.   **c** No problem.

Language at work

Complete these sentences with verbs from the list. There is one extra verb.

will be able to   can't   won't be able to   can
were able to   couldn't   haven't been able to

25 I _____ let you know until next week.

26 We _____ find a solution for a long time but then someone in R&D came up with a great idea.

27 Do you know what the problem is? I _____ access anything on this computer today!

28 They _____ reduce their prices for over a year but they promise to on this order.

29 We were lucky because we _____ see a gap in the market before anyone else.

30 The new changes next year mean that our customers _____ check their details online.

Result _____ / 30 marks

Speaking test

Role card

This *Speaking test* has only one role card because each student has to give an individual presentation. Copy this page and cut out the role card for the student. Then use the *Speaking test results* form to evaluate the student's performance. You can then cut out the results and give them to the student.

Cut along this line

You work for a company called EyeScan. You are about to launch a product which scans someone's eye to identify them. However, you need further investment to start manufacturing on a large scale and for marketing.

You have three minutes to convince a potential investor. Here are some key points to mention (you can also include your own ideas).

Key users are

- airports
- government organizations
- large companies.

Benefits compared to other forms of security are

- no password or other form of identity needed
- every eye is different and cannot be copied
- it's fast and can handle large amounts of people in a short time.

Remember to

- introduce yourself
- preview the talk
- introduce the new business idea
- explain the future benefits to the user.

You can use visual aids, if necessary. You will also need to answer two questions at the end.

Cut along this line

Speaking test results

Use this form to evaluate the student.
Note that you will need to ask two questions at the end to check the final criteria.

Cut along this line

Can the student …	Didn't do this (0 points)	Yes, but with some mistakes (1 point)	Yes, did this very well (2 points)
introduce himself / herself?			
preview the talk?			
introduce the new business idea?			
explain future benefits to the user?			
answer two questions convincingly?			

Result _____ / 10 marks

Cut along this line

Working with words

Complete these sentences with words from the list.

> responsive repeat existing loyal high-quality
> attentive courteous sub-standard discourteous

1 It's important to train our staff to give a _____ service – customers will expect them to be polite and respectful.

2 It takes less effort to keep _____ customers than to find new ones.

3 Lisa has been named 'Employee of the month'. Customers comment on how _____ she is to their personal needs – she's always very helpful.

4 If you treat people well, you'll always get _____ business with customers coming back time and time again.

5 They offer such _____ care and service – it would be hard to find a supplier with better standards.

6 The woman at the desk was so _____ when she spoke to me! I've taken my complaint to the manager.

7 One way to make sure customers remain _____ is to introduce a card where they receive points every time they shop with you.

8 I phoned yesterday about the fault and an hour later the technician was here. Now that's what I'd call a _____ service.

9 The hotel was rather _____. We won't go there again.

Complete the missing verbs in these sentences.

10 How do you m_____ the needs of your customers?

11 Finding out how many customers come back year after year is one way to m_____ the level of customer satisfaction.

12 We don't aim to match our customers' expectations. We aim to e_____ them!

13 We g_____ feedback by asking clients to fill in this form.

14 With so many problems, they'll l_____ lots of customers to their competitors.

Business communication skills

Complete the three conversations with phrases a–j. Write the letters in the spaces.

a How can I help you
b I'll look into it straightaway
c Let me get this straight
d By Thursday at the latest
e Talk me through
f You mean
g Could you give
h Can you tell me
i What I'll do is
j As soon as

1 A Hello. [15]___?
   B I asked for a double room but it only has a single bed.
   A Really? [16]___ which room you're in?
   B 101.
   A Let me check … Our records say you wanted a single. [17]___ put you in a double on the first floor and …

2 A Hi. It's me again. My computer has crashed again.
   B [18]___ what happened.
   A Well I switched it on and it stopped.
   B [19]___. Did you switch it on and it didn't work?
   A Not exactly. The screen just says 'Error dxx.l. This program is not available' and then it goes blank.
   B [20]___ it switches off or there's nothing on it?
   A The computer's still on but the screen doesn't work.
   B [21]___. Which office are you in? I'll be up in a minute.

3 A We ordered it two weeks ago and nothing has arrived.
   B I see. [22]___ me the order number?
   A IO11-7
   B Yes, there's been a mistake. When do you need it?
   A [23]___.
   B OK. [24]___ I've checked with our warehouse, I'll arrange for another box to be sent out by courier.

Language at work

Put these words in the correct order to make direct or indirect questions.

25 can when they you are tell me arriving?

26 did she when call?

27 let me could called you know why he?

28 you his email got address have?

29 is this it why doing?

30 this you who message took know do?

Result _____ / 30 marks

Speaking test

Role cards

Copy this page and cut out the role cards for the students. Students should do both role-plays. Then use the *Speaking test results* forms to evaluate each student's performance. You can then cut out the results and give them to the students.

Cut along this line

Student A

1 You are a supplier of office stationery and receive a call from an unhappy customer.

   - Begin and end the call appropriately.
   - Request information about the problem.
   - Establish the facts about the order (number, date).
   - Clarify and check facts.
   - Promise action.

2 You work in Sales and need help from your colleague in IT Support.

   - You installed new software yesterday and now when you switch on the computer, you only get the error message 'dvv.331-T' and after a few seconds the screen goes blank.
   - You need access to the database straightaway.

Student B

1 You ordered a supply of paper and envelopes three weeks ago with these details.

   - Order number AI33E
   - Date of order: 25th May
   - 2,000 sheets of paper
   - 2,000 envelopes

   You received 4,000 envelopes and no paper. The delivery firm left the box outside. It rained so the envelopes were damaged.

2 You work in IT Support and receive a call from a colleague in Sales.

   - Begin and end the call appropriately.
   - Request information about the problem.
   - Establish the facts about the error message.
   - Clarify and check facts.
   - Promise action.

Cut along this line

Speaking test results

Use these forms to evaluate the students.

Cut along this line

Student A

Can the student …	Didn't do this (0 points)	Yes, but with some mistakes (1 point)	Yes, did this very well (2 points)
start and end the call appropriately?			
request information about the problem?			
establish the facts?			
clarify and check facts?			
promise action?			

Result _____ / 10 marks

Student B

Can the student …	Didn't do this (0 points)	Yes, but with some mistakes (1 point)	Yes, did this very well (2 points)
start and end the call appropriately?			
request information about the problem?			
establish the facts?			
clarify and check facts?			
promise action?			

Result _____ / 10 marks

Cut along this line

Working with words

Complete these sentences with verbs from the list. Change the form of the verb if necessary.

| act comply share reduce take donate stay |

1 We've always _____ true to our principle of fairness to the customer and the supplier.

2 Companies in the 21st century which don't _____ responsibly are likely to receive bad publicity.

3 How about _____ more time to helping a charity?

4 All our employees _____ an active part in our fund-raising activities.

5 If we did more videoconferencing and less flying, we'd _____ the impact we have on the environment.

6 Currently, this factory doesn't _____ with regulations on the disposal of waste water.

7 All our subsidiaries _____ a strong commitment to supporting the local community.

Each headline refers to ethical or unethical behaviour. Choose the noun from the list which describes the action.

| bribery generosity greed fairness discrimination |

8 Company agrees to pay workers from other countries an equal amount. _____

9 CEO paid colleagues to take part in illegal financial activities. _____

10 Woman to prosecute company for paying her less than male colleagues doing the same job. _____

11 Business owner leaves fortune to charity. _____

12 Shareholders take profits while workers receive no pay rise. _____

Decide if the word in each sentence is an adjective or noun and complete the word.

13 We are not involved in the corrup_____ scandal.

14 Customers will ask questions about our credib_____ if we don't do something quickly.

15 He says he isn't prejud_____ against older applicants, but he never employs anyone over 40.

16 We want to be described as an ethic_____ business.

17 Appearances can be decept_____ – he seems friendly, but be careful!

Business communication skills

Complete the conversations with phrases a–g. Write the letters in the spaces.

a we'd be delighted to see you   e You're welcome
b it would be a good idea to   f That would
c That sounds really   g That makes sense
d It's well worth a visit

1 A We'd like to invite you to the theatre this evening.
  B ¹⁸___ be great. What's on?
  A It's a Russian theatre company performing *Hamlet*.
  B ¹⁹___ interesting.

2 A If you're free, ²⁰___ at dinner this evening.
  B Sorry, but I'm meeting someone for drinks at six.
  A Oh well. ²¹___ to come later if you change your mind.

3 A While you are in Italy, ²²___ visit our supplier in Salerno. It will save time and money later on.
  B ²³___.
  A Ask them to show you round their factory. ²⁴___.

Language at work

Choose the correct answer from the verb forms in *italics*.

25 You can check the details with Amalie. She *'s coming / will come* in later this afternoon as arranged.

26 One day, when I have enough money, I *start / 'm going to start* my own business.

27 A When are you back in the office?
   B I'm not sure. I *'ll let / 'm letting* you know before I leave.

28 The flight from Jakarta *is going to land / lands* at 5 p.m. your time according to my e-ticket.

29 We've booked places and we *stay / 're staying* at the Westin Hotel.

30 Sorry about the late delivery. Let me call the warehouse to check and I *'m calling / 'll call* you straight back.

Result _____ / 30 marks

Speaking test

Role cards

Copy this page and cut out the role cards for the students. Students should do both role-plays. Then use the *Speaking test results* forms to evaluate each student's performance. You can then cut out the results and give them to the students.

Cut along this line

Student A

1 Call your colleague to confirm this revised schedule for a group of journalists visiting your company.

9.30 Arrival. Coffee and introductions in conference room
10.00 Tour of factory
12.30 Lunchtime presentation by CEO
13.30 Press launch of new 'End Child Poverty' project

Invite your colleague to come along for lunch and recommend that he / she attends the press launch.

2 A journalist is visiting your resort in the Pacific. Your partner will call to confirm the schedule. Make notes on any changes to time or information.

Monday: Flight arrives at 8 p.m.
Tuesday: 8 a.m. Breakfast meeting
10 a.m. Show eco-friendly huts on the beach
11 a.m. Take bus round the island
12 Lunch
2 p.m. Visit mountain resort

You are free for lunch. In the afternoon, you have a meeting with staff.

Student B

1 Your colleague will call to confirm the schedule for a group of journalists visiting your company. Make notes on any changes to time or information.

9.00 Arrival. Coffee and introductions in reception area
9.45 Tour of factory
12.15 Lunch
13.00 Presentation by CEO
13.30 Press launch of new 'End Child Poverty' project

You are free to meet journalists at lunchtime. You have a meeting with a client at 13.30.

2 A journalist is visiting your resort in the Pacific. Call your partner to confirm this revised schedule.

Monday: Flight arrives at midnight
Tuesday: 9 a.m. Breakfast meeting
10 a.m. Take bus round the island
11 a.m. Show eco-friendly huts on the beach
12.30 Lunch
After lunch: Water skiing and diving

Invite your partner to come for lunch and recommend the water skiing in the afternoon.

Cut along this line

Speaking test results

Use these forms to evaluate the students.

Cut along this line

Student A

Can the student ...	Didn't do this (0 points)	Yes, but with some mistakes (1 point)	Yes, did this very well (2 points)
start and end the call appropriately?			
explain plans and arrangements?			
clarify any changes to plans and arrangements?			
invite?			
recommend?			

Result _____ / 10 marks

Student B

Can the student ...	Didn't do this (0 points)	Yes, but with some mistakes (1 point)	Yes, did this very well (2 points)
start and end the call appropriately?			
explain plans and arrangements?			
clarify any changes to plans and arrangements?			
invite?			
recommend?			

Result _____ / 10 marks

Cut along this line

Working with words

Match the adjectives from the list to the descriptions.

> methodical   outgoing   creative   tactful   impulsive
> pragmatic   detached   conventional

1 He loves socializing and meeting people. That's what makes him a good marketing manager. _____

2 We need someone who takes a practical and realistic attitude to any kind of task. _____

3 The reason for her success is that as soon as she hears a good idea she takes action – she doesn't wait to hear what the problems might be. _____

4 If you work in design you need to be a person who likes to come up with original ideas. _____

5 I like a traditional approach to decision-making. _____

6 The CEO is diplomatic and good at talking to people about difficult matters. _____

7 He's good at staying out of office politics and doesn't get involved. _____

8 Our accounts manager does things step by step. As a result, she never makes mistakes! _____

Choose the correct answer from the words in *italics*.

9 I suggest you weigh up all the *options / judgements* before you make a final decision.

10 Sometimes you just have to trust your own *perspectives / instincts* rather than spend more time analysing facts.

11 As long as everyone else has *feelings / confidence* in your decisions, then things will probably work out OK.

12 I simply can't *decide / consider* between the two options. Which do you think is better?

Business communication skills

Complete the missing words in this meeting extract.

A ^{13}L_____ at the facts. They're here in black and ^{14}w_____. We are overspending.

B ^{15}W_____ you say is right, but there are some good reasons. We've had to invest in more advertising and marketing in order to grow.

A Yes, but that was budgeted for last year. What I ^{16}m_____ is we've spent money on unplanned items. A ^{17}c_____ example is this list of expenses. I'm ^{18}n_____ convinced that all these are necessary. Look at this restaurant bill for over $200!

B Exactly. But that is a marketing cost. Clients have to be taken out.

A In other ^{19}w_____, you're saying our staff should go to the most expensive restaurants they can find.

B Obviously I think it would be ^{20}c_____ for an employee on a business trip to only choose expensive places on their own. But with clients it's important.

A Jens, what's your ^{21}p_____ on this?

C As ^{22}f_____ as I'm concerned, until we set clear limits and give our staff written guidelines on travel expenses, we'll always have this discussion …

B … but the drawback is that every trip is different. It's hard to say there's one rule for every type of expense.

A Hang ^{23}o_____. Let's hear what Jens has to say.

C In my ^{24}o_____ we need to define what they can and can't do.

A Good idea. Let's draw up some ^{25}a_____ points …

Language at work

Match 26–30 to a–e.

26 Too few … ____

27 Don't spend too much … ____

28 Hardly anyone … ____

29 Lots of … ____

30 I'd like to spend a little … ____

a time on this. It isn't important.

b less time in meetings and more time actually doing some work.

c people have applied for the post. We don't have enough good candidates.

d internally has applied. They are nearly all external.

e time has been spent on this. Too much in fact.

Result _____ / 30 marks

Speaking test

Role cards

Copy this page and cut out the role cards for the students. Students should do both role-plays. Then use the *Speaking test results* forms to evaluate each student's performance. You can then cut out the results and give them to the students.

Cut along this line

Student A

1 Recently, employees in your department have been arriving late for work. They complain about traffic and lack of parking facilities, e.g. one person arrived at lunchtime because he said a road was closed. This problem is costing money.

- Present the problem to the company owner.
- Give an example.
- Argue that these ideas might help.
  - introduce flexitime so staff can arrive later or earlier
  - encourage staff to share cars
  - suggest staff cycle to work twice a week

2 A manager in your company wants to discuss the problem of employees often going on courses – this means they're out of the office when needed. You think training is important for quality but you'd also like to save money on the training budget.

- Listen, respond and ask for clarification as necessary.
- Draw up some action points at the end.

Student B

1 A manager in your company wants to discuss the problem of employees often arriving late for work. You don't want to spend money solving the problem. You also believe many employees are just lazy.

- Listen, respond and ask for clarification as necessary.
- Draw up some action points at the end.

2 Employees in your department often go on courses – this means they're out of the office when needed, e.g. the IT engineer was away for a week so the computers weren't fixed. You lost days in working time. This problem is costing money.

- Present the problem to the company owner.
- Give an example.
- Argue that these ideas might help.
  - staff can take online courses
  - they could study in the evenings
  - the training manager needs to know when is a good / bad time of year to send staff away

Cut along this line

Speaking test results

Use these forms to evaluate the students.

Cut along this line

Student A

Can the student …	Didn't do this (0 points)	Yes, but with some mistakes (1 point)	Yes, did this very well (2 points)
present an argument?			
give an example?			
give an opinion?			
respond to arguments and / or clarify?			
agree action points with the other person?			

Result _____ / 10 marks

Student B

Can the student …	Didn't do this (0 points)	Yes, but with some mistakes (1 point)	Yes, did this very well (2 points)
present an argument?			
give an example?			
give an opinion?			
respond to arguments and / or clarify?			
agree action points with the other person?			

Result _____ / 10 marks

Cut along this line

Working with words

Choose the correct answer from the words in *italics*.

Journalist Will the fact that so many companies are now outsourcing [1]*lead to / free up* major job losses over here?

Politician Certainly jobs in [2]*infrastructure / sectors* such as telecommunications and IT could be affected.

Journalist But this means [3]*skilled / offshore* workers are out of work. Where will they find new jobs?

Politician Well, of course, companies will retain their core [4]*activities / facilities* which will always need well-qualified people with [5]*expertise / growth*. I also want to add that outsourcing is necessary for companies to [6]*gain / get through* a competitive edge. Without [7]*streamlining / achieving* their operations they won't survive in the global economy.

Business communication skills

Complete these sentences with words from the list.

| turn | notice | look | move | show | send |
| leave | mention | relates | see |

8 Statistics _____ that export growth is at 5% this year.

9 You will _____ on this chart how many jobs have been lost.

10 Have a _____ at these figures.

11 A further point to _____ is that Bangalore has a highly-trained workforce.

12 Let's _____ our attention to the effects of this.

13 Looking at this slide, we can _____ the reason for the fall.

14 We've looked at India, so let's _____ on to China.

15 This next part _____ back to what I was saying earlier.

16 Before I go today, I'd like to _____ you with some food for thought.

17 The message I'd like to _____ you away with today is this.

Put these phrases in the right order to make a dialogue.

I completely forgot the time

I was busy too

I'm really sorry

No problem

A [18]_____ . [19]_____ .

B [20]_____ . [21]_____ .

Language at work

Rewrite these sentences using the passive or active form.

22 A business award has been given to him.
He _____ .

23 We expect he will leave straightaway.
It is _____ .

24 You are being fired. I have made the final decision.
You are being fired. The final decision _____ _____ .

25 Sue still hasn't fixed the problem with all the computers.
The problem with all the computers _____ _____ .

26 Everyone knows that the CEO will retire next year.
It _____ .

27 Employees will answer all customer complaints within five working days.
All customer complaints _____ _____ .

28 Somebody locks up the warehouse at ten.
The _____ .

29 You were phoned while you were out.
Somebody _____ .

30 They are promoting you to office manager.
You _____ .

Result _____ / 30 marks

Speaking test

Role card

This *Speaking test* has only one role card because each student has to give an individual presentation. Copy this page and cut out the role card for the student. Then use the *Speaking test results* form to evaluate the student's performance. You can then cut out the results and give them to the student.

Cut along this line

Prepare a presentation to persuade a company to open a new offshore production facility in Poland. Use the slide and article to prepare your short presentation. When you make your presentation, remember to

- present the advantages of choosing Poland
- refer to the slide showing the advantages of Poland
- move from the slide to giving the example of Michelin in Poland
- present the facts about Michelin
- conclude on a strong note.

Slide

Advantages of Poland
- Skilled labour force
- High percentage of workforce speak English
- Tax incentives for overseas businesses
- Positive attitude to new business in Poland

Article

Michelin to expand operation in Poland

Michelin has a manufacturing site in Olsztyn, Poland and due to its success has recently invested another $342 m in the construction of a logistics and warehousing centre. This is Michelin's largest investment programme in Europe and will create more than 500 new jobs.

Cut along this line

Speaking test results

Use this form to evaluate the student.

Cut along this line

Can the student …	Didn't do this (0 points)	Yes, but with some mistakes (1 point)	Yes, did this very well (2 points)
present the advantages (of Poland)?			
refer to the slide?			
move from one point to another?			
present factual information (about Michelin)?			
conclude on a strong note?			

Result _____ / 10 marks

Cut along this line

Working with words

Choose the correct answer from the words in *italics*.

1 They're offering people over 55 the chance to take early *retirement / redundancy*.

2 They've asked me to move to Sales, but it seems like a *transferable / sideways* move.

3 Many women in my position reach a *corporate / glass* ceiling and can't go any further.

4 If I take this course, it's a quick way to *update / train* my computer skills.

5 It's only a temporary *secondment / relocation* for six months while a colleague goes on maternity leave.

6 1,300 workers have been *laid off / unemployed* from a factory in Marseille.

7 To *appoint / retain* our key staff, it may be necessary to offer additional incentives.

8 We found that bringing in flexitime reduced staff *development / turnover* and in fact increased applications from skilled people.

9 Many employees prefer plenty of job *mobility / vacancy* to staying in one place for the whole of their career.

10 In order to get *in / on* in life, it's who you know, not what you know.

Business communication skills

Complete this negotiation with phrases a–k. Write the letters in the spaces.

a One option would be to	g Let's look at
b The areas we need to	h what I propose is
c you guaranteed	i That sounds like
d If I	j I'm happy
e What we need to decide	k supposing
f it just wouldn't work	

A ¹¹___ on today is what to include in the repatriation package. ¹²___ discuss are salaries, education for children and the request for loans to buy houses. ¹³___ what our options are. ¹⁴___ offer a basic package to everyone.

B Sorry, but ¹⁵___ if we offered everyone the same. For example, you have some people with no children and some with five. Then you have people already with a house and those with nowhere to live when they get back.

A Well, ¹⁶___ we gave everyone the same salary rise as a percentage?

B That's a good start. And then ¹⁷___ that we take each person case-by-case. So if ¹⁸___ equal pay rises, I think they'd let you bargain more easily with other incentives.

A Good. ¹⁹___ a plan. So, a recap. ²⁰___ look at realistic figures for the rise, you'll spend some time looking at each individual's needs. OK?

B ²¹___ with that. I can even talk to each of them by phone before the official meeting …

Language at work

Complete these sentences with the correct form of the verbs in brackets to make first or second conditionals.

22 If I ask Lisa, you _____ (ask) Tish.

23 But if I _____ (give) you my best people, who would I have left?

24 We _____ (not / have) a high turnover, if we paid a decent salary.

25 If we decide before Friday, then everyone _____ (know) by Monday.

26 What _____ (you / offer) if I could pay you in cash?

Choose the correct answer from the words in *italics*.

27 I won't do anything *supposing that / unless* everyone wants me to.

28 *In case / As long as* you keep quiet about your deal, no one else will ask about a remuneration package.

29 *Provided that / Unless* I have use of IT support all next week, there'll be no problems with installing the new software.

30 *Supposing / In case* we stretch the budget, then we can take on a trainee.

Result _____ / 30 marks

Speaking test

Role cards

Copy this page and cut out the role cards for the students. Students should do both role-plays. Then use the *Speaking test results* forms to evaluate each student's performance. You can then cut out the results and give them to the students.

Cut along this line

Student A

1 You need to negotiate a repatriation package with an employee returning from relocation in Sweden. Make the following offer.

   - a 10% pay rise
   - private education for their two children.

   When you negotiate the package, remember to

   - outline the main point for discussion
   - put forward your proposals
   - bargain
   - reach agreement
   - summarize the situation.

2 Your manager wants you to train 15 new trainees next month. However, you have already booked time off. You will do it on certain conditions.

   - The company pays for the holiday you've already booked.
   - You get two weeks' extra holiday as compensation.
   - You'd like paid overtime for this course (which you wouldn't normally receive).

   Your manager will begin the negotiation.

Student B

1 You are returning from relocation in Sweden and would like your repatriation package to include

   - a 15% pay rise
   - private education for your two children
   - an interest-free loan to pay off your mortgage (€40,000).

   Your manager will begin the negotiation.

2 You have 15 new trainees next month. You need your employee to train them. You know that he / she has booked time off. Make the following offer.

   - The company pays for the holiday he / she booked and will give one week's extra holiday as compensation.

   (Note that you do not have the budget to pay overtime for any extra hours on this course.)

   When you negotiate the package, remember to

   - outline the main point for discussion
   - put forward your proposals
   - bargain
   - reach agreement
   - summarize the situation.

Cut along this line

Speaking test results

Use these forms to evaluate the students.

Cut along this line

Student A

Can the student ...	Didn't do this (0 points)	Yes, but with some mistakes (1 point)	Yes, did this very well (2 points)
outline a point for discussion?			
put forward proposals?			
bargain?			
reach an agreement?			
summarize the situation?			

Result _____ / 10 marks

Student B

Can the student ...	Didn't do this (0 points)	Yes, but with some mistakes (1 point)	Yes, did this very well (2 points)
outline a point for discussion?			
put forward proposals?			
bargain?			
reach an agreement?			
summarize the situation?			

Result _____ / 10 marks

Cut along this line

Working with words

Complete these sentences with a word from each list.

return	financial
business	start-up
gap	network
venture	

investment	capital
market	contacts
backing	capitalist
plan	

1 In a competitive business, you can only succeed if you see a new _____ in the _____.

2 I think you'll need about €50,000 as _____ _____ to launch your new company.

3 If you look at our _____ _____, you'll see it contains our financial estimates.

4 I'd rather borrow the money from my parents than have to share the profits with a _____ _____.

5 If I lend you €30,000 to set up the business, what do you expect will be the _____ on my _____?

6 A business angel could give you some extra _____ _____, until you start making a profit.

7 We made use of our large _____ of _____ and found people who could help us.

Choose the correct answer from the words in *italics*.

8 This project is *totally / extremely* risky. Be careful!

9 My new member of staff is *totally / hugely* useless.

10 You've been *incredibly / completely* helpful. Thanks a lot.

11 Their plan is *extremely / absolutely* ridiculous.

12 This system is *really / absolutely* complex.

Business communication skills

Complete the conversations with phrases a–k. Write the letters in the spaces.

a Send me the details
b Could you do me a favour?
c since you're
d Actually, that's the reason why
e What have you been up to?
f Then let's talk about it over dinner.

g Could you put me in touch with
h How's life treating you?
i The thing is
j When was the last time we saw each other?
k I'll certainly think about it.

1 A Jose, I don't believe it!
  B Tonya! How are you?! **13**___
  A Oh, the same old things … still working for TTB. What about you?
  B I've had a couple of jobs since I left TTB but I've just set up on my own. Which reminds me. **14**___
  A Sure.
  B **15**___, I've been looking for a document recently on website insurance. I think I left it at TTB.
  A Well, I'm not sure. **16**___ and I'll see what I can do.

2 A It's good of you to meet me this morning.
  B Don't mention it. **17**___
  A At that conference in Lisbon.
  B That's right. **18**___
  A Not bad, though I've had problems with my employer. **19**___ I asked to meet. **20**___ anyone who might have a position, **21**___ well known in the business?
  B **22**___ Why don't we have a drink first. **23**___

Language at work

Choose the correct answer from the words in *italics*.

24 I've *called / been calling* her all afternoon and she still hasn't got back to me.

25 They've *sent / been sending* me the final report. I just need to check it.

26 I've *worked / been working* in this department while two of their staff are away.

27 I hope they've *kept / been keeping* you busy. How much longer are you on secondment here?

28 We've finally *agreed / been agreeing* the deal and the contract has been signed.

29 She's *applied / been applying* for a new job. I think the interview for it is next week.

30 Hello! I haven't *seen / been seeing* you for ages!

Result _____ / 30 marks

Speaking test

Role cards

Copy this page and cut out the role cards for the students. Students should do both role-plays. Then use the *Speaking test results* forms to evaluate each student's performance. You can then cut out the results and give them to the students.

Cut along this line

Student A

1 You are at a conference and meet an old school friend who now owns his / her own company. You don't like your current job so ask him / her a favour.

- Greet your friend.
- Ask about work / life.
- Respond to questions about work / life.
- Change the subject to introduce a favour.
- Ask about possible job openings at his / her company.

2 You are at an airport. By chance, you meet an old colleague who used to work for your company but went to work for a competitor. Be prepared to respond to a request for a favour.

- Greet your colleague.
- Ask about work / life.
- Respond to the request for a favour.

Student B

1 You have your own successful business. You are at a conference and meet an old school friend who asks a favour.

- Greet your friend.
- Ask about work / life.
- Respond to the request for a favour.

2 You are at an airport. By chance, you meet an old colleague from your previous company. You left a list of contacts there and need the details for a client called Mason Richards. Ask your colleague to find this information out for you.

- Greet your colleague.
- Ask about work / life.
- Respond to questions about work / life.
- Change the subject to introduce a favour.
- Ask your colleague to get the client's details.

Cut along this line

Speaking test results

Use these forms to evaluate the students.

Cut along this line

Student A

Can the student …	Didn't do this (0 points)	Yes, but with some mistakes (1 point)	Yes, did this very well (2 points)
greet the other person?			
ask about work / life?			
respond to questions about work / life?			
change the subject to introduce a favour?			
ask a favour?			

Result _____ / 10 marks

Student B

Can the student …	Didn't do this (0 points)	Yes, but with some mistakes (1 point)	Yes, did this very well (2 points)
greet the other person?			
ask about work / life?			
respond to questions about work / life?			
change the subject to introduce a favour?			
ask a favour?			

Result _____ / 10 marks

Cut along this line

Working with words

Complete these sentences with the correct preposition.

1 Teleconference technology allows us to interact _____ people from all over the world.

2 Now, I'd like to focus _____ how to improve this system.

3 What kind of websites do you subscribe _____?

4 Currently, I'm involved _____ a project to improve communication across departments.

5 The developments in mobile technology have probably had the biggest impact _____ the way we work in recent years.

6 Sorry, but I don't have access _____ that part of the system.

7 The building project is going well. We're currently waiting to be connected _____ the main power network.

8 We also collaborate _____ another telecommunications firm in Chenai.

Complete these sentences with the words in brackets in the correct form (personal noun, noun or adjective).

9 Nelson Mandela is a great _____ (communicate).

10 You need quite an _____ (analyse) brain to work in logistics.

11 I'd like to take a gap year and do some _____ (volunteer) work.

12 With all your experience, you could leave this firm and go freelance as a _____ (consult).

13 Many _____ (economy) are warning us that there may be a recession next year.

14 You'd be surprised how many of your skills are _____ (transfer) to other areas of business and management.

15 How many _____ (participate) did you have at yesterday's training session?

Business communication skills

Replace the words in bold in these sentences with a–j so that the meaning stays the same. Write the letters after the numbers.

16 ___   18 ___   20 ___   22 ___   24 ___

17 ___   19 ___   21 ___   23 ___   25 ___

a 've got that   f catch
b you must   g faint
c do you mean   h are … with
d wait   i speed up a little
e you're back   j run through

16 You're very **quiet**.

17 **Hang on** … is that better?

18 Yes, I **understand**.

19 **It's essential to** tell them how to use the website.

20 What exactly **are you saying**?

21 Can you **explain** that again?

22 **Do** you **understand** me?

23 **I can hear you** again now.

24 Can we **discuss this more quickly**?

25 I'm afraid I didn't **hear** that last bit.

Language at work

Tick the modal, a or b, that can replace the modals in bold in these sentences.

26 You **don't have to** stay late tonight.
   a mustn't   b needn't

27 We **ought to** ask everyone how they feel about the plan.
   a should   b can

28 They **weren't allowed** the time off for all that overtime they did.
   a didn't have to have   b couldn't have

29 We **can't** run over time today. The room is only booked until 3.00.
   a don't need to   b mustn't

30 **Have you got** to pay for all your calls?
   a Do you have   b Do you need

Result _____ / 30 marks

Speaking test

Role cards

Copy this page and cut out the role cards for the students. Students should do both role-plays.
Then use the *Speaking test results* forms to evaluate each student's performance. You can then
cut out the results and give them to the students.

Cut along this line

Student A

1 Explain this new procedure to your partner.

Complaint about a superior at work
1 The employee must write down what happened.
2 This document is given to the HR Manager.
3 The complaint must be responded to within three working days.

Remember to check the listener understands, answer questions and clarify any procedures.

2 You have the following procedure, but it is out of date.

Arranging time off
1 The employee must request the dates from Human Resources a week before.
2 Human Resources checks with the line manager.
3 Human Resources confirms this in writing.

- Listen to your partner's explanation.
- Make notes on any changes to the procedure.
- Ask for clarification.
- Show you understand.

Student B

1 You have the following procedure, but it is out of date.

Complaint about a superior at work
1 The employee must speak to another manager.
2 The manager must speak to the superior and then speak to the employee within five working days.

- Listen to your partner's explanation.
- Make notes on any changes to the procedure.
- Ask for clarification.
- Show you understand.

2 Explain this new procedure to your partner.

Arranging time off
1 The employee must write down the dates requested three weeks before.
2 This document is given to the line manager.
3 The line manager confirms this in writing within five working days.

Remember to check the listener understands, answer questions and clarify any procedures.

Cut along this line

Speaking test results

Use these forms to evaluate the students.

Cut along this line

Student A

Can the student ...	Didn't do this (0 points)	Yes, but with some mistakes (1 point)	Yes, did this very well (2 points)
explain point 1 of the new procedure?			
explain point 2 of the new procedure?			
explain point 3 of the new procedure?			
check the listener understands?			
answer questions and clarify any procedures?			

Result _____ / 10 marks

Student B

Can the student ...	Didn't do this (0 points)	Yes, but with some mistakes (1 point)	Yes, did this very well (2 points)
explain point 1 of the new procedure?			
explain point 2 of the new procedure?			
explain point 3 of the new procedure?			
check the listener understands?			
answer questions and clarify any procedures?			

Result _____ / 10 marks

Cut along this line

Working with words

Write the missing first syllable of the verbs in these sentences.

1 Opponents tend to ___sist change whenever possible.

2 Expect that people will ___act differently to the plans.

3 Staff want to know how this will ___fect them.

4 If you can't ___cept the change, you ought to leave.

5 Don't ___pose everything. Some ideas might be good.

6 I find it hard to ___dapt to all this new technology.

Choose the correct answer from the words in *italics*.

7 They ran *into / out / with* a few problems last year but the consultant's report helped to solve them.

8 My company regularly puts *off / on / out* training courses for its staff. There's something every week.

9 It's my job to deal *with / for / of* customer queries and sometimes they are complaints.

10 At first I was worried by the plans to mix the two departments but it has all worked *off / into / out* well.

11 We brought this policy *in / on / into* five months ago. There was resistance at first but now everyone's happy.

12 We'll be taking *out / with / on* new clients in the spring, hopefully, if the expansion continues.

13 Personally, I'm in favour *about / on / of* this strategy.

14 How keen are you *on / towards / of* the car-sharing plan?

15 It isn't surprising that so many of them are resistant *of / to / on* the cuts. It will mean longer hours with less money.

Business communication skills

Complete the memo with phrases a–f. Write the letters in the spaces.

a We'd like to assure you
b Hopefully, the new system
c Many of you have recently asked about
d It's crucial that
e Over the next few
f Starting from next

To: All Staff   **From:** Judy
Subject: Changes to working hours

¹⁶___ improving the system of fixed hours of 9–6, which apply to most staff. ¹⁷___ months, therefore, we will be looking at ways of changing the current system of working hours. ¹⁸___ month, we'll be holding a series of meetings with line managers and staff. ¹⁹___ that everyone's views will be taken into account. However, this will only work with your participation. ²⁰___ you attend meetings. ²¹___ will be in place by the end of October.

Language at work

Complete these sentences with the future continuous or future perfect form of the verbs in brackets.

22 Decisions will definitely _____ (make) by the end of April.

23 Over the next few days, we'll _____ (meet) each of you individually.

24 I'll _____ (travel) to New Zealand on that day, so can we speak the day after?

25 By next year, we predict that the company will _____ (recover) most of its losses.

26 In twenty years' time, a lot of people will _____ (use) robots in their everyday life.

Complete the two missing words so the second sentence has the same meaning as the first.

27 It'll definitely change the way we work.
It's b_____ t_____ change the way we work.

28 It's likely that we'll expand.
There's a g_____ c_____ that we'll expand.

29 We probably won't be going to Germany.
It's d_____ t_____ we'll be going to Germany.

30 Maybe they're coming later.
They m_____ b_____ coming later.

Result _____ / 30 marks

Speaking test

Role card

This *Speaking test* has only one role card because each student has to give an individual presentation. Copy this page and cut out the role card for the student. Then use the *Speaking test results* form to evaluate the student's performance. You can then cut out the results and give them to the student.

Cut along this line

Your company is currently losing money and needs to become more efficient. It plans to

- cut 5% of the workforce (in the next six months)
- consider moving a factory overseas (maybe in two years' time)
- stop any overtime (from next week)
- introduce changes to the hierarchical system of management (probably sometime next year).

You must present these plans to a line manager who will tell his / her staff.

Remember to

- explain the planned future events
- make informed predictions about the timing
- refer to the line manager's knowledge and concerns
- give a call to action.

You will also have to answer a question at the end.

(Note that in this role-play, the line manager is your teacher who will ask you a question at the end.)

Cut along this line

Speaking test results

Use this form to evaluate the student.
Note that you will need to ask a question at the end to check the final criteria.

Cut along this line

Can the student ...	Didn't do this (0 points)	Yes, but with some mistakes (1 point)	Yes, did this very well (2 points)
explain the planned future events?			
make informed predictions about the timing?			
refer to the line manager's knowledge and concerns?			
give a call to action?			
answer a question convincingly?			

Result _____ / 10 marks

Cut along this line

Working with words

Write these figures in full. See the example.

3,000 nm _three thousand nanometres_

1 36.6 kbps _____

2 31st _____

3 121.8% _____

4 $\frac{1}{20}$ _____

5 598,000,000 _____

Read the figures and choose the correct answer from the words in _italics_.

6 $505: The final cost was a _little / great deal_ more than five hundred dollars.

7 53%: _Roughly / Exactly_ fifty per cent of the people said they liked it.

8 28.8kbps → 42.2kbps: The Internet speed was increased _marginally / substantially_.

9 98: Just _under / slightly_ a hundred people voted for the idea.

Complete these headlines with words from the list.

shoot	level	rapidly	stay	plummet	slight

10 House prices _____ to an all time low.

11 Upward trend in oil prices starts to _____ off.

12 Concerns as shares suffer _____ fall.

13 Interest rates will _____ the same for another month.

14 Unemployment set to _____ back up to high levels of the 1970s.

15 Sales of downloads continue to grow _____.

Business communication skills

Match 16–22 to a–g.

16 Could you give ... ____

17 What's that in ... ____

18 Roughly ... ____

19 According ... ____

20 The bottom ... ____

21 Overall, I'd say things are looking ... ____

22 The overriding ... ____

a up and very positive.

b us the low-down on this?

c trend is towards downloads instead of CDs.

d to a recent survey, more people are buying it.

e line is that we need to make some huge cuts.

f speaking it's about 5% more.

g terms of growth?

Language at work

Rewrite the sentences using the words given.

23 'I'll call her back.'
He said / he / her / back

_____

24 'When are you flying back?'
My secretary / ask / when / flying back

_____

25 'Have you seen Frank?'
They / ask / if / Frank

_____

26 'Check my messages, please.'
She / told / to / messages

_____

27 'Thank you for all the hard work you've done.'
Miles / thank / hard work / done

_____

28 'This product doesn't work properly!'
A customer / complain / the product / work properly

_____

29 'I'll look into it for you.'
The sales assistant / promise / look into it / me

_____

30 'Sorry for being late. My train was delayed.'
Peter / apologize / late and said / delayed

_____

Result _____ / 30 marks

Speaking test

Role card

This *Speaking test* has only one role card because each student has to give an individual presentation. Copy this page and cut out the role card for the student. Then use the *Speaking test results* form to evaluate the student's performance. You can then cut out the results and give them to the student.

Cut along this line

1 You will give a short presentation to your teacher which summarizes the key factual or numerical information in this article. First, read the article and underline any parts which report figures and the main findings.

Podcasts are sound files, often made up of speech and music, that can be downloaded and listened to on a computer, or transferred to a mobile MP3 player. Increasingly, they are automatically delivered using software. Originally, they were put together by people good at using computers and posted on the Internet. Topics varied from the sensible to the bizarre. But now, in addition to these home-grown shows, media organizations like National Public Radio in the US and the BBC in the UK use podcasting as an alternative way to distribute their content. As a result, podcasting has exploded. Here are some recent findings on the trends for podcasting.

Fact 1: A survey by the Pew Internet and American Life Project has found that only 12% of US people online had downloaded a podcast in the last 12 months. Earlier this year, a survey by the same research group found that just 7% of online Americans had downloaded a show.

Fact 2: Podcast Alley, a website that acts as a directory of shows, listed just 1,000 podcasts in November 2004. Today, it lists more than 26,000 different podcasts with more than one million episodes. 'While podcast downloading is still an emerging activity primarily enjoyed by early adopters, the range of content now available speaks to both mainstream and niche audiences,' said Mary Madden, senior research specialist at Pew. 'We are at a crossroads of a major change in the way media content is delivered and consumed.'

Fact 3: Last year, a forecast by research firm The Diffusion Group suggested that podcasts could have a US audience of 56 million by 2010.

Source: BBC News

2 Now make notes on the text and prepare your summary presentation. In your presentation
- introduce what the report is about
- report the three main pieces of factual or numerical information in the report
- summarize the overall trend for podcast use in the future.

You have 3–4 minutes to present. You will not be allowed to read from the article above. Only refer to your notes – don't read them aloud.

Cut along this line

Speaking test results

Use this form to evaluate the student. Note that in this test you might wish to tell students that you will deduct marks if their presentation lasts for more than 4 minutes.

Cut along this line

Can the student …	Didn't do this (0 points)	Yes, but with some mistakes (1 point)	Yes, did this very well (2 points)
introduce the presentation?			
report the first piece of factual / numerical information?			
report the second piece of factual / numerical information?			
report the third piece of factual / numerical information?			
summarize the overall trend?			

Result _____ / 10 marks

Cut along this line

Working with words

Replace the words in **bold** in these sentences with words from the list.

> cautious   strict   liberal   collectivist
> hierarchical   egalitarian

1 In countries like Malaysia and Indonesia, companies tend to be **organized in levels**. _____

2 I think the company would be more effective if the system was more **equal**. _____

3 You don't need to be so **careful**. Take a risk! _____

4 At meetings, I don't feel comfortable with the way they are so **free** with their opinions. _____

5 In my culture, people like to be able to express their own views. It's individualistic rather than **one where everyone must agree as a group**. _____

6 When I first moved here, I found it very hard because all the rules were so **rigid and had to be obeyed**. _____

Match 7–11 to a–e.

7 Are you aware … ____

8 Do I need to inform … ____

9 Are you familiar … ____

10 Have you found that they aren't very sensitive … ____

11 What aren't you used … ____

a them about how they should greet each other?
b to eating?
c to the way other cultures behave?
d of the importance of small talk with people from the UK?
e with their attitude to time?

Business communication skills

Complete these sentences with the words / phrases from the list.

> Go   Luckily   That's   Despite   All in   That
> It came   While

12 _____ all, it turned out well.

13 _____ about because of cultural differences.

14 _____, I'd read that being on time is important in this country.

15 _____ arriving on time, we still didn't start the meeting for fifteen minutes.

16 _____ we were talking, he looked uncomfortable with the topic of politics.

17 _____ on. I'm listening.

18 _____ understandable.

19 _____ was when I was aware we had a problem.

Choose the correct answer from the words in *italics*.

20 This new film is a real *blockbuster / page turner*.

21 It's slow to start but there's a great *unwind / twist* at the end.

22 This is a great *book / film*. I couldn't put it down.

23 It's a box office *cast / hit*.

Language at work

Complete these sentences with the past perfect, past continuous or past simple form of the verbs in brackets.

24 While they _____ (wait) for a taxi, a colleague stopped in his car and gave them a lift.

25 By the time I arrived, the meeting _____ (already / start).

26 Just as I _____ (leave), I received a call to say I didn't have to go.

27 It was raining so we _____ (not / walk). We took the subway.

28 At the end of the project, my boss gave me a gift for all the hard work I _____ (do).

29 A … Then on the way the car broke down!
    B So what _____ (happen) next?

30 A As a result of his comments, they asked him to leave.
    B Why? What _____ (he / say)?

Result _____ / 30 marks

Speaking test

Role card

This *Speaking test* has only one role card because each student has to tell an individual story. Copy this page and cut out the role card for the student. Then use the *Speaking test results* form to evaluate the student's performance. You can then cut out the results and give them to the student.

Cut along this line

Study this critical incident and tell the story to your teacher. Remember to

- introduce the story
- link the narrative
- use time expressions
- use a variety of narrative tenses
- summarize the narrative.

A time-keeping problem

Northern European businesspeople tend to be punctual and not spend too much time making small talk. Brazilians have a more relaxed attitude to time, and making social conversation is an important part of the business process.

Study the following situation where a German and British business delegation attended a meeting in Brazil and discovered a problem with time!

12:00 Two businessmen from the UK and Germany arrived on time in a meeting room for their Brazilian counterparts. But the room was empty. They wondered if they had the right place.

12:08 Their Brazilians colleagues arrived and warmly greeted them.

12:20 They all made small talk. By 12.20 the German and British businessmen were getting impatient.

13:00 The meeting ended on time. Both sides were happy and agreed a deal. They went for lunch to celebrate.

Cut along this line

Speaking test results

Use this form to evaluate the student.

Cut along this line

Can the student ...	Didn't do this (0 points)	Yes, but with some mistakes (1 point)	Yes, did this very well (2 points)
introduce the story?			
link the narrative?			
use time expressions?			
use a variety of narrative tenses?			
summarize the narrative?			

Result _____ / 10 marks

Cut along this line

Working with words

Complete this text with the words from the list.

> scale   criteria   tool   views   appraisal
> performance   issue

I had my half-yearly staff [1]_____ last week. Some people don't like them, but I think they're a good development [2]_____. Anyway, it was fine. We began by discussing the assessment [3]_____ so I understood them. Then my boss allowed me to express my [4]_____ on the way things had gone since I joined the company. We rated my skills and abilities using a [5]_____ of one to ten. There was only one [6]_____ we really needed to address. One of the people in my department had criticized me for using a new supplier. Actually, the criticism was probably fair, but I'm not sure about using colleague's comments as part of [7]_____ management. After all, what if they aren't true!

Complete these sentences with the missing particles.

8 We ended _____ with an agreement to meet again in six months' time to see if things improve.

9 Mark comes _____ as being confident, but in fact he's quite unsure of himself.

10 It's time to move _____ from this and discuss the next criteria.

11 Could you hand _____ this form to all your staff?

12 Let's start by going _____ each of the points you've mentioned on the form.

13 I'm afraid you can't possibly carry _____ in the same way. Your criticism of the others is affecting the team.

Business communication skills

Complete these sentences with the pairs of words.

> areas + improve   put + list   identify + goal
> positive + could   must + happy
> consider + success   constraints + performance

14 What do you _____ was your biggest _____?

15 Are there any _____ you feel you need to _____ on?

16 Can we _____ that as a personal _____?

17 I _____ say, we're very _____ with all you've done on this project.

18 On a less _____ note, you _____ have thought more about how your actions affect others.

19 Let's _____ that on your _____ of goals.

20 Were there any _____ that affected your _____?

Language at work

Each sentence contains one mistake. Rewrite the sentences correctly.

21 You should have do that course.

_____

22 If Sandra had left, I probably would applied for her job.

_____

23 If I'd known, I might do something about it.

_____

24 If they'd listened to my instructions, there wouldn't been a problem now.

_____

25 We'd have enough staff for next week's conference, if we would have planned properly in the first place.

_____

Choose the correct answer from the words in *italics*.

26 I *could / should* have joined you for a drink if my train hadn't been delayed.

27 She *should / might* have complained about the way he did her appraisal. He mustn't speak to people like that.

28 If I'd followed my mother's advice, I *would have / would* become a doctor.

29 They still aren't here. They *ought to / might* have decided to work late.

30 You *ought to / would* have waited to hear other offers before accepting the first one you received.

Result _____ / 30 marks

Speaking test

Role cards

Copy this page and cut out the role cards for the students. Students should do both role-plays. Then use the *Speaking test results* forms to evaluate each student's performance. You can then cut out the results and give them to the students.

Cut along this line

Student A

1 Conduct an appraisal with your partner whose performance has been very good this year. There has been only one problem. Staff in his / her team have said they ask for help with the new database but receive none. You plan to suggest a course in Effective Communication Skills.

Remember to

- make your partner feel relaxed
- ask about his / her overall performance
- give feedback on general performance
- give advice and suggest the training
- suggest the course is completed by the end of May.

2 You are the appraisee. Overall, you realize you have had problems at work. Your department has a new manager and you find it hard to work with him. You disagree with many of his decisions because you think they are bad for the company.

- Answer your partner's questions.
- Justify and explain any of your actions.

Student B

1 You are the appraisee. Overall, you are happy with your performance this year. However, you think some of your staff need to work harder. They often make mistakes with the database because they never read the instruction manual you gave them.

- Answer your partner's questions.
- Justify and explain any of your actions.

2 Conduct an appraisal with your partner whose performance this year has been below average. One problem is the new manager who says this member of staff has a 'negative attitude'. You plan to suggest a move to a new department and more responsibility in other areas.

Remember to

- make your partner feel relaxed
- ask about his / her overall performance
- give feedback on general performance
- give advice and suggest changes
- suggest a meeting next week to discuss the changes.

Cut along this line

Speaking test results

Use these forms to evaluate the students.

Cut along this line

Student A

Can the student ...	Didn't do this (0 points)	Yes, but with some mistakes (1 point)	Yes, did this very well (2 points)
make partner feel relaxed?			
ask about performance?			
give feedback on performance?			
give advice?			
set goals / agree actions?			

Result _____ / 10 marks

Student B

Can the student ...	Didn't do this (0 points)	Yes, but with some mistakes (1 point)	Yes, did this very well (2 points)
make partner feel relaxed?			
ask about performance?			
give feedback on performance?			
give advice?			
set goals / agree actions?			

Result _____ / 10 marks

Cut along this line

Working with words

Match 1–10 to a–j.

1 My career break gave me a new perspective … ___

2 The best piece of … ___

3 When you leave university, don't put … ___

4 I really feel my week off recharged … ___

5 He's feeling a little … ___

6 I'm not convinced that a gap year broadens … ___

7 It taught me to be grateful … ___

8 After the break, my career headed … ___

9 The new policy of flexiwork has improved staff … ___

10 Working there allowed me to develop some soft … ___

a uncertain about the whole project.
b for the things I have got.
c retention at our company.
d advice I ever had was to take a gap year.
e off applying for a job. In fact, it's a good idea to start looking before you leave.
f on life, and I balance work and leisure time more effectively.
g skills like leadership and communication.
h your horizons. It's more of a long holiday.
i my batteries. I feel much more motivated about work.
j off in a completely new direction.

Business communication skills

Complete the personal case with phrases a–h. Write the letters in the spaces.

a you have some misgivings
b there are other benefits
c It's a once-in-a-lifetime
d I've been inspired by
e the experience I'd gain
f it's been a long-term goal
g I'd like to do
h it's a win-win situation

The thing is, ^{11}___ of mine to travel round the world, but obviously I'd like to do something useful. Anyway, ^{12}___ a friend who is working for an educational charity in Laos. ^{13}___ this as well because it would help children in the area. They are setting up a school to educate local children. I'd help with administration, setting up computers and I might do some teaching as well. ^{14}___ opportunity. I understand if ^{15}___ about letting me go for three months, but ^{16}___ for you. For example, you could sponsor me and print photos in the local paper. I also thought some of the staff here could raise some money for the school. And then, of course, ^{17}___ would be invaluable for my department. It's much better than the typical training course. So ^{18}___ for us all. What do you think?

Complete these phrases with the missing prepositions.

19 I took a day _____ last week.

20 We finally caught _____ on all that paperwork.

21 They managed to get away _____ a few days.

22 We were _____ a three-day spa break.

23 It was great to be away. I totally switched _____ .

Language at work

Choose the correct answer from the words in *italics*.

24 I'd really like *taking / to take* a gap year.

25 They enjoy *working / to work* abroad.

26 It's worth *asking / to ask* them what they think.

27 I look forward to *seeing / see* them.

28 It would be invaluable for *improving / to improve* my IT skills.

29 I'm worried about *having / to have* so much time.

30 One day I plan *running / to run* my own company.

Result _____ / 30 marks

Speaking test

Role cards

Copy this page and cut out the role cards for the students. Students should do both role-plays. Then use the *Speaking test results* forms to evaluate each student's performance. You can then cut out the results and give them to the students.

Cut along this line

Student A

1 You have arranged a meeting with your line manager to request a six-month career break. You would like to take part in a conservation project in the rainforests of the Amazon. It involves monitoring local animals and helping with a variety of conservation initiatives. You would work alone and with a team of five.

   When you present your case

   • state what you want
   • state motivation
   • explain benefits
   • argue persuasively
   • deal with objections.

2 An employee has arranged a meeting with you. You think he / she intends to ask for a career break.

   • Find out the details.
   • Find out the benefits.
   • Make the objection that it doesn't help the company.
   • Decide if you are convinced.

Student B

1 An employee has arranged a meeting with you. You think he / she intends to ask for a career break.

   • Find out the details.
   • Find out the benefits.
   • Make the objection that it doesn't help the company.
   • Decide if you are convinced.

2 You have arranged a meeting with your line manager to request a year-long career break. You would like to work for a charity in Nepal, which helps new businesses get started. Volunteers give advice and training in their area of business expertise. You would be in charge of ten projects and have a team of five. You would also take an intensive course in the Nepalese language.

   When you present your case

   • state what you want
   • state motivation
   • explain benefits
   • argue persuasively
   • deal with objections.

Cut along this line

Speaking test results

Use these forms to evaluate the students.

Cut along this line

Student A

Can the student …	Didn't do this (0 points)	Yes, but with some mistakes (1 point)	Yes, did this very well (2 points)
state what he / she wants?			
state motivation?			
explain benefits?			
argue persuasively?			
deal with objections?			

Result _____ / 10 marks

Student B

Can the student …	Didn't do this (0 points)	Yes, but with some mistakes (1 point)	Yes, did this very well (2 points)
state what he / she wants?			
state motivation?			
explain benefits?			
argue persuasively?			
deal with objections?			

Result _____ / 10 marks

Cut along this line

Progress test answer key

Unit 1

1 reputation
2 principles
3 professionalism
4 extravagance
5 innovation
6 rapport
7 tradition
8 wary
9 practical
10 over confident
11 positive
12 suspicious
13 (an) expensive
14 complex
15 I **was** given your name by a colleague of mine.
16 Hello, I'm **calling** about the email I sent you.
17 I wanted to see if you are still interested **in** my proposal.
18 I suggest we **meet** to discuss things further.
19 Can you tell me how I **get** to your office?
20 c
21 a
22 e
23 b
24 d
25 're currently updating
26 leaves
27 is becoming
28 get
29 is working
30 remember

Unit 2

1 motivate
2 achievement
3 recognition
4 morale
5 performance
6 schemes
7 rewards
8 valued
9 car
10 feedback
11 plan
12 insurance
13 h
14 a
15 f
16 d
17 b
18 c
19 g
20 e
21 Have you spent much time in China?
22 Who told you?
23 Do you know Jem?
24 Was that with Randall and Sons?
25 ... you're from India, aren't you?
26 Where did she come from?
27 isn't
28 was
29 have
30 didn't

Unit 3

1 ahead of
2 over
3 upfront
4 miss
5 out of
6 accurate
7 out of
8 b
9 e
10 a
11 f
12 d
13 c
14 How are
15 How's the
16 How far
17 What do
18 What you're
19 How about
20 Why don't
21 've changed
22 didn't know
23 've just won
24 had
25 played
26 Have you booked
27 a
28 b
29 c
30 b

Unit 4

1 breakthroughs
2 practical
3 cutting-edge
4 benefit
5 major
6 state-of-the-art
7 proposition
8 with
9 round
10 up
11 up
12 about
13 out
14 off
15 down
16 b
17 a
18 c
19 b
20 a
21 c
22 c

23 b
24 b
25 won't be able to
26 couldn't
27 can't
28 haven't been able to
29 were able to
30 will be able to
can is the extra verb.

Unit 5

1 courteous
2 existing
3 attentive
4 repeat
5 high-quality
6 discourteous
7 loyal
8 responsive
9 sub-standard
10 meet
11 measure
12 exceed
13 get
14 lose
15 a
16 h
17 i
18 e
19 c
20 f
21 b
22 g
23 d
24 j
25 Can you tell me when they are arriving?
26 When did she call?
27 Could you let me know why he called?
28 Have you got his email address?
29 Why is it doing this?
30 Do you know who took this message?

Unit 6

1 stayed
2 act
3 donating
4 take
5 reduce
6 comply
7 share
8 fairness
9 bribery
10 discrimination
11 generosity
12 greed
13 corruption
14 credibility
15 prejudiced
16 ethical
17 deceptive
18 f

19 c
20 a
21 e
22 b
23 g
24 d
25 's coming
26 'm going to start
27 'll let
28 lands
29 're staying.
30 'll call

Unit 7

1 outgoing
2 pragmatic
3 impulsive
4 creative
5 conventional
6 tactful
7 detached
8 methodical
9 options
10 instincts
11 confidence
12 decide
13 Look
14 white
15 What
16 mean
17 classic
18 not
19 words
20 crazy
21 position
22 far
23 on
24 opinion
25 action
26 c
27 a
28 d
29 e
30 b

Unit 8

1 lead to
2 sectors
3 skilled
4 activities
5 expertise
6 gain
7 streamlining
8 show
9 notice
10 look
11 mention
12 turn
13 see
14 move
15 relates
16 leave

17 send
18 I'm really sorry.
19 I completely forgot the time.
20 No problem.
21 I was busy too.
22 He has been given a business award.
23 It is expected (that) he will leave straightaway.
24 You are being fired. The final decision has been made.
25 The problem with all the computers still hasn't been fixed.
26 It is known that the CEO will retire next year.
27 All customer complaints will be answered within five working days.
28 The warehouse is locked up at ten.
29 Somebody phoned you while you were out.
30 You are being promoted to office manager.

Unit 9

1 retirement
2 sideways
3 glass
4 update
5 secondment
6 laid off
7 retain
8 turnover
9 mobility
10 on
11 e
12 b
13 g
14 a
15 f
16 k
17 h
18 c
19 i
20 d
21 j
22 'll ask
23 gave
24 wouldn't have
25 will know
26 would you offer
27 unless
28 As long as
29 Provided that
30 Supposing

Unit 10

1 gap, market
2 start-up capital
3 business plan
4 venture capitalist
5 return, investment
6 financial backing
7 network, contacts

8 extremely
9 totally
10 incredibly
11 absolutely
12 really
13 e
14 b
15 i
16 a
17 j
18 h
19 d
20 g
21 c
22 k
23 f
24 been calling
25 sent
26 been working
27 been keeping
28 agreed
29 applied
30 seen

Unit 11

1 with
2 on
3 to
4 in
5 on
6 to
7 to
8 with
9 communicator
10 analytical
11 voluntary
12 consultant
13 economists
14 transferable
15 participants
16 g
17 d
18 a
19 b
20 c
21 j
22 h
23 e
24 i
25 f
26 b
27 a
28 b
29 b
30 a

Unit 12

1 re (resist)
2 re (react)
3 af (affect)
4 ac (accept)
5 op (oppose)

6 a (adapt)
7 into
8 on
9 with
10 out
11 in
12 on
13 of
14 on
15 to
16 c
17 e
18 f
19 a
20 d
21 b
22 have been made
23 be meeting
24 be travelling
25 have recovered
26 be using
27 bound to
28 good chance
29 doubtful that
30 might be

Unit 13

1 thirty-six point six kilobits per second
2 thirty-first
3 one / a hundred and twenty-one point eight per cent
4 a / one twentieth
5 five hundred and ninety-eight million
6 little
7 Roughly
8 substantially
9 under
10 plummet
11 level
12 slight
13 stay
14 shoot
15 rapidly
16 b
17 g
18 f
19 d
20 e
21 a
22 c

Note that in some sentences below the pronoun might be changed to *I*, *you* or *we*. Allow for this when marking.

23 He said he'd call her back.
24 My secretary asked when I was flying back.
25 They asked if we'd seen Frank.
26 She told me to check her messages.
27 Miles thanked me for all the hard work I'd done.
28 A customer complained (that) the product didn't work properly.

29 The sales assistant promised to look into it for me.
30 Peter apologized for being late and said (that) his train had been delayed.

Unit 14

1 hierarchical
2 egalitarian
3 cautious
4 liberal
5 collectivist
6 strict
7 d
8 a
9 e
10 c
11 b
12 All in
13 It came
14 Luckily
15 Despite
16 While
17 Go
18 That's
19 That
20 blockbuster
21 twist
22 book
23 hit
24 were waiting
25 had already started
26 was leaving
27 didn't walk
28 'd done
29 happened
30 did he say (or) had he said

Unit 15

1 appraisal
2 tool
3 criteria
4 views
5 scale
6 issue
7 performance
8 up
9 across
10 on
11 out
12 through
13 on
14 consider + success
15 areas + improve
16 identify + goal
17 must + happy
18 positive + could
19 put + list
20 constraints + performance
21 You should have **done** that course.
22 If Sandra had left, I probably would **have** applied for her job.

23 If I'd known, I might **have done** something about it.
24 If they'd listened to my instructions, there wouldn't **be** a problem now.
25 We'd have enough staff for next week's conference, if we'**d** planned properly in the first place.
26 could
27 should
28 would have
29 might
30 ought to

Unit 16

1 f
2 d
3 e
4 i
5 a
6 h
7 b
8 j
9 c
10 g
11 f
12 d
13 g
14 c
15 a
16 b
17 e
18 h
19 off
20 up
21 for
22 on
23 off
24 to take
25 working
26 asking
27 seeing
28 improving
29 having
30 to run

Practice file answer key

Unit 1

Working with words

Exercise 1
2 a   3 f   4 d   5 e   6 c

Exercise 2
2 trustworthy   5 successful
3 ineffective   6 wary
4 functional

Exercise 3
1 rapport   4 innovation
2 creativity   5 tradition
3 professionalism   6 principles

Business communication skills

Exercise 1
1 I'm calling about
2 responding so quickly
3 I wondered if you'd
4 I suggest we meet to
5 would you like to meet
6 Let's say
7 Whatever's best
8 in from France, won't you
9 Can you tell me how
10 Let me know where
11 I'll email you a map
12 See you

Exercise 2
1 My name's James Sims and I work for UB.
2 I was given your details by Jill Sander.
3 I wanted to see if you are still interested in our offer.
4 Is it best by taxi or public transport?
5 I'll get my assistant to call you later today to confirm.

Language at work

Exercise 1
1 buys, sells
2 goes
3 does the last flight to New York leave
4 's taking
5 's having
6 'm seeing
7 get back
8 're developing

Exercise 2
Example answers
2 What does he look like?
3 Do you prefer tea or coffee?
4 What does it taste like?
5 Who does this belong to?
6 Do you own your apartment?

Exercise 3
1 catch   4 complete
2 'm designing   5 check
3 'm staying

Unit 2

Working with words

Exercise 1
1 b   2 b   3 a   4 c   5 a
6 b   7 b   8 c

Exercise 2
2 appreciation   6 commission
3 incentive   7 fulfilment
4 bonus   8 loyalty
5 morale

Business communication skills

Exercise 1
2 e   3 d   4 l   5 j   6 f   7 h
8 c   9 i   10 k   11 g   12 a

Exercise 2
1 I don't think we've met.
2 Nice to meet you.
3 What a coincidence!
4 Apparently
5 Really?
6 Well
7 So
8 Catch you later.

Language at work

Exercise 1
1 Is anyone coming in tomorrow?
2 How much could we save?
3 What are you talking about?
4 Who did you come with?
5 How long have you been working with Diana for?
6 Who did you send to the exhibition?
7 Hasn't Guy gone to the conference?
8 Should we ask our manager for help?

Exercise 2
1 Why **didn't you** come to me for help?
2 How much **does a new one cost**?
3 Don't **you work** for MT Electrics?
4 What **will you do** first?
5 How long **have you been** working for Cisco?
6 Who **did you** see at the sales meeting?
7 What **does** 'This program has performed an illegal operation' **mean**?
8 What **does** UNESCO **stand for**?

Exercise 3
1 aren't you   5 have you
2 could you   6 will you
3 doesn't it   7 have they
4 did you   8 was it

Unit 3

Working with words

Exercise 1
2 ran out of money
3 were ahead of schedule
4 allocating funds
5 resolve conflicts
6 prioritize tasks
7 miss the deadline
8 keep track of

Exercise 2
1 keep   4 check
2 make   5 stay
3 runs   6 set
Hidden word = perhaps

Business communication skills

Exercise 1
1 b   2 d   3 c   4 d   5 a   6 c
7 b   8 a

Exercise 2
1 d   2 c   3 g   4 f   5 b   6 h
7 e   8 a

Language at work

Exercise 1
1 's decided   8 Have you finalized
2 've already spoken 9 've fixed
3 did you see   10 spoke
4 called   11 Have you arranged
5 did he say   12 've just organized
6 hasn't made   13 booked
7 haven't arrived   14 've been

Exercise 2
1 c   2 a   3 d   4 e   5 f   6 b

Unit 4

Working with words

Exercise 1
1 set up   5 carried out
2 bring down   6 pay off
3 come up with   7 got round
4 taken up   8 taking forward

Exercise 2
1 revolutionary   5 state-of-the-art
2 practical   6 advantage
3 features   7 potential
4 technology

Business communication skills

Exercise 1
2 a   3 e   4 c   5 j   6 b   7 d
8 h   9 i   10 f

Exercise 2

1 whereas
2 The other major advantage
3 is another great thing about
4 At the moment
5 This means
6 The biggest potential benefit of
7 in the future

Language at work

Exercise 1

1 can / will be able to
2 be able to
3 haven't been able to
4 can
5 can
6 be able to
7 can't / won't be able to
8 can't
9 Has she been able to
10 can

Exercise 2

1 could	5	were you able to
2 did you manage to	6	couldn't
3 was able to	7	managed to
4 was able to	8	Were you able to

Unit 5

Working with words

Exercise 1

1 repeat	6	high-quality
2 sub-standard	7	responsive
3 discourteous	8	existing
4 dissatisfied	9	efficient
5 loyal	10	attentive

Exercise 2

1 b 2 a 3 c 4 b 5 b 6 c
7 a

Business communication skills

Exercise 1

1 How can I help you
2 Could you explain exactly what the problem is
3 Let me get this straight
4 by tomorrow
5 Could you give me
6 Once I've looked into it I'll call you back
7 You mean
8 in time for the

Exercise 2

1 What can I do **for you**?
2 If I understand you **correctly** …
3 I'll look **into** it straightaway.
4 We need the goods in time **for** …
5 … I'll get **back to you**.
6 … by Friday **at** the latest.

Language at work

Exercise 1

3 Do you know why **he left** the company?
4 Could you let me know **if Sam is** working today?
5 Correct
6 Could you tell me who **you spoke** to?
7 Do you know if **the meeting has** started?
8 Correct
9 Do you know whether **we can** leave early today?
10 Could you tell me where the **information office is**?

Exercise 2

1 Do you think he will take the job?
2 Could you find out when Amanda sent them the catalogue?
3 Do you know if this is the train for Munich?
4 Do you know where the bus for Place de la Concorde goes from?
5 Could you tell me if / whether you have had anything from the minibar?
6 Do you know who left this package here?
7 I'd be grateful if you could tell me what time you'll be arriving.
8 Please let us know if you have any special dietary requirements.

Unit 6

Working with words

Exercise 1

1 d 2 f 3 c 4 e 5 g 6 a
7 b

Exercise 2

1 Ethical	6	discrimination
2 responsible	7	prejudice
3 credibility	8	bribery
4 generosity	9	corruption
5 fairness	10	deception

Business communication skills

Exercise 1

2 i 3 b 4 d 5 a 6 e 7 j
8 c 9 h 10 f

Exercise 2

1 We're going to provide you
2 You'll get the opportunity to
3 is well worth a visit
4 It would be a good idea to
5 We'd like to invite you to
6 It's just the kind of thing we need
7 Alternatively, we'd be delighted to show you

Language at work

Exercise 1

Incorrect answers are:

1 I see	5	We'll lose
2 I'll take	6	I'm being
3 I'll meet	7	I'm going to get
4 they're falling		

Exercise 2

1 'm going to pick up	7	Are you staying
2 will be	8	aren't flying
3 'm seeing	9	are you getting
4 'll take	10	leaves
5 'll make sure	11	only takes
6 're going to go back	12	'll have

Unit 7

Working with words

Exercise 1

1 indecisive	5	determined
2 conventional	6	methodical
3 outgoing	7	creative
4 impulsive	8	thoughtful

Exercise 2

1 perspective	5	rely
2 consider	6	confidence
3 weigh up	7	delay
4 between		

Business communication skills

Exercise 1

1 They're here in black and white …
2 I think it would be crazy to …
3 If you ask me, we should …
4 Could you give us some detail, please?
5 Hang on, let's hear what Clare has to say.
6 What John says is right.
7 If we look at the facts, we'll see …

Exercise 2

1 Today, I'd like to
2 what's your position
3 As far as I'm concerned
4 I don't think we
5 The fact is
6 what you're getting at is
7 I'm not convinced
8 it'll mean we
9 that's my view
10 In other words
11 Let's draw up some action points
12 I don't want to spend too long

Language at work

Exercise 1

countable	uncountable
table	furniture
hotel room	accommodation
week	time
letter	correspondence
computer program	software
fax / photocopier	equipment
lesson	training
euro	money

Exercise 2
1 is
2 were
3 don't
4 is
5 has
6 aren't
7 was
8 is

Exercise 3
1 more
2 a
3 is very little
4 too many
5 very few
6 some
7 a little
8 a morning paper

Unit 8

Working with words

Exercise 1
1 activities
2 process
3 employment
4 facility
5 workers
6 growth
7 location

Exercise 2
1 leads to job losses
2 improved the quality of life for
3 take cost-cutting measures
4 streamline our operation
5 free up resources
6 created 980 new jobs
7 gain a competitive edge

Business communication skills

Exercise 1
1 data
2 has resulted in
3 look at
4 move on
5 Due
6 notice on
7 a result
8 looked at
9 turn our attention to
10 the facts
11 Have a
12 leave

Exercise 2
1 to   2 of   3 to   4 at   5 in   6 on
7 to   8 of   9 to   10 for

Language at work

Exercise 1
1 All my important files have been lost.
2 my flat had been broken into
3 to be promoted
4 being told
5 Our computer system must have been hacked into.
6 we are not being told
7 I'm being sent
8 the chairs were being put away
9 Microsoft's latest operating system was unveiled
10 will the Olympic Village be used

Exercise 2
1 accuses
2 are paid
3 don't recognize
4 are often forced
5 visited
6 was told
7 were
8 were given
9 made
10 was packed
11 have had
12 have been made
13 have always produced
14 have benefited
15 will be raised
16 'll get
17 'll keep up
18 will finally be done

Unit 9

Working with words

Exercise 1
1 h   2 f   3 a   4 d   5 g   6 c
7 e   8 b

Exercise 2
1 retain
2 resource
3 redeploy
4 appoint
5 mobility
6 invest
7 key
8 promote
Hidden word = turnover

Business communication skills

Exercise 1
1 c   2 b   3 d   4 c   5 d   6 b
7 a   8 c   9 d   10 b

Exercise 2
1 The areas we need to discuss are
2 One option would be to
3 Why don't we take on
4 So who have we got so far?
5 That sounds like a plan

Language at work

Exercise 1
1 comes, will
2 wanted, would
3 were, would
4 would, had
5 will, give
6 would, spoke
7 made, would
8 want, will

Exercise 2
1 likely situations: 1, 5, 8
2 unlikely situations: 2, 3, 4, 6, 7

Exercise 3
1 in case
2 unless
3 Provided
4 if
5 As long

Exercise 4
Example answers
1 I would take a year off.
2 I knew I could get my job back.
3 I'll go for a ride.
4 we'll start without him.

Unit 10

Working with words

Exercise 1
1 c   2 b   3 a   4 c   5 c   6 b
7 b   8 c   9 a   10 b

Exercise 2
1 totally
2 a really
3 absolutely
4 incredibly
5 clever
6 really
7 impossible
8 hugely

Business communication skills

Exercise 1
1 What **are you doing** here?
2 I **haven't seen** you for ages.
3 How**'s life treating** you?
4 How**'s business with you**?
5 … could you **do** me a favour?
6 The thing is, I**'m looking** for …
7 That**'s** not something I can **decide** on right now.
8 I'll **certainly** think about it.

Exercise 2
1 j   2 e   3 i   4 c   5 d   6 b
7 h   8 a   9 g   10 f

Language at work

Exercise 1
1 've known
2 's been staying
3 has been using
4 've been negotiating
5 've read
6 've been going sailing
7 've had
8 have you been waiting
9 've been trying
10 's been raining

Exercise 2
1 d   2 b   3 g   4 e   5 i   6 h
7 f   8 c   9 j   10 a

Unit 11

Working with words

Exercise 1
1	with	4	in	7	to
2	to	5	on	8	with
3	on	6	to	9	with

Exercise 2
1	analyst	6	participants
2	analytical	7	consultative
3	communicative	8	consultants
4	communication	9	transfer
5	participation	10	transferable

Business communication skills

Exercise 1
2 a   3 c   4 f   5 d   6 h
7 e   8 b

Exercise 2
1 d   2 a   3 e   4 b   5 f   6 c

Language at work

Exercise 1
1	must	4	mustn't	7	mustn't
2	must	5	needn't	8	mustn't
3	needn't	6	must	9	needn't

Exercise 2
1	aren't allowed to	4	don't have to
2	aren't allowed to	5	have to
3	have to	6	don't have to

Unit 12

Working with words

Exercise 1
1	try out	5	ran into
2	taken on	6	dropped out of
3	putting on	7	dealt with
4	brought in	8	worked out

Exercise 2
2 antagonistic towards
3 critical of
4 ambivalent about
5 receptive to
6 optimistic about
7 concerned about
8 enthusiastic about

Business communication skills

Exercise 1
1 as you all know
2 Starting from February next year
3 We'd like to assure you
4 we're calling on you to
5 we are fairly certain everyone
6 You may be wondering
7 I'd like to pass this point over to
8 let's digress for a moment and

Exercise 2
1 Starting from next month we'll be learning
2 We're well aware of your concerns regarding
3 Over the next few weeks we'll be nominating
4 We're also proposing to introduce
5 will now deal with
6 Later this month we'll be recruiting

Language at work

Exercise 1
1	'll be talking	6	will be giving
2	'll have finished	7	won't have agreed
3	'll be analysing	8	'll be visiting
4	'll have produced	9	'll be attending
5	'll also be holding	10	won't have got back

Exercise 2
2 I probably won't get the job.
3 They are quite likely to cancel the whole order.
4 There are certain to be some changes in the final design.
5 They are unlikely to accept these terms.
6 I might be offered promotion.
7 We may face some opposition to these changes.
8 If this goes ahead, there will definitely be some job losses.

Unit 13

Working with words

Exercise 1
Answers supplied on page.

Exercise 2
1 eighteenth
2 forty-eight
3 one thousand and ninety-three
4 nineteen seventy-two
5 five point seven
6 three hundred and thirty thousand
7 ten to the power of six
8 a hundred and eighty billion

Exercise 3
1	substantially	6	fractionally
2	levelled	7	significant
3	gradual	8	gradually
4	shot	9	somewhere
5	approximately		

Business communication skills

Exercise 1
1	speaking	5	interpret
2	According	6	low-down
3	figures	7	general
4	bottom		

Exercise 2
1 Can we look at the figures
2 In general
3 According to
4 What's that in terms of
5 Stani assured us that
6 Apparently, figures from
7 show
8 overall things are looking

Language at work

Exercise 1
1 the plan would work
2 doesn't believe in working at weekends
3 to send the letter immediately
4 if I'd been waiting long
5 they'd had a great time on holiday
6 what I thought about the proposal
7 a lot of people are unhappy about the changes
8 not to let anyone see the plans
9 if I'd ever been skiing
10 he'd be back on Friday

Exercise 2
1 b   2 d   3 a   4 e   5 c   6 f

Exercise 3
a He denied being responsible.
b He encouraged me to apply for the job.
c He refused to let me use his computer.
d He offered to help me.
e He apologized for being late.
f He agreed to lend me the money.

Unit 14

Working with words

Exercise 1
1	individualistic	6	cautious
2	liberal	7	formal
3	egalitarian	8	strict
4	hierarchical	9	open
5	accepting	10	collectivist

Exercise 2
1	to	3	about	5	of	7	to
2	of	4	with	6	to	8	of

Business communication skills

Exercise 1
1 in the end
2 It came about because of
3 That was the first problem
4 So what did you do?
5 It seems that
6 What happened next?
7 That was when I felt really uncomfortable
8 As time went by

Exercise 2

1 At first
2 What's more
3 It wasn't until
4 Despite
5 Luckily
6 It really surprised me, but it worked.

Language at work

Exercise 1

1 didn't recognize, 'd changed
2 was waiting, called
3 was, was raining
4 met, was working
5 got, 'd left
6 arrived, had broken
7 jumped, ran, smashed
8 noticed, was reading

Exercise 2

1 was doing	12 turned
2 went	13 ran
3 arrived	14 looked
4 decided	15 was racing
5 was walking	16 was chasing
6 saw	17 reached
7 stopped	18 dived
8 'd never come	19 looked
9 didn't know	20 was
10 jumped	21 had disappeared
11 came	22 were laughing

Unit 15

Working with words

Exercise 1

1 monitor	5 express
2 conduct	6 constructive
3 address	7 agree
4 objective	

Exercise 2

1 Performance	4 criteria
2 appraisals	5 value
3 tool	6 peer

Exercise 3

1 out	3 on	5 on
2 through	4 across	6 with

Business communication skills

Exercise 1

1 successes	5 improve
2 failures	6 best way
3 have been	7 ought
4 happy	

Exercise 2

1 **Feedback** from …
2 How **should I do this**?
3 Can we **identify** that as
4 we could **do** with some …
5 you **demonstrated** good
6 … I **wouldn't** have organized
7 While we're talking **about** money …

Language at work

Exercise 1

1 'd bought, would have made
2 would have missed, 'd driven
3 'd studied, wouldn't need
4 had gone on, would have shut down
5 hadn't brought, wouldn't be talking
6 'd packed, would have happened
7 'd left, would be
8 'd been, would have done

Exercise 2

1 You could have been dismissed.
2 You could have seen Anne.
3 You shouldn't have spoken
4 You might have let me know
5 You should have sent
6 We could have lost
7 You might have called

Unit 16

Working with words

Exercise 1

1 perspective	5 put off
2 appreciate	6 charity
3 hesitate	7 revitalized
4 tip	

Exercise 2

1 enthusiasm	5 broaden
2 Soft	6 head off
3 development	7 policy
4 retention	

Hidden word = holiday

Business communication skills

Exercise 1

1 a	2 c	3 c	4 b	5 d
6 b	7 d	8 b		

Exercise 2

1 It's been a long-term goal of mine to finish my university course.
2 The plus points are skills development and more leadership experience.
3 My motivation for this comes from my volunteer work with the Red Cross.
4 I'll never be satisfied unless I do it.
5 That's hardly fair – I've never refused to do overtime.

Language at work

Exercise 1

1 to tell	10 to give
2 to do	11 to keep
3 to think	12 taking
4 finding	13 working
5 to be sent	14 to check
6 to oversee	15 collaborating
7 to be	16 to discuss
8 to explore	17 hearing
9 letting	

Exercise 2

1 a	2 f	3 c	4 h	5 d
6 e	7 g	8 b		

Material used in the DVD

Business Result Upper-intermediate Student's Book, Unit 4, pages 26–27, exercises 2–6
PowerPoint slide created by student

Part 1 | Why do we teach presentation skills?

1 Do you ever ask your students to give presentations in class? Do they enjoy this? What do they find difficult? Why can it be useful?

2 These four kinds of presentation are taken from units in *Business Result Upper-intermediate*.

- presenting an idea, service or product
- presenting factual information
- presenting plans and arrangements
- presenting the case for something

Which of these presentations do you think each of these people might need to give?

1 a Sales Representative _____

2 the Head of Administration _____

3 a Finance Director _____

3 Do you think your current students would have to give any of the four presentations listed in 2?

4 ▶ Watch this section and make notes on questions 1–2.

1 Rebecca (the co-author) says that in general there are two types of presentations. What are they? Which do you think are more common for your students?

_____

_____

2 What types of presentation does Melissa (one of the students) need to give in her job? How formal do you think these will be?

_____

_____

Part 2 | What do we teach in a presentation skills lesson?

5 ▶ Watch this section where Simon (the teacher) begins the lesson.

1 How does he introduce the topic?

_____

2 How will he structure the two lessons?

_____

3 Does his plan sound logical? Are there alternatives to this structure?

_____

Lesson 1 | The language of presentations

6 ▶ Watch this section, which is part of the first lesson. The students listen to the recording of the presentation twice.

1 What do you think is the teacher's aim in the first listening task?

_____

2 What kind of language does the teacher ask the students to listen for in the second listening task?

_____

7 Make a list of other types of phrases you would need to teach in a lesson on presenting. For example, referring to visual aids: _take a look at this slide._

Lesson 2 | Student presentations

8 ▶ Watch this section.

1 What task does Simon give the students who are listening to Melissa's presentation? Why do you think he does this?

_____

2 In the extracts from Melissa's presentation, how well do you think she uses the phrases for presenting?

_____

Feedback

9 As well as commenting on language, some teachers also believe it is their job to comment on non-linguistic aspects of a presentation. Other teachers disagree. Would your business English students expect you to comment on the following?

- eye contact
- structure (for example, was there a clear introduction?)
- body language
- delivery (pace, clarity)
- visual aids

10 ▶ Watch this section showing the feedback stage following Melissa's presentation.

1 Which non-linguistic aspects of presenting do the students comment on?

_____

2 How does the teacher organize feedback? How much does he comment?

_____

3 How does Melissa feel about her presentation and the feedback she received?

_____

Material used in the lesson

Business Result Upper-intermediate Student's Book, Unit 2, page 16, exercise 1

Part 1 | Why do students choose one-to-one lessons?

1 Read the quotes relating to why students choose a one-to-one course.

   a "Seniority in the company often means a student chooses one-to-one."

   b "For me, one-to-one is a more intensive way of learning."

   c "There's far more flexibility with one-to-one learning."

   d "It responds to my specific needs or interests which a group course can't do."

   e "You get individual attention from the teacher."

   f "The whole lesson can be learner-centred and personalized."

   g "Many students perceive that it is a more effective way of learning."

   1 Do any of the quotes include reasons why your students choose one-to-one?

   _____

   2 What are some other reasons that your students have for choosing one-to-one?

   _____

   3 Do you think the views in c, d and f are always true?

   _____

2 ▶ Watch this section.

   1 Which three reasons from 1 does Rebecca (the co-author) mention?

   _____

   2 Which reasons does Stephan (the student) mention for choosing one-to-one?

   _____

Part 2 | What are the benefits of one-to-one teaching?

3 Look at the first column in the table below. It lists some of the benefits of a one-to-one lesson for the teacher. Do you think all of these benefits do <u>not</u> apply to group lessons?

The teacher can ...	Rebecca	Penny
a make the lessons very learner-centred		
b address the student's needs directly		
c select materials of interest and relevance		
d get to know the student personally		
e go at the pace of the student		
f work out a course programme together		

4 ▶ Watch this section. Rebecca (co-author) and Penny (teacher) describe some of the benefits for the teacher. Tick the reasons in the table that they each give.

5 ▶ Watch the final section and make notes on questions 1–4.

1 In the previous part of the DVD, Penny and Stephan were looking at question forms for social situations. In this part of the lesson, how does Penny make the language point relevant to Stephan's job?

_____

2 Who inputs the questions that Stephan will ask in a social situation, the teacher or the student?

_____

3 What error correction techniques does Penny use during the lesson? How does she try to improve Stephan's English?

_____

4 At the end, Penny describes her approach to error correction with Stephan. Which of the following (a, b or c) best summarizes her approach? Which tends to be your approach in one-to-one teaching?

a "My students choose one-to-one so that I have time to correct all their errors. So that's the most important thing."

b "I'm trying to strike a balance between helping the student to be accurate but also to be fluent."

c "It's more important that the student can communicate effectively and fluently, so I tend to keep correction to a minimum."

6 Look at the roles (right) that are often used to describe a teacher.

1 Tick the roles which you think best describe Penny, the teacher, in this one-to-one lesson.

2 How do you think our role(s) changes in the one-to-one classroom compared with a group lesson?

language expert

observer

prompter

administrator

performer

corrector

facilitator

provider of input

controller

coach

7 The final screen in the DVD suggests that one-to-one teaching lets you

• Target the student's specific needs

• Personalize classroom activities

• Go at the student's own pace

• Adapt and tailor materials to suit

• Deal with individual errors

• Teach the way they like to learn

Imagine the screen begins with '_One-to-one teaching_ **doesn't** _let you ..._'.

1 Think of three bullet points to explain the disadvantages of one-to-one teaching.

_____

_____

_____

2 Are there ways to deal with these drawbacks in one-to-one lessons?

Materials used in the lesson

Business Result Upper-intermediate Student's Book, Unit 2, page 17, Case study

!!! Note that the case study you watch in this DVD lasted approximately 60 minutes in real time.

Part 1 | What is a case study?

1 Look at the case study used by the teacher on page 17 of *Business Result Upper-intermediate Student's Book*. Read the *Background* and make notes on the following.

- Consider each stage of the case and what problems students might have.
- Think about the language you expect students will need for the discussion stages during the *Task*.

2 Based on the case study about Palmate Hellas and on your own experience of using case studies, complete the following statements in your own words.

A case study is a _____

The purpose of using case studies with our students is to _____

_____

3 ▶ Watch this section.

1 Compare your answers in **2** with Rebecca's (the co-author's) comments.

2 At the beginning of the lesson, how does Simon (the teacher) check that students understand what the topic of the case study is?

Part 2 | How do you stage a case study?

4 Read the comments made by teachers on some problems they have had using case studies. How do you think the teachers could solve these problems?

1 "The students weren't interested in the topic."

2 "They took ages to understand the context and background to the case study."

3 "At the end, the main discussion only lasted about five minutes and they didn't use any of the phrases I taught last week."

4 "They couldn't agree at the end."

5 "Two students dominated the final discussion."

6 "At the end, one student asked me if they could do a proper lesson next time."

7 "The students liked it but we ran out of time."

5 Read the following tips for staging case studies.

- Generate students' interest and personalize the topic for them.
- Concept-check to be sure students have understood each stage of the case.
- Give plenty of preparation time (for reading and dealing with questions).
- Allow even more time for the discussion stages.
- The discussion during the task needs to be student-led.
- Monitor and take notes on language problems during the task.
- Give feedback on the language and the task.

▶ Watch this section and tick the tips that Rebecca (the co-author) mentions. Can you think of any more tips?

Part 3 | Set the scene | Input key content | Resolve the case

6 ▶ Watch this section showing the different stages of the case study. Here are four incorrect statements about what Simon does during the lesson. As you watch, rewrite the sentences to make them correct.

1 As a lead-in, Simon tells the students what some causes of low morale at work can be.

2 Simon doesn't spend much time on the background reading so there is more time for speaking at the end.

3 While students are resolving the case, Simon interrupts from time to time in order to keep them on track and help with corrections.

4 During the feedback stage, Simon focuses on correcting the students.

7 How you manage student interaction and organize the classroom can really affect a case study. Look at these six diagrams of classroom layout during the lesson in the DVD (T = teacher, S = student).

1 What order were these layouts used in? Number them 1–6.

2 In diagrams C, E and F, what is the teacher's role?

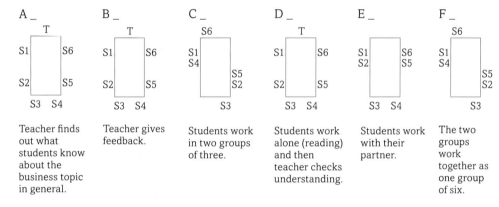

A _
Teacher finds out what students know about the business topic in general.

B _
Teacher gives feedback.

C _
Students work in two groups of three.

D _
Students work alone (reading) and then teacher checks understanding.

E _
Students work with their partner.

F _
The two groups work together as one group of six.

▶ Watch all three stages of the case study again and check your answers. (Note that the final part of the lesson is only referred to.)

8 Look at a similar case study on page 35 (Unit 5) of *Business Result Upper-intermediate Student's Book* and complete the following.

- Sketch a set of diagrams (similar to those in **6** above) for each stage.
- Imagine you have 60 minutes for the case study. How many minutes would you allocate to each part of the lesson? Write the amount of time next to each diagram.
- If possible, compare and discuss your plan with other teachers using *Business Result*.

DVD Worksheet answer key

Presentations

1 Answers will vary. Many will find giving presentations in class extremely daunting since they have to deal with their language issues as well as the usual problems associated with public speaking. It can be useful as it gives students the chance to practise in a fairly relaxed environment and they can get feedback on how they can improve their presentations.

2 1 A Sales Representative might present a new service or product to potential customers. It is likely to be semi-formal, depending on the type of product and target market.

2 The Head of Administration could give information about new plans or arrangements to be implemented around a company.

3 A Finance Director is likely to give factual information or report on figures. As a result of the figures he or she could also present a case for a certain strategy.

3 Answers will vary.

4 1 Rebecca describes presentations as 'formal' (for example, to large audiences such as clients) or as 'less formal' (for example, internal presentations at a meeting).

2 Melissa presents at national and international meetings as well as to companies. She needs to present information on products for medical research so they are probably quite formal.

5 1 He simply tells the students what the topic is.

2 He plans to input the language and then students will present using the new language.

3 Simon's plan is logical, although at this level he could try asking students to give a presentation first. Then he could give feedback and do remedial work on the presentations before finally asking them to present again. It will depend on various factors, such as how familiar your students are with giving presentations, or if you already know they lack the necessary expressions and skills.

6 1 The aim is for students to understand the main content of the presentation.

2 He asks students to listen for phrases used to introduce and preview the talk, and also for phrases to introduce the product.

7 Some possible answers are as follows.

Types of phrase	Example phrases
moving to the next part of the presentation	*Let's move on to …*
checking the audience understands	*Is that clear?*
sequencing information	*Firstly …, Secondly …*
conclude	*So, to sum up …*
invite questions	*Are there any questions?*
handle questions from the audience	*That's an interesting question.*

8 1 Simon asks the other students to think of one question to ask in order to encourage them to listen intently to the presentation and so that Melissa will gain practice dealing with questions at the end of her presentation. He also asks them to write one thing they liked about the presentation. This is so that he can elicit peer feedback afterwards and so that students become accustomed to commenting on each other's work. (Note that he also gives his rationale towards the end of the DVD.)

2 Melissa successfully uses quite a few fixed phrases for presenting. Her words are a little broken up, and note that later in the feedback section Simon talks about contracting speech (*I would = I'd*) to make her sound a little more fluent.

9 Many teachers do not feel it is their job to comment on non-linguistic issues. In many ways your students may be more experienced than you, so use their expertise and get them to comment on these issues. However, it is often hard to separate the skill from the language. If a student has a poor visual aid with incorrect English, the teacher is as qualified as anyone to comment.

10 1 The students comment on Melissa's body language, how clearly she spoke, and that she looked confident.

2 The teacher lets other students comment first. He tends to concentrate his own feedback on the language problems only. The feedback really focuses on the positive overall.

3 Melissa says she was scared and tried to avoid unnecessary or distracting gestures with her hands. She appreciated the feedback from her peers.

One-to-one teaching

1 Answers will vary.

2 1 Rebecca refers to quotes a, d and g.
  2 Stephan refers to quotes b, d and e.

3 Possible comments are as follows.

It is less likely that a group lesson will allow a teacher to get to know a student personally or to go at the pace of one particular student. However, it may be possible to address all students' needs and select relevant materials if a group consists of students from the same company, working in the same department and of a similar level. It is certainly possible to make a group lesson learner-centred, through the use of pair work and group work.

4 Rebecca: a, b, c, e   Penny: b, d, f

5 1 Penny asks about Stephan's job and finds out what kind of visitors he meets. In this way she shows the student how question forms for socializing are useful and relevant to him.

  2 Penny elicits questions from Stephan so that he inputs the language he needs. Her role is to prompt and if necessary correct any of the language.

  3 Penny corrects the following.

  Missing preposition – she asks him to provide a preposition (but doesn't say what it is) and she also asks him to repeat it so that it sounds natural.

  Word stress on *comfortable* – she says it and he repeats it.

  Intonation – she asks him to listen to the recording and repeat a sentence which needs improving.

  * Note that she uses the recorder so that he can also self-correct his language. Also note that she gives positive feedback on good sentences.

  4 Penny would probably say approach b best summarizes her view of error correction in this lesson. However, one-to-one lessons allow you to vary your approach according to the student. Many students will ask you to correct every mistake whereas others don't mind about some mistakes as long as they can communicate their message.

6 1 In this lesson, Penny demonstrates roles which are typical of the business English one-to-one teacher: in particular, language expert, prompter, corrector, facilitator, provider of input, coach.

  2 In a one-to-one lesson, a teacher is probably less likely to take on the role of performer or controller than in a group lesson.

7 1 Disadvantages could include the fact that group work is not possible and pair work can only be achieved with the teacher taking on the other role, meaning that it is more difficult to monitor the student. One-to-one

lessons can also be demotivating for students who enjoy a competitive element to learning, since there would be no other student to compare themselves to. It is also possible that the teacher becomes so accustomed to the student's language that they become immune to the student's errors, and so do not correct.

  2 It is helpful to devise a course plan and to review this frequently so that you can be sure the student is making progress. It's also worth discussing the issue of error correction frequently with your student – make sure your student knows when and why you correct or don't correct (e.g. depending on whether the focus of an activity is fluency or accuracy) and find out the student's personal preferences regarding correction. Adapt pair work and group work activities where possible and record the activities so that you can participate, monitor and promote self-correction.

Case studies

1 Answers will vary. Possible comments could be that students will need plenty of time when reading the *Background* and may need extra help with unknown vocabulary. Language for reporting back, for making suggestions, for offering opinions and for agreeing / disagreeing could be useful in the *Task* section.

2 Answers will vary.

3 1 The co-author says: a case study is a typical business situation or problem which requires students to analyse, discuss, problem-solve or to find a suitable outcome. The purpose of using case studies with our students is to put them in a credible business situation in order to use their English. In *Business Result*, the case studies aim to recycle the language from the unit.

  2 Simon tells students who the company is and what will happen. He writes the topic (morale) on the board and asks a student to define it.

4 There are no exact answers or solutions to these problems. The following are possible reasons.

  1 "The students weren't interested in the topic."

  It may be that the teacher didn't raise their interest at the beginning or make it apparent how the issues in the case study related to their work.

  2 "They took ages to understand the context and background to the case study."

  Teachers need to predict difficulties that students will have with some vocabulary. However, teachers should plan for the fact that this early stage of a case study will require plenty of time and they shouldn't feel pressured into rushing students onto the next stage.

3 "At the end, the main discussion only lasted about five minutes and they didn't use any of the phrases I taught last week."

This suggests that the early stages were not completed properly so students hadn't explored all the different issues. Note that you can never guarantee that students will use all the language taught. A case study is also an opportunity for them to use other strategies and language, and therefore develop fluency and communication skills. However, it is sometimes helpful to begin the case study by reminding them of key phrases to use or to mention phrases which would have been helpful in the feedback stage at the end.

4 "They couldn't agree at the end."

This doesn't matter as long as students have practised target language, understood the concepts and, hopefully, enjoyed the case study.

5 "Two students dominated the final discussion."

This is a particular problem with group discussions. Some students will talk more during the pair work or closed group discussion and then not feel comfortable about speaking in the final discussion. One strategy to solve this is to make sure the more confident students are on the same side at the end and quieter students work together and have to present arguments.

6 "At the end, one student asked me if they could do a proper lesson next time."

This is probably because the value of the case study and the fact that language was being recycled from previous lessons wasn't apparent to the student. This relates back to comment 3 above. If necessary, state your rationale for doing the case study at the beginning.

7 "The students liked it but we ran out of time."

This is a classic problem. Teachers often underestimate the time needed and so the final student-centred discussion at the end is cut short. A well-planned case study can often last the whole lesson.

5 The co-author mentions the following.

Generate students' interest and personalize the topic for them.

Concept-check to be sure students have understood each stage of the case.

Give plenty of preparation time (for reading and dealing with questions).

Give feedback on the language and the task.

6 Possible rewrites are as follows.
1 As a lead-in, Simon asks students what some of the causes of low morale at work can be.

2 Simon spends a great deal of time on the background reading as well as giving plenty of time for speaking at the end.

3 While students are resolving the case, Simon is silent, monitoring and taking notes.

4 During the feedback stage, Simon focuses on correcting the students and giving praise.

7 1 The pattern for this case study is: A 1, B 6, C 4, D 2, E 3, F 5. Note that this pattern moves the lesson from being teacher-led to one that is student-led (and student-centred). It ends with the focus back on the teacher when he is giving feedback. However, the students could also give peer feedback or analyse their own performance if the case study discussion is recorded on video.

2 In diagrams C, E and F the students are working in pairs or groups so the teacher's role is to monitor, ensure the students stay on track, answer queries about language or the content, and prompt with ideas where necessary.

8 For more ideas on how to plan this case study, see the notes on page 17 of the *Teacher's Book*.